"**The Buy Side takes the reader on an extremely wild ride so eloquently and honestly that we never want it to end.** Cocaine wants everything you love and everything that loves you. Turney Duff had everything and nothing while trading billions of dollars on a razor's edge. His book takes you from Wall Street to Skid Row to the Thompson Hotel—and then, mercifully, back to sanity and finding a place in the world. **Hang on, The Buy Side is gonna move you around, and there are no seatbelts to keep you from getting hit hard.**"

—Brian O'Dea, author of
High: Confessions of an International Drug Smuggler

"**The Buy Side is Wall Street meets Breaking Bad—except that this book is fact not fiction.** Turney Duff yields to temptation at every turn, and the sheer volume of criminal behavior he saw, and even participated in, is astonishing. . . . If you want to see Wall Street's seamy underbelly firsthand, read this book."

—Frank Partnoy, bestselling author of
F.I.A.S.C.O. and *Infectious Greed*

"If you took Gordon Gekko, Bud Fox, a copy of *Bright Lights, Big City*, and threw them in a blender with an ounce of cocaine, a bottle of Patrón Tequila, and your favorite teddy bear, you'd have yourself a *Buy Side* smoothie. **Turney's my kind of guy; a madman with heart. I couldn't put the book down.**"

—Colin Broderick, author of *Orangutan*

THE BUY SIDE

A Wall Street Trader's Tale of
Spectacular Excess

TURNEY DUFF

CROWN
BUSINESS
NEW YORK

Published in the United States by Crown Business, an imprint of the
Crown Publishing Group, a division of Random House, Inc., New York.
www.crownpublishing.com

Crown Business with colophon is a trademark of Random House, Inc.

Library of Congress Cataloging-in-Publication Data

Duff, Turney.
The buy side : a Wall Street trader's tale of spectacular excess / by Turney Duff. —
First edition.
pages cm
1. Duff, Turney. 2. Stockbrokers—United States—Biography.
3. Investment advisors—United States. 4. Finance—United States. I. Title.
HG4928.5.D84A3 2012
332.6092—dc23
[B]   2012046852

ISBN 978-0-7704-3715-2
eISBN 978-0-7704-3716-9

Printed in the United States of America

Book design: Ellen Cipriano
Jacket design and photograph: Michael Nagin

2 4 6 8 9 7 5 3 1

First Edition

To

LOLA,

with love

AUTHOR'S NOTE

I wanted to write an honest book, so I've tried to keep all of the names and places real. In certain cases, however, owing to considerations of privacy and a desire to not embarrass those whose intentions were honorable (and some not so honorable), I've chosen to alter certain identifying details and make use of pseudonyms. A complete list of these pseudonyms appears on this book's last page. Dialogue and events have been re-created from memory and in some cases have been compressed to convey the substances of what occurred or was said. I've done my best to keep the time sequence in order, but it's possible that events occurred either earlier or later in reality than they occur in this story. Otherwise, this book is a candid account of my experience on Wall Street as I remember it.

PROLOGUE

I'M READY. The early darkness falls as we make our way across Tribeca, our shoes clicking on the cobblestones. At this hour the Bugaboo strollers have yielded to the coming Saturday-night revelry. My roommates and inner circle—six men and three women, all fashionably dressed as if they're attending a red-carpet premiere—surround me. They mirror my every move, like a school of night fish. Our pace increases as we stride the few blocks to West Broadway and Canal. I wear a flannel shirt that has the sleeves ripped off, my favorite pair of worn jeans, and baby blue tinted sunglasses with studded fake jewels around the lenses.

Marcus, the owner of the Canal Room, meets us outside the club's door. When he sees me, a smile stretches across his face. "They're with me," I say, flicking a thumb at my trailing companions. The doorman unhooks the red velvet rope and we follow Marcus into the club. It's nearly empty, but not for long. Marcus is smiling for good reason. He calls me the Pied Piper—King of the Night. And soon my following, the royalty of young Wall Street, will fill his club.

By eight p.m. the line outside the Canal Room stretches to more than a hundred people. By eight thirty it's almost doubled. When the doors finally open it's as though someone has pulled a stopper in a marble sink filled with champagne. Dressed in Armani and Prada, the excited throng pours inside. I stand by the door, playing the role of greeter, accumulating lipstick impressions on my cheeks and, occasionally, a small gift—a perk of the buy side. One friend, Brian, gives me ten ecstasy pills. I have no intention of taking them—well, maybe just one or two. I shove them into my pocket to use as party favors later. I'll walk up to anyone who I know is down with it and, with a devilish grin, ask, "Breath mint?" When they open their mouth I'll pop one in. Tonight, there are no limits.

I've arranged everything: the space, the bands, and the guest list. The invites were sent out by my alter ego, Cleveland D. The club has just been remodeled with a brand-new sound system, the best in New York City, and now, appropriately, it's blaring Missy Elliott's "Work It." If any of the guests thought this night was just another average Wall Street bash featuring some overpriced DJ or a retro band like the Allman Brothers or Foreigner, that notion is put to rest when Lisa Jackson, a cross-dressing glam singer, takes the stage. When she breaks into "Purple Rain" and then "Ring My Bell," it's as though she's just grabbed a handful of every guy's well-tailored crotch. And she's only the foreplay.

By nine thirty the place is throbbing. Liquor flows. People dance or sway to the music, drinks held high. I make my way to the bar, but it takes me five minutes to move five feet. I can't talk to anyone for more than a few seconds before feeling a tug at my back or a hand on my shoulder. I can see people across the room flashing a nod or toasting me with their drink. It seems all of Wall Street is here, at least all of Wall Street that *matters*. Every brokerage firm is represented: other buy side traders, sell siders, bankers, fixed income traders, and the rest.

On the stage the group Naughty by Nature begins their hip-hop version of the Jackson 5 hit "ABC." It takes just a few notes for the entire crowd to erupt, realizing they're hearing the song "OPP." Multiple rotating strobe lights frantically stripe the fist-pumping revelers. Treach, Naughty by Nature's lead rapper, has the microphone in his hand and is pacing back and forth onstage. The energy surges, plateaus, then builds some more. The area in front of the stage is a pulsating mob, and as the space between the swaying bodies draws closer and closer, escape becomes impossible for anyone in front. The musical loop continues, spurring the crowd to beg for more, and then Treach finally puts the microphone to his mouth. "You down with Cleveland D?" he shouts as he points the microphone toward the crowd. "Yeah, you know me," they shout back.

I stand next to the stage, the thump of the bass hammering my eardrums as I shout the lyrics: "Army with harmony . . . Dave drop a load on 'em . . ." I sing along with Treach as if we're one, as if the words are as much mine as his. In front of me, four hundred guests—sexy, attractive, drunk, intelligent, powerful, and all with fat wallets—jump and sing with as much gangsta as they can muster. They're a tribe doing a triumphant war dance. I know this room will earn hundreds of millions of dollars combined in annual income this coming year— what the Street likes to call "fuck-you money." And on this night, I have all these princes and princesses of finance in my front pocket.

Then the flush of ecstatic excitement I'm feeling subsides and in its place comes a curious and discomforting thought. In a distended moment that suddenly opens like a chasm, it strikes me: I've just turned thirty-four; this party is meant to celebrate that. But it's meant to celebrate something more. Somehow, against the odds, I've become a hedge fund trader—a job description that is the envy of Wall Street. I'm at the very pinnacle of my career, a career powered not by an Ivy League MBA or some computer-like dexterity (a common skill set among the youthful and moneyed dancing in front of me) but by an odd Wall Street truth: what happens *after* the closing bell is as important as anything that happens during the day. It's during those hours after office lights have been turned out that I shine.

But as I consider what I've accomplished, something gnaws at my satisfaction—bores a deep hole in my happiness. I can't put my finger on it . . . it's just, as I stand there, right beside the stage, looking out at this sea of privilege, I'm *empty*. And, for the first time in a long while, I don't know what can fill me.

PART ONE

JANUARY 1984
KENNEBUNK, MAINE

IT'S SNOWING. Our blue and gray Cape house, which sits on the edge of a wildlife preserve, is covered with two feet of snow. Through the foggy kitchen window, I can see my forty-four-year-old father shoveling the driveway in the dimming light. He's in better shape than most men half his age. He looks like a young William Shatner dressed for an L.L.Bean catalog photo shoot. As the heavy flakes fall on him, he methodically digs, scoops, and tosses the snow from his shovel. Never missing a beat, no breaks, no pauses, just dig, scoop, toss. Dig, scoop, toss. His icy breath is a carbon copy of the exhaust spitting from the Green Machine, our '77 Ford LTD station wagon. The car warms up while he shovels around it. Slowly but surely, my father is carving out a path. Dig, scoop, toss.

I sit at the long wooden kitchen table, eating my cereal. Dig, scoop, eat. Dig, scoop, eat. The wood plank floor and white stucco walls absorb the heat from the woodstove. It's the warmest part of the house.

I'm wearing my Boston College sweats, a Christmas present from my sister Kristin, a freshman there. She's in the living room watching television with Debbie, my oldest sister, who is attending the University of Maine. They're both home from school on winter break. Kelly, the youngest of the Duff girls, is doing her homework across from me. I hold my bowl with both hands and bring it up to my lips. I look at Kelly over the rim. She's focused on the textbook open in front of her. All of my sisters have my father's determination and the trademark Duff nose, so small and perfectly shaped that it looks like it belongs in some plastic surgeon's catalog. Kelly is a junior in high school and the homecoming queen. She's also a track and field state eight-hundred-meter champion. All of the Duff children have inherited my dad's athletic ability. I slurp the sweet milk and Cheerios. Kelly looks up from her textbook with mild contempt, which instantly dissolves. She feels bad for me. She knows I don't want to go with my dad. I smile back at her.

My mother sits at the far end of the kitchen working on her cross stitch, for which she has won magazine contests, and sipping a glass of wine. Her hair is shoulder-length and frosted, and she wears an apron over her golf shirt. "You'd better finish before your father sees you eating cereal for dinner," she says. I tilt up the bowl and pour the rest of the milk and what's left of the cereal into my mouth.

"I really don't want to go," I say, wiping my lips with the back of my hand. She already knows I don't. Although there have been times when she successfully advocated for me, on this night my father's mind is made up. When he gets to this point, it's like a Supreme Court decision. And not even two feet of snow can stop my dad. Dig, scoop, toss.

My father has decided that I have the potential to be a great high school wrestler. And tonight, despite the snowstorm, despite all my protests, despite the alliances of my sisters and mother, and even though

I'm only in eighth grade, he's taking me to the high school gym to attend a wrestling practice and, perhaps, show the coach what I can do.

He himself was something of a wrestling superstar. All these years later, people in his hometown, Mt. Lebanon, Pennsylvania, still talk about his exploits on the mat. He was offered no fewer than three college scholarships. None of those schools, however, offered a mechanical engineering degree, on which he had his heart set. So his wrestling dreams were pinned by his career aspirations.

But it wasn't as if he was trying to recapture high school glory through me—at least, I don't think he was. Partly, he saw wrestling as a way to make a man out of me. With three older sisters and a doting mom, I needed the burn of the mat and the smell of the locker room, he thought, to toughen me up a bit. But most of all, he didn't want to repeat the relationship that his father had with him. Though my father was a star wrestler and a record-holding pole-vaulter in high school, my grandfather never once attended any of his events. My father saw wrestling as something we could share, just us Duff guys. There's only one little problem with my father's plan: I don't want to be a wrestler.

I used to want to be a chef. A friend's mother once snuck us into the White Barn Inn, the fanciest restaurant in Kennebunk. When the chef came out of the kitchen, all of the customers looked at him. I liked the attention and deference he garnered. If not a chef, maybe I'll become a conman. I always loved those characters in the movies. In sixth grade I tried to blackmail a girl named Kelli. I threatened that if she didn't leave a dollar in the book *Backboard Magic* on page 13 in the library, I would tell everyone at recess who her boyfriend was. She told the teacher and I got in trouble. But now I think I'd like to attend either UNLV or Cornell for hotel management. I want to run the show. I want to help other people have a great vacation. Plus, it doesn't seem that difficult. Maybe I just don't want to be like my father.

For him, there is no shortcut, no easy money. Everything he does is analyzed and planned down to the last detail. He leaves nothing to chance. He knows which gas station has the cheapest fuel in town, he follows the most accurate weatherman on television, and he gets up at two in the morning when daylight saving time occurs to reset every clock in the house. Though we have the same name and unusual bluish-green eyes that sometimes look gray—and, of course, the signature Duff nose—we're nothing alike. He tries to instill in me a work ethic, discipline, and a rigid schedule, and I resist at every turn. He wants me to be a man. He wants me to be more like him. It's for that exact reason that I'm sitting at the kitchen table with a huge pit in my stomach.

I hear the door from the garage open and close. I know it's him. "Car's out," he announces to the house. "Let's go, Turney." I bow my head and glance at my mom. I want her to see the sadness in my eyes. She forces a sympathetic smile and I know I have to go.

We're the only car on the road. The flakes hit the windshield like snowballs as we sit in silence. This is brilliant. We're risking our lives so we can attend a high school wrestling practice. Someone please kill me. Maybe we'll slide off the road into a ditch and get stuck. I should only be so lucky. Then I see headlights slowly approaching. It's a black Corvette. It can only be one person. The New York license plate confirms it. As we pass each other at about ten miles per hour, I spot his thick bushy mustache. "That's Uncle Tucker," I say.

"He left eight hours ago," Dad says as we drive right by the Corvette. I guess we aren't turning around. I love when Uncle Tucker visits. He always teaches me a new card trick. He's thirty-two years old and makes a ton of money; he goes on exciting trips and vacations. He's in town to take my two oldest sisters skiing tomorrow. I watch until his brake lights disappear in the blizzard. We approach our first stop sign and have to start slowing down about a hundred yards in advance so we can be sure to stop. My father takes his eyes off the road to look at me. "You know, when you were an infant you learned how to bridge before you could crawl," he says.

"I know," I say. It's only the nine hundred and fifty-sixth time I've heard the story. He breaks into how important it is to bridge when you're wrestling. He explains to me it's the only way to avoid being pinned when you're on your back. He lifts his neck back to show me how it's done. I know how it's done. I did it in my crib.

"You raise your shoulders and support your body with your neck," he says anyway. I turn my head to look at the road. "The coach invited us. We're just going to observe," my father says, sensing my displeasure.

The gymnasium floor is covered with a giant blue wrestling mat. I follow my dad over to the one set of bleachers that are pulled out as we try to shake the snow off our hair. I look across the floor. Guys are everywhere, running, stretching—a few are already wrestling. If I hadn't figured out that I haven't reached puberty yet, I realize it now. These guys are huge; some even have facial hair. I feel worse than I did before. The pit in my stomach grows. I don't want to wrestle. My father smiles at the coach when he sees us.

The coach waves to us and makes his way over. He's in his early forties, short but solidly built. He wears tan pants, a blue shirt with KENNEBUNK WRESTLING on the breast, and a whistle around his neck. He sticks out a beefy hand to shake mine and introduces himself as "Coach." I muster a smile and tell him it's nice to meet him.

"So you like wrestling?"

Every fiber in my body wants to say no, but I know my dad will kill me if I do. I just nod and say, "I like it okay." Luckily, the coach turns his attention to my dad. They start swapping wrestling jargon. I hear words like "rip back" and "undercup" and I want to puke. But there's a joy in my father's face that I don't normally see. He's a balloon and every bit of wrestling terminology blows him up a little bit more.

The next thing you know, I'm wearing headgear and wrestling shoes. I drew the line at putting on the singlet. My BC sweats will suffice. Someone hands me a mouthpiece. I'm standing off to the side of the mat. Across from me is a freshman named Brian. He's a year older than I am but I knew him from junior high. I'm surprised he's on the wrestling team. I never saw him play any sports. He was more the science club type—he was the only one who knew how to use the computer in the school and was always playing Atari or some other video game. I can see he's scared, and not from the prospect of having to wrestle my menacing five-foot-four, 110 pounds of massive destruction, but from the possibility of losing to a kid in junior high. His teammates start to ride him. They're already cheering me on before we start. He has everything to lose. His peers will never let him live it down if I beat him. Then Coach blows the whistle.

Though I might have my dad's wrestling DNA, I have none of his technique. The only thing I know how to do is bridge, which is just fine. I figure if I don't get pinned, everyone will be happy and we can just get out of here. Brian comes toward me and we lock arms and try to maneuver each other to the ground. I can tell right away that he's slower than I am. His attention is on proper form and making sure he's in the right position. While he does that, I slide behind him and grab him by his waist and throw him to the ground. Before Brian realizes it, I have him on his back and Coach is slapping the mat. The small crowd of wrestlers who are watching us let out a unified "Whoa." It's over. Thank god—I can go home. But Coach has something else in mind. He wants me to wrestle a sophomore. Now the crowd of onlookers swells to a dozen or more. I pin the sophomore in less time than it took me to pin Brian.

I should have tried to lose. The third time I'm told to wrestle, it's against a senior named Mark who's expected to follow in the footsteps of his older brother, a state champ. The crowd has now switched sides. It was okay for an eighth grader to beat a couple of guys who aren't on the varsity team this year, but it's not okay for me to beat their captain. He puts his arm on my shoulder and I knock it off. He shoots for my leg, but I pull it away just in time. We lock head-to-head, ear-to-ear, and then both tumble to the ground. I think I might have leverage on him, but we go back and forth for a minute. Now I *know* I have leverage. I can feel his arms getting weak and I'm going to go for it. I grab the arm that's planted on the ground and attempt to collapse it. I hear him giggle. All of a sudden I feel like I'm rolling down a mountain in one of those cartoons. My body parts are being tangled in a way I haven't experienced. I'm still in that full pretzel position when I hear the coach slam his hand on the mat to announce my defeat. It takes me a second to untangle my body.

I never did wrestle again. And, true to his word, my father only brought it up one more time, when I was a freshman in high school. I just shook my head no and he knew. Instead, I played football, which my father told me I was too small to play—a comment that only made me try harder. I wanted to be a star on the biggest stage. I wanted to see my name in the headlines in the local paper, which I would eventually get to do. I was voted MVP and all-conference my senior year. My father never missed one of my games. He even told me I had far exceeded his expectations. I only took one thing from his comment: his expectations for me were way too low.

When our station wagon pulls into our snow-covered driveway, right next to my uncle's Corvette, I jump out and run to go see Tucker. My father grabs the shovel to finish the rest of the driveway. As I reach the house I can already hear the dig, scoop, toss. Dig, scoop, toss.

JANUARY 1994
KENNEBUNK, MAINE

TEN YEARS on, same driveway, same amount of snow. The Green Machine has been replaced by a red '87 Ford Explorer. My father buys a car every decade or 200,000 miles. He also repainted the house, but with the same colors. The last of the U-Haul is packed. I look at the giant lobster on the side of it and the script *America's Moving Adventure—MAINE*. I glance at my best friend, Jayme, who's talking to my parents. We're both five-foot-nine, dark hair, unshaven. Our skin is pasty white from the winter months, and we both wear jeans, baseball hats, and J.Crew jackets. We'll be perfect roommates. He's already moved most of his stuff, but he came up to make the drive with me.

My journalism adviser from Ohio University had called me six months after graduation. He told me if I want to work in New York, I have to be in New York. In the month of December I'd sent over thirty blind résumés and cover letters to newspapers, magazines, and public relations firms. Getting zero responses, I decided to knock on doors. The U-Haul is ready to go. My mother gives me a hug that makes me feel like I'm going off to war. My father reaches out his cold hand to give me a handshake. His technique is perfect, firm and solid, while he looks directly into my eyes, exactly how he taught me.

"Good luck," he says. If there was ever an opportunity to hug my father for the first time, it's now. I'm sure he hugged me as a child, but I don't remember. He should hug *me,* I think. I release from his handshake to break the awkward moment. We're off.

It's still snowing. Ten hours later we're done moving my stuff into the apartment on Eighty-Fifth and Columbus. There'll be three of us living here. A friend of a friend of Jayme's named John, who is a banking analyst and works eighty hours a week, is getting the large bedroom. Jayme has dibs on the smaller bedroom. And I'm going to sleep on a couch in the room that connects the small bedroom with the living room. My rent is four hundred dollars a month. The wood floors and white walls look nice—it's just small. This is going to work, I think. Tomorrow I'll get a job.

I can't even get past the front lobby. Apparently *Sports Illustrated* doesn't appreciate unannounced guests. The security guard squints his eyes and leans in closer when I tell him I want to go up and introduce myself. "No, I don't have an appointment," I admit. "I just want to drop off my résumé and see if I can talk to someone."

"Mail it," the guy says.

When I get home I decide to make some phone calls. I figure if I'm going to call a public relations firm I should ask to speak with the president. No one calls me back, ever. After weeks of this activity, I find myself in a headhunter's office. I've heard the word "temp" used several times while sitting next to her desk. It's depressing. The office is old. The walls are dirty and the carpets are stained. Four women, each with a smoker's hack, sit at their desks hidden behind stacks and stacks of paper. Darlene, who has high hair and wears a purple pants suit, tells me to follow her. She's the one I booked the appointment with from the ad in the newspaper. She leads me to a small empty desk with a typewriter.

"Here," she says with a flick of a piece of paper. "You have one minute to type."

I look at the page; it's a few paragraphs about some guy named Bobby who wants to buy a new car. When I spoke to Darlene on the phone she didn't mention anything about a typing test. I roll a blank piece of paper into the typewriter. I neatly place the story about Bobby on what resembles a music stand. Darlene stares at her watch.

"Go!" she shouts.

I took a typing class my freshman year in high school, and as a journalism major I typed in college, but I was never fast. And I'm rusty. I begin slowly. I figure it's better to not make any mistakes than to try to rush. I finish the first sentence and give it a once-over to make sure there are no mistakes. *Fuck.* I put a space between *dealer* and *ship*.

"Time," Darlene says behind my back.

"Are you serious?" I say. It was the fastest minute in all of my twenty-four years. She takes one look at my one sentence and tells me I failed. I glance up at her with puppy-dog eyes, the same expression that usually works on my mom.

"Sorry," she says without a single drop of compassion. "Can't help ya."

She doesn't even walk me to the elevator, but instead slinks back to her desk and sits behind her stacks. I grab my coat and leave.

I'm sitting in the apartment alone. Jayme and our other roommate, John, are at work. I stopped by the Gap on my way home and got an application. At least they were friendly there. I decide to file it away in my closet. I don't want my roommates seeing it, and I don't want to work at the Gap. But I need a job. I pick up the phone to call my mom for some comforting, and she suggests I call her brother for guidance. I've only seen Uncle Tucker twice in ten years, both times at my sisters' weddings. All I know is, he moved to San Francisco with his second wife. He still works in finance. He shaved his mustache and traded in the Corvette for a navy blue Mercedes 560 SL that he calls the Boesky Benz. He named the car after his biggest client, Ivan Boesky, who was at least partly the inspiration for *Wall Street*'s Gordon Gekko. Because of Uncle Tucker, the Wall Street world has always seemed magical to me. But the idea of working there has never even entered my mind. He must know successful, influential people, even in the world of journalism. I jot down his number and say goodbye.

Tucker answers the phone on the first ring. "Trading," he says. I tell him it's his nephew Turney and he's surprised but happy to hear from me. He waits for me to speak. I haven't planned what I'm going to say. My throat is dry and my brain feels empty. I try to get my words out, and somewhere in between all of my *um*s, *ah*s, and dead silence, I manage to tell him I need help finding a job.

"Gotcha," he says.

I try to elaborate, but I keep repeating myself.

"Call you back in ten," he says before I'm able to tell him what kind of a job I'm looking for. I set the phone down and sit on the couch also known as my bed. Twenty minutes later the phone rings. "You have ten interviews this week," he says.

"For what?" I ask.

"Just tell them you want to get into sales," he says.

When Jayme gets home from his paralegal job I tell him about the lead from my uncle. As we sit on the couch eating a pizza, Jayme tells me about Dave, his college friend from BC whom I remember from my visits there. "Dude, he got a call to interview at Goldman Sachs," Jayme says, and his words hang in the air while he waits for my response. But I have no idea what Goldman Sachs is. It sounds like a fancy department store.

"Is he gonna work there?" I ask.

"Nah," Jayme says, wagging his head. "Blew it off. He's movin' to Prague to try to play professional basketball." Good for him, I think. Better than selling ladies' perfume.

A few days later I'm wearing my Filene's Basement suit and standing in front of Three World Financial Center. Behind me, the Twin Towers soar to the sky. It's 8:45 a.m., and a stream of suits file past. I muster my courage and push through the door. The guard at the front desk calls my contact and directs me to take the elevator to the eighth floor. There, the receptionist smiles and shows me to a windowed room filled with sleek modern furniture and tables strewn with *Wall Street Journals* and financial magazines. I decline her offer of something to drink and sit on the edge of one of the stainless steel and leather chairs. Five minutes later, a man in his early forties, short but fit, with a receding but still black hairline, walks into the waiting room. He wears dark suit pants and a white dress shirt with the sleeves rolled up. His tie is loose around his collar, like he's been at work for hours.

"Mike Breheny," he says pumping my hand.

Apparently already super caffeinated, he begins to talk a mile a minute. He has a New York or Jersey accent, which along with a quick delivery makes him a little hard to understand. I think he's telling me something about the history of Lehman Brothers, and then he asks me what I'm interested in doing.

"Sales," I say. "I want to get into sales."

I'm sure my uncle must have left something out. But it seems enough of an answer for Mike. He nods and takes me out to a big, open room lined with long desks on which sit computer screens and telephones. On the trading floor, there are maybe a hundred mostly young men, all of them talking, either on the phone or to one another. The energy they emit is kinetic. My heart, already beating quickly, begins to thump in my chest. Mike leads me down one of the aisles and seats me between two young traders.

"Get a sense of what we do here," he says, patting me on the back. Although I've only known Mike for a few minutes, I don't want him to leave. But one of the traders allays my fear with a friendly smile.

"Where'd you go to school?" The young, sharply dressed trader has the phone receiver cradled in the crook of his neck as he looks at me. "Ohio," I answer as he punches the lit-up button on the phone and barks something about needing a look in Bristol Myers. "When didya graduate?" I feel like I'm intruding, but somehow he's able to carry on both conversations simultaneously and seemingly with equal interest. All of a sudden, he bolts straight up from his chair. "Bristol's opening at fourteen and a half on two fifty," he yells over to another coworker some twenty feet away. I have no idea what just happened, but I love it.

Once the opening bell rings, it's controlled chaos. Everyone is screaming, punching tickers into the keyboard. A trader in his chair rolls down the aisle and ducks to avoid a phone cord that stretches twenty feet. Crumpled balls of paper are shot into wastebaskets. Everyone commands attention: Some stand and some sit. Some have phones on one ear and then both while shouting across the room to their coworkers. The frenzy of movement seems as well choreographed as a fight scene in *West Side Story*.

A few minutes later, the young trader plugs in a phone for me and tells me to listen in to his conversations. "When I hit the light, you hit yours," he says. One right after the other, he calls clients, the floor of the New York Stock Exchange, and other traders. I understand none of it. It's like he's talking in code and at light speed. But in the midst of this litany, one call has a slightly different tone than the rest. The guy talking on the other end is saying something about plane tickets and hotel reservations in Vegas. A plan for a bachelor party is apparently in the works. Midway through the conversation, the young trader realizes I'm still monitoring his line. He holds his hand over the receiver. "Um, you don't need to listen to this one," he says. As he talks with his friend I look around. I see a pool of people I want to be with. I'm swept up by the energy, intensity, and utter grandness of it all. I want in.

I'm pulled from my thoughts by Mike. He walks me over to meet the big boss, a fellow named Donald Crooks, who glad-hands me and asks a quick battery of questions: What school did I go to? Did I play football? What he doesn't ask is anything that might indicate if I'm right for the job. In fact, I don't remember, in any of my Wall Street interviews, being asked a question that might qualify me for a job in finance.

My next eight interviews at such firms as Merrill, KBW, Jefferies, Smith Barney, and UBS are more of the same. All feature modern reception rooms and shirtsleeved managers. All have the energy Lehman had. But each interview seems perfunctory. The fast-talking guys Uncle Tucker steered me to take my résumé and tell me to keep in touch.

Then I'm at Morgan Stanley on the thirty-third floor, the trading floor. I'm almost at the point when the manager takes my résumé and tells me to keep in touch when the phone on his desk rings. "There's someone on thirty-seven who wants to meet you," he says.

She introduces herself as Stephanie Whittier. She might be forty, but if she is, it's a nice forty. With raven hair and a figure that fills the dark business suit she wears, she looks a bit like Demi Moore circa *A Few Good Men*. We get on the elevator and go up four floors.

"I love Tucker," she says. "We go way back." As she walks me to her office we make the usual small talk. Her desk is clean. She has stacks of folders, but they are in perfect order. She has a few items on her desk—a rubber-band ball the size of a grapefruit, a yellow smiley face stress ball, and some chopsticks. I also notice a photo of her and O. J. Simpson—standing on the trading floor, it appears. Out of exactly nowhere she mentions she missed the previous night's episode of *Melrose Place*. Conveniently, *Melrose* is a guilty pleasure of mine. I saw the show, so I tell her about Sydney's ploy to hire a prostitute to seduce Robert and how she videotaped the whole thing and how Michael mailed the videotape to Jane—crazy stuff. Stephanie thumps the desk with her hand.

"No way," she says.

I nailed it.

Twenty minutes or so later, she tells me she has two stacks of résumés for the job she's going to fill. "One's this high," she says, holding her hand a few feet over her desk. "And the other's this high," she says, lowering her hand to a couple of inches. Then she smiles and says: "You're in the second one." Twenty-four hours later, she calls and offers me a job.

It's a few days before my first day on the job and I decide to take a walk instead of going back to my apartment. I happen to have twenty-two dollars in my pocket, a fortune! I start walking west over to Amsterdam Avenue. I think there's a movie theater on Eighty-Sixth and Broadway. When I'm alone I love to escape. There's nothing better than spending two hours staring at a screen getting lost in someone else's world. I prefer a thriller, but I'll see any movie. When I get to Amsterdam, I see a bar. There, in front of a saloon called the Raccoon

Lodge, is a sign that announces draft beers $2, ALL DAY. I pull out my money and do some quick math: eleven beers without tipping, and approximately eight to nine beers with tipping. I allow the magnetic pull of the Raccoon Lodge to gently tug me. I've also found that a few beers help me escape and are usually better than a movie. The first beers taste like dirty bathwater, but the third and fourth taste just fine. Just around then, I notice a middle-aged man looking at me from the end of the bar. He has on a brown suit that has had one too many trips to the dry cleaner. It shines like a new penny. He's also wearing an ugly, pastel-colored tie and sneakers. He's obviously had a few. He sees me looking at him and I quickly look away. But I'm too late. He picks up his draft and slides it down to the stool next to me. He throws his Marlboro Reds on the bar in front of me.

"Have one," he says.

"I don't smoke," I say.

"You don't smoke?" he asks. I shake my head. "Live in this city long enough and you will," he says.

If he'd approached me during my first beer I would have turned my back. But after four beers, I'm feeling rounded at the edges. He looks like a Larry, I think. He has a lopsided grin and his hair sticks out on the sides of his head. He asks me where I'm from.

"Born in Cleveland, but grew up in Maine," I say.

"Maine!" he says, rolling his eyes. I sit quietly, expecting him to tell me why my home state warrants such an animated reaction, but no explanation comes. Instead he asks me how old I am. When I tell him, he just shakes his head at the injustice of anyone being twenty-four years old. Finally, he asks what I do for work.

"I'm starting at Morgan Stanley next week," I tell him. "It's my first job."

"Whoa!" he says with a whistle. "The bigtime! You must be some kind of genius or related to someone." Larry lights another butt. "Listen to me, kid," he says. "I used to work at a place called Sands Brothers—ever heard of them?"

"No," I say as I take a pull on my beer. "I really don't know much about Wall Street."

"They're a piece of shit, that's what they are," he says. "They fucked me." Larry flicks the ash off the cigarette onto the floor and then takes a drag. "I got some advice for you, kid." His words come on a carpet of white smoke. "There are three things you need to always remember if you're gonna make it in this business." Watching Larry is like viewing bad television. I really want to turn the channel, but there's something about him that holds my attention. I nod my head ever so slightly. "First, always, and I mean always, work the day after Thanksgiving. It's only half a day and it makes you look like a hero." I signal the bartender for another beer. I can feel Larry's stare boring in on me. He leans in close. "Second," he says in a smoky whisper, "you need to get in with all the ten-five-Ws."

"The what?" I say, afraid to ask.

"The Eskimos," he says. I'm really confused. "Keep 'em close—they run the business. Sure, the Merrills, Morgans, and Montgomerys are all stacked with guys like you and me." I look at him and wonder what he means by guys like me and him. I'm nothing like him. "But who do you think is in upper management, who's pulling all the strings? It's the ten-five-W's."

"Ten-five-what?" I ask.

"What's the tenth letter in the alphabet? The fifth letter in the alphabet?" I use my fingers to count out the letters, J and E. *Jews?* I grew up in a town without any Jewish or black people. The only thing we knew about racism was what we saw in the movies. I drink what's left of the beer in front of me, pick up all but two bucks of my cash. As I turn to go, I feel his hand on my shoulder.

"Wait," he says. "I didn't tell you the third thing." I turn back and look at him. His eyes are rheumy, his teeth are crooked and the color of a school bus. He pulls on his cigarette so hard that his cheeks sink. "Attach yourself to revenue," he says while pointing his cigarette at me. "If you do that, then nobody can touch you." He exhales and disappears behind the billow of smoke. "It's that simple," he says. I escape to the street and try to figure out which direction the movie theater is.

FEBRUARY 1994

THERE'S ONE empty chair. Conference room A is on the inside of the building so there are no windows. Seven women and two men, all of whom are, more or less, my age, are already seated around the sleek oval table with comfy black chairs. The women all look attractive and alert. Most have notebooks out and pens uncapped. The two other men in the room seem a little bit more relaxed. They're dressed just like me, in bargain suits and ties. I take the empty chair and look up at Stephanie. The smile I remember from my interview is gone. She looks stern, almost angry. She allows the silence to settle in the air. It cues the two other guys to sit up a little straighter and focus on our boss. "Welcome to Private Client Services," she says. My uncle told me PCS is as close to the trading desk as I can get. These brokers manage high-net-worth individuals' money instead of institutions. They are re-tail brokers, but their client lists aren't your mom-and-pops down the street. They only manage money for people with ten, twenty, thirty million plus. "I know a few of you have already been at Morgan Stanley for a couple of weeks now and some of you"—she looks directly at me—"are starting today."

She begins to walk around the room. "It's my job to train and develop you into the best sales assistants on the planet." She stops for a moment and begins to laugh. "It's also my job to make sure you don't cry." I look around to see if anyone else is laughing but no one is. She's serious again—it's like she has an on-off laugh switch. She continues her slow circle around us.

"Do you know how long I've worked at this firm?" she asks. She's looking directly at one of the other guys. "Twenty years. Wanna know why I've worked here for twenty years? I'll tell you why . . . because there's Morgan Stanley and then everybody else." It's as though she's channeling the voice of Henry Morgan or Harry Stanley: "You only get to leave Morgan Stanley once."

She takes a moment to let her words soak in. I notice a couple of the women are writing this down in their notebooks. I don't think I belong here. I want to be on the trading floor, where it seems like a bunch of guys having a good time. This is serious. She starts to walk again. I feel like I'm in some kind of sinister game of duck, duck, goose. "Most of you are going to be floaters," she says. She is now standing right behind me. "Last year's MBA training program was our largest yet, and they'll be looking for sales assistants soon. Some of you will find positions and the rest of you will find the door." I feel like she might tap me on the head at any moment. "So when you're floating, you have to prove your worth to these brokers. They'll be the ones deciding whether they want you as their assistant or not."

For the next five minutes, Stephanie explains that we need to pass two tests, the Series 7 and the Series 63, learn how to use the phones and computers, read research, and also introduce ourselves to the people in the mail room and back office. I try to absorb everything she's saying, but I don't feel like a sponge. I look over at the two other guys and they seem confident, even arrogant. They don't look anything like I feel. The seed that maybe I'm not cut out for this starts to grow roots.

It's our turn to introduce ourselves. And as each of my new coworkers does, the group starts to sound like a *Who's Who* of the talented and gifted and their alma maters like a *Princeton Review* top ten colleges list. Duke, Stanford, and Harvard all get mentioned. I've never felt embarrassed by where I went to school. I love Ohio University. I think it's the greatest college in the world. But when I say, "I'm Turney Duff, from Kennebunk, Maine, and I attended Ohio University," the guy on the end, from the University of Virginia, yells out, "Buckeyes!"

"Ohio University, not Ohio State," I say.

"It's Miami of Ohio," someone else interjects, but they're wrong too.

"In Athens," I say. "Bobcats? Green and white?"

Everyone is looking at me with a perplexed expression. My moment in the spotlight now feels like a police flashlight shining in my eyes. I hope to salvage it in part two of "getting to know each other," which involves offering an interesting comment about ourselves. "I like to write," I say. I think the group will find that nugget at least as interesting as the compost volunteered by my peers: high school yearbook superlatives, favorite pets, and the kiss-ass from Virginia telling Stephanie he likes to trade stocks in his own account. But instead my comment sits there, a non sequitur, like a meatball on an ice cream sundae. I can feel the perspiration gathering on my forehead. Stephanie smiles, but I can't tell if it's out of compassion or if she's enjoying my discomfort.

"Come on, everybody," she says as she turns to lead us out the door. "Let me show you where the cafeteria is." I fall in toward the back of the group close to the girl from Duke.

"What's a floater?" I whisper to her.

The office is as wide as a city block and the length of a football field. All of the brokers and assistants sit out in the open. The desks are arranged in clusters of six, and they line the whole floor. Every desk looks the same, with a computer screen, a phone, an inbox and outbox mail holder, and a keyboard, along with family photos, cute sayings, and memorabilia. At any one time, there are two to three hundred people on the floor. For the most part it's men in their thirties and forties, and women in their twenties. Offices, occupied by men in their fifties with very serious looks on their faces, ring the floor.

Floaters, I find out, come to work every day and get placed with any group missing an assistant or a group that might be looking for an assistant. We report to Stephanie's office first thing and she finds a place or a need for our services that day. It's just a little better than being a temp. The idea is, after moving around for a while, eventually a broker or a team of brokers will like you and ask you to join their group.

On my second day, I'm asked to send an eighteen-page fax of bond prices to a broker's client, which I do. But the client calls the broker and tells him he didn't receive it. I resend it. This time the client calls and says he has thirty-six blank fax pages—I'd put them all in upside down. The broker doesn't talk to me for the rest of the day. A few days later they have me answering phones for another group. The system works like this: The phone rings and I pick it up. Then I write down the information that's coming from the trading floor, then stand up and yell it to the two brokers and three assistants sitting behind me. It's only a little more advanced than two soup cans and a string, but this is 1994 and that's how it's done. The first time the phone rings I pick it up and the voice on the other end begins to rattle something off. I try to scribble it down as fast as I can. Before I know it, they've hung up. I look down at the piece of paper I've written on. It says: *Fred Governor rhetoric is dubbish.* What am I supposed to do with this? I feel ill. The brokers and assistants are all looking at me; I pretend to still be writing so I don't have to look back at them. But I know I have to face them sooner or later, so I stand and hold the paper like I'm about to recite a poem. "Fred Governor," I say with as much courage as I can muster. "Rhetoric is dubbish." There is a collective pause. Then the group busts into a roar. I try to laugh with them, but my face feels hot and I know it's as red as a stop sign. Finally, the head assistant walks up to my desk.

"I think they might have said, 'The Fed governor is dovish,'" she says, trying to keep a straight face. "But I could be wrong."

My days, weeks, then months as a floater become one of those montages in romantic comedies, the ones where you see the protagonist go on bad date after bad date: there's the crazy broker who randomly shouts profanities at nobody; the team of brokers who want a hot chick as their assistant and not a dude; the Latin American brokers whose clients don't speak English; the female broker who hates me and anyone with a penis; the broker who is getting a divorce and cries all day (he wants me to go to dinner with him after work to talk about his ex-wife); the broker who doesn't talk to me and whispers things into the phone because he thinks I might be a Russian spy trying to steal secrets; the broker I'd love to work for, but who already has two assistants. All I want to do is find a team, but as the days go by, it seems like I never will.

My work life would be easier to deal with if the rest of my life was manageable. But it's not. New York City is an even bigger mystery to me. Like, West Broadway isn't the part of Broadway that goes west. There's nothing express about the subway that takes you to the Bronx. Mysteriously, cabdrivers and food delivery guys never have change when all I have is a twenty. The guy without legs outside my subway stop must have used the money I gave him to buy a pair, because he plays basketball down the block. The umbrellas that sell for two bucks when the sun's shining go for ten when it's raining. Nursery schools can be prestigious. You're supposed to say "Happy Holidays," not "Merry Christmas." Doormen don't appreciate candy canes for their year-end tip. Channel 35 has some very interesting late-night programming. Girls in the Meatpacking District who ask me if I want a "date" might not be girls. Bus drivers don't care if you're on the wrong bus. Bars stay open until four a.m. Twenty-Third Street is not downtown.

It takes some time, but by December 1994, things finally start to break my way. First, Stephanie calls me into the conference room. I'm not in trouble, but I still have anxiety. Everybody has anxiety around bonus time. Whether you're in a white shoe firm or a here-today-gone-tomorrow mutual fund, the same scene is replayed countless times on the Street. Your name is called and everybody in the office watches as you march to hear your fate. The walk is like a cross between a bride heading down the aisle and an overmatched challenger heading into the ring—expectation and fear course through your bloodstream. In an otherwise empty conference room, your boss or bosses sit stone-faced. They've worn their best bonus-day outfits, ones that are always somber and conservative. Though it's Christmastime—I mean holiday time—they pretend there's nothing festive in what's about to happen.

Stephanie tells me the firm is giving me a two-thousand-dollar bonus and then asks if I'm happy. I try to smile, but all of a sudden it's hard for me to catch my breath. The emotion of the moment hits me all at once. Two grand is a big deal. I wag my head back and forth, trying to get the word "Thanks" out. It must look to her like I'm shrugging her off, because she says, "How about three?" so quickly that it takes the rest of the air out of my lungs. In looking back, I've often thought I might have gotten ten if I choked to death. Later that same day I'm in the mail room with all of the other floaters. When we start comparing bonuses, which I later find out is a no-no, I realize I'm the only one who got the extra grand. From now on I'll shrug at every bonus I'm ever offered.

A few months later, I get a bigger break. Stephanie wants me in her office. When I walk in, two brokers, Andy and Josh, with whom I'd floated for a couple of weeks, are already seated. Andy has a florid face and he wears thick glasses. He's never afraid to tell you that he comes from money:

"Hey, Andy, how was the Knicks game last night?"

"Oh, it was good. On my way to the Garden before tip-off I had my driver stop by my apartment on Park Avenue to pick up my floor seats," he might say.

Josh is olive-skinned and wears similar glasses. He's almost too nice for Wall Street. Andy takes advantage of Josh's gentle demeanor. But together, they're the golden boys of the firm. They get the hottest leads, the best allocations, and all the resources they need. "We'd like to offer Turney a position with our team," Andy tells Stephanie.

Sometime in the mid-1990s, high-net-worth departments, like Morgan Stanley's Private Client Services, underwent a seminal shift in their approach. It used to be that these brokers primarily helped their clients trade. Brokers were instructed to generate revenue by commission trades. The new model is to gather "assets under management," using the heft of $10, $20, even $100 million parcels in investments and charge a fee to manage the money. Although individual client trading still makes up a fair percentage of the business, assets under management is where the big money lies. Andy and Josh want to focus on pounding the pavement and raising more capital to collect their management fees. But they still need someone to be in the office trading for clients. Actually, it's more Andy's offer. He's the alpha dog of the team, a guy's guy, and in me he sees a potential protégé. When he tells me they want me for the position, my pulse races. I think back to my first interview and the trading floor at Lehman Brothers. Although it won't be nearly the same, I *will* be trading.

But maybe more important to me is that the permanent position comes with a raise. Fifty thousand. Twice what I was making as a floater. This is life-changing money. No longer will I need to borrow money from Jayme every other Thursday to buy a subway token to get to work. Maybe I'll even start taking a cab. What a luxury! Sleeping in an extra twenty minutes, never worrying about a service shutdown, not standing all the way to work, no one stepping on my feet. Maybe I'll buy a new suit at Brooks Brothers over the weekend. And on Monday I'll be holding a Dr Pepper and a *Wall Street Journal* I pick up at the newsstand. I'll tell the cabbie the address of my office and sit back and enjoy the ride. I feel like I have a career.

My desk—I can call it that now—is next to Andy's. All of the desks are clustered together, including those that belong to Gail and Michelle, the other two assistants. A mother of two, Gail has poofy brown hair and rosy cheeks and knows the ropes—and all the gossip. She's been with the firm for years. Michelle is my age and hot (though she goes out of her way, with frumpy outfits and thick glasses, to hide it). She's also frighteningly smart and the most detailed-oriented person I've ever met. I'm sure I'll get along with both of them. Josh and Andy seem excited to have me on their team and couldn't be nicer. Then the opening bell rings.

Andy starts reeling off numbers to me: "ITG, I bought fifty at a half, twenty-five at five-eighths, and twenty-five at three-quarters. I need my average," he says. I don't even have a pen in my hand. What? He can tell I'm struggling, so he says it again but only faster. Michelle, who watches the scene unfold out of the corner of her eye, starts jotting something down on a piece of paper. I'm still trying to remember what Andy said when Michelle hands me the note. It reads: "50k at a half, 25k at 5/8 and 25k at 3/4" in perfect penmanship. I'm still not sure what to do with it. I start to multiply 50k times .50 and then I multiply 25k times .75, but I'm not sure what five-eighths is. I start to divide eight by five to figure out what the decimal is. Andy yells over, "I need my average now." Michelle hands me another note with the answer on it while I'm still doing long division.

That night at home I wonder what it would be like to go back to Kennebunk and put my application in for a job as the high school football coach. It's not a pretty thought, but it's safe. I'm not about to quit, though. I've never quit anything in my life. Or at least at anything I wanted to do. Maybe it's the thought of going back to Kennebunk High that gives me the idea. I make a cheat sheet of the fractions and decimal points, which I plan to tape into my desk drawer at work in the morning. It's funny. In school, I thought fractions were meaningless, and here they're the most important thing in my life. If I'd known I was going to be in this position I'd have paid more attention in math.

It takes time, but each day I get a little better, and in six months I'm able to spit an average out to Josh and Andy without looking at my cheat sheet. I'm as fast at my job as any of the assistants—well, maybe not Michelle.

By 1995, in my second year at Morgan Stanley, the biggest change in doing business has occurred. The Internet is now on everyone's computer, and it brings with it both opportunity and fear. The world around us begins to speed up; trades that used to take five days are settled in three. The upside is that the advent of technology and email levels the playing field for someone like me, and maybe even gives me an advantage.

Now I type emails to fix problems. Maybe having my fingers on the keyboard awakens my dormant writer's imagination, but having a way with words can come in handy. For example, there's something called a "cancel and correct" form, which we use when we have to fix an error on a trade. If you have to rebook more than three trades a month, the back office, the operations guys, will charge fifty bucks for each subsequent ticket. Andy and Josh get upset with me every month we get charged, because it's my fault. One day, when I'm emailing a fourth cancel and correct form, I put "Personal Ads" in the subject line. Then I type, "Single White Male sales assistant with an athletic build looking for an operations guy who can help me with my cancel and correct. Must also enjoy gourmet cooking, movies, and long walks on the beach." The response from the back office comes immediately. They don't charge us for the cancel and correct. Right then, I begin to realize that social skills might be as important on Wall Street as an Ivy League MBA.

Though things get better in PCS, three years somehow pass and still there's no sign of a job on the trading floor. I go over to the floor once or twice a month, just to say hello and hang around a bit. I want them to know who I am. That way, if a job opens up maybe they'll think of me. I want to be around the Uncle Tuckers of the Wall Street world; I don't want to become like Andy. The trading floor isn't stiff like PCS. It's glamorous, flashy, filled with young guys my age. Though I do *some* trading, most of the work I do is administrative. I decide to ask Stephanie for help.

When I lightly rap on her office door, the door I'm already standing inside of, she greets me with a terse "What?" Stephanie is, as usual, wearing a black suit. If she ever had to go to a last-minute funeral, she'd be all set. She tries to smile but seems annoyed that I'm in her office.

"I just wanted to check in with you. I'm into my third year and I always thought the plan was for me to get a job on the trading floor." She stands up and moves by me to close her door.

"It's not my job to find you a new job," she says. I feel a rush of blood to my face. "If you don't want to be here I have hundreds of résumés to choose from to hire someone else."

"I'm grateful for my job," I say. "I'm sorry. Just . . ."

"Just what?" she asks. "Just wave my magic wand and create a million-dollar trading job for you? Do it on your own." I need to do damage control. I tell her I understand. "You have to make a difference," she says, calming down just a little bit. "Opportunities aren't given, they're made." Though her statement sounds like something stitched on a pillow, she seems very proud of it. I sense an opportunity for a semi-dignified exit. I have to show her I'm a team player—she likes toughness.

"You're right," I say. "Thank you for the words of encouragement." I get up to leave her office and open the door. "Would you like me to leave this open or close it?" I ask.

"Leave it open," she says.

I'm a few steps outside her office when she says, "Go make friends with Matt DeSalvo or David Slaine. Buy them a drink." She follows this with a cackle. "That'll show 'em."

The idea of chumming around with DeSalvo or Slaine hadn't entered my mind. As managing directors on the trading desk, they exist at a level far above the social circles with which I'm familiar.

JULY 1996

I'M SURROUNDED by women. The bar Cite is across the street from our office and is a favorite. I've only recently begun going out after work with my peers. I'm not really all that comfortable with the suit-and-tie Wall Street hangouts. Give me a pair of jeans and a sawdust floor any day. Cite is primarily a restaurant, and, I must admit, with the curved bar and intimate space, the place has its merits. The wineglasses are gigantic and bartenders pour heavy. On a typical night at Cite, pronounced "sit-tay," as in "par-tay," there are ten to fifteen women from our floor at the bar and five to ten men from the trading floor. The spot isn't a secret. Many a six-hour love story has started here.

I'm standing at the bar next to Drea and Keryn. They both run the syndicate desk on our floor. Drea is short for Andrea. She has piercing blue eyes and a tiny gap between her front teeth, which on her is very sexy. She's almost as naïve as I am. She sees the good in everyone. I love hanging out with her. We giggle all the time. Her assistant is Keryn, whose eyes are even bluer than Drea's. She has a deep tan and jet black hair. Guys are drawn to her like mosquitoes to a bug zapper. And on this night her voltage is on high.

Just down the crowded bar a few stools sits Dave Slaine. Everyone on Wall Street knows him. Six feet tall and muscle-bound, Slaine has the body of a professional football player. But his wispy brown hair gives him an almost boyish appearance. Don't be fooled. His hair-trigger temper is legendary on the floor. He's the head of the over-the-counter desk; he runs the entire trading operation. When he's angry, which seems like most of the time, he talks to people in grunts. If a trade doesn't go his way, you can practically see the steam come out of his ears. There's a story often told about Slaine that has several versions. Whether it was that he was eating french fries and someone kept bothering him for them, or that someone wouldn't give him any of the fries they were eating, or that he just got mad at the computer terminal really doesn't matter. All of the versions end in the same way, with him ripping the keyboard out of the computer and flinging it across the room. Dave scares me. He scares just about everybody. But when Keryn calls him over, I remember Stephanie's stitched-pillow suggestion.

Slaine buzzes over to Keryn. When she introduces me, he does a kind of a sideways nod in my direction without taking his eyes off her. I've met him before, not that he'd remember. I sit on my stool waiting for my chance to make a comment or add to the conversation. I know I have to do something, or say something. I chug my drink.

Down the bar, I see my coworkers Heather and Nora, both of whom are just as attractive as Drea and Keryn. Heather is the blond rebel cheerleader type—anything goes. Nora has the Latin-infused exotic look. I wave them over. One of the advantages of growing up with older sisters is that I know how to connect with females. It just comes naturally. I know just about every woman who works in PCS. I know where they grew up, their boyfriend's name (if they have one), and how to make them smile. That they all happen to be beautiful says more about Wall Street's hiring practices than any selectiveness on my part.

"This is Dave," I say to Heather and Nora. And just like that, Dave and I are surrounded by some of the most beautiful women in the bar.

"You guys need a drink?" I ask. I can feel the group's attention on me. Even Dave has begun to realize I'm standing next to him. "Heather wants a boob job," I say. "Dave, what do ya think?" Heather playfully slaps me on the shoulder, then sticks out her friendly B-cups with a smile. Dave has one of those slack-jaw, I-can't-believe-this-guy-just-said-that expressions. But his eyes are wide and twinkling. I can feel my stock rise. I chug more.

"They look great to me," he says.

Heather chimes right in. "I'm thinking D-cups," she says, holding out what they might look like with her two hands. Everyone laughs. I try to get Drea and Nora to stick out their chests, but they're not having it. I order a round of drinks and call over a couple of other girls from our floor, Angelia, Liz, and then Lauren, an almost six-foot-tall beautiful girl from Texas. I've worked with them for almost three years. It's somewhere around this point that I realize I'm in my element. I feel in total control and at ease. Only in looking back can I see how seminal this moment is. I would never be able to stand out at my job. There I'm out-experienced, out-connected, and out-degreed. But here, with a glass in hand, I have as good a chance as any to move and shake. Maybe even a better chance than most. When someone suggests we hit another bar, I pipe right up.

"Then grab your coats," I say.

Seven of us, Dave and I and five of the seven women with us at the bar, hop in two cabs. I tell the driver the address: Tenth Avenue and Seventeenth Street. I'm sure Dave and Keryn can handle the place I have in mind, but the other girls might be a little horrified. It's one of my favorite bars; I go there almost every weekend. Our cab drops us off first. Along with Drea, Lauren, and Keryn, I stand outside a wooden door covered with stickers for bike shops, booze, and gangs. There are no lights on the street corner; the only illumination comes from the neon bar sign. We're on the outskirts of the Meatpacking District. Seventeenth Street is as dark as an alley. We can hear the rumblings of a good time coming from inside the bar. The black banner emblazoned in red with RED ROCK WEST above the windows looks like it may fall down any minute. The girls want to know where I'm taking them.

"You'll see," I say.

A few minutes later, Heather, Nora, and Dave hop out of their cab. As I open the door to the bar, lyrics from a Def Leppard song slam us in the face: "Do you like sugar?" the song asks. "One lump or two!" the crowd of bikers, party girls, and cowboys bellows in response.

The place is packed. The medium-size bar is dark, but glows blues and reds from the neon beer signs. Behind the bar are more stickers, license plates, Harley signs, hula hoops, postcards, lanterns, and bras hanging from a huge mirror. Lots of bras. The air is thick with the smell of stale beer. Two female bartenders dressed in skimpy leather tops and jeans stomp around in their black shit-kicking boots. As the speakers blare "Pour Some Sugar on Me," a girl lies on top of the bar with her shirt pulled up to her neck revealing Victoria's Secret, a pretty pink push-up, while a bartender pours whiskey into her belly button. The head bartender sees me and waves me over. She plants a kiss on my lips, then hops up on the bar, straddles the patron, and sucks the whiskey out of the girl's innie. The crowd is delirious. They raise their Buds, PBRs, and Rolling Rocks as suds fly everywhere. The jukebox is blasting. People are singing. The two female bartenders begin making out as the crowd eggs them on. I order eight longneck Buds and turn to hand them back to my group. The girls stand there, mouths wide open, in absolute disbelief. Dave clinks his longneck to mine.

JUNE 1997

I'M SUMMONED into Stephanie's office. I think I'm in trouble. She looks very stiff, like something's wrong. She tells me to sit down and close the door. I know what I did. I might be fired.

Morgan Stanley recently has had mice problems. We've received several emails reminding us not to leave food on our desks at night. My desk-mate Michelle is terrified of mice. So last week when she went to lunch, I snuck under her desk. It was too tight under there, so I had to slide open the black metal door under her desk to crawl into the area where we hide our computers and all of the phone wires. I barely fit. When Michelle returned from lunch, she kicked off her shoes. I knew it. A perfect pink glossy pedicure. I bet she wears sexy outfits and open-toe high heels on the weekends. I took my index finger and thumb and started giving her little mouse bites on her feet. It was the loudest scream I'd ever heard. She jumped up from her desk screaming. Her lunch flew into the air. This must be why Stephanie called me into her office. Everyone had to have heard the scream.

Stephanie looks like she's shooting arrows from her eyes. She picks up the phone and dials a number. "Hey, John, I just want to confirm what we talked about," she says.

I don't like the sound of this. But as she hangs up, her serious expression melts to a big, shiny white grin. "I want you to plan a party," she says. It takes me a second to realize I'm not in trouble. Meanwhile, Stephanie has begun to go into detail about the morale on the floor, which, she says, is too low. Apparently the department is allocating three grand to boost it.

"I'm in," I tell her. I know how to throw a great party. I majored in it at college. When I get back to my desk I realize Stephanie must have been talking with John Straus on the phone. He's the head of the department, my boss's boss's boss, the very top of the food chain. I don't even think he knows my name. I admire him. He's like a general, but willing to stand on the front line. He's a family man with values. His hints of gray hair show his age and make him look distinguished.

I find a bar near Thirty-Seventh Street and Third Avenue. It has a narrow room with a long wooden bar, exposed brick, and a jukebox. There's really nothing to it, except the huge outdoor space they have in back. After one trip there, two phone calls, and three emails, the entire night is planned. Now all I have to do is to make sure the party is a success. I know both Stephanie and John Straus plan to attend. I don't want to end up looking like a complete failure in front of two of the most important people in the office. I come up with a plan. On a Sunday I call up my high school friend Chris Arena, who moved to the city before I did. He works for the NBA in their main office in Midtown, and he has a computer program in his office I want to use. He meets me at the side entrance of Saint Patrick's Cathedral off Fifth Avenue; his office is across the street. As we make our way through his lobby and into his elevator bank, I explain to him what I have in mind: a newsletter. In Chris's office, I sit in front of his computer looking at the blank screen. I love a blank screen. All I want to do is fill it up.

The whole purpose of my newsletter is to get people excited about the party, but I also want it to be fun to read. The who, what, when, where, why, and how of the party fills the whole first page. I add some cheesy champagne bottles and flying streamers clip art, and also a table of contents—a teaser of what's inside. I know I can't provide any of my coworkers with market knowledge or insight that they don't already know. This has to be straight-up supermarket checkout lit. Water cooler talk. When I realize this, the stories begin to fly out of me. I title the first story "So . . . You Want to Be a Porn Star?" Eight hours later—an interval that goes by in the blink of an eye—I finish the last of the blind items. All that's left is to give the newsletter a name. I write *The Turney Tape* in large, bold font across the top.

I decide to wait until Tuesday to hand it out. I figure my audience should receive it close enough to the party so they won't forget. That morning I wake up an extra thirty minutes early so I can get to the office and make 250 photocopies of *The Turney Tape*. I need to print it on longer paper so it looks like a real newsletter or miniature newspaper. I get the guy in the mail room to show me how to print it. I decide lunch is the best time to distribute them—I don't want them to get buried in the morning research and client requests.

At noon, I look at the stack of newsletters and begin to wonder if this is a huge mistake. There's at least a fifty percent chance I'm coming out of this looking like a joke. What if nobody laughs? When I stand up, my trepidation gets even worse. It would have been hard enough distributing some type of business-related research I'd done. Even that would have left me wide open to snide remarks and criticism. But an office gossip newsletter? What was I thinking?

In front of me stretches the block-long open office. Though most of the brokers and many of the assistants are still working, on the phone or intently studying the computer screens, there's also the first sign of lunchtime on their desks: paper take-out bags and cafeteria salads and sandwiches. I take a deep breath and begin my march. One by one, I hand out copies of *The Turney Tape*. I stop at every desk. It's easier to give them to the sales assistants, because I know them all. The brokers seem a little more skeptical. I guess they assume it's official Morgan Stanley business, information on a new product we're launching or something. But with each copy I hand out I become a bit more emboldened. I tell myself I don't care anymore. I'm doing it.

It's right about this time when I hear the first giggle behind me.

I turn and see an assistant holding the newsletter up, pointing out an article to another person in her group. I watch and confirm that they're both smiling. Then I hear someone from another group laughing. Another laugh comes from a desk a few steps away. Then a broker comes up and asks me for a copy.

Once I finish with all of the brokers, assistants, and back office and portfolio guys, I start to make my way to the windowed offices, the managing directors. I tiptoe into office after office, smile politely, and leave the newsletter on the desk. When I reach the biggest corner office on the entire floor, I peek in. Thankfully it's empty. I'm not sure I'd have the courage to hand John Straus a copy if he were there. I drop the newsletter on his desk and dart out of his office.

As I return to my desk, I turn to look back out on the floor and it seems like everyone is reading it and laughing. That afternoon, I receive a steady stream of assistants and brokers congratulating me. More important, almost all are excited about the party. *The Turney Tape* is a hit.

A little later I hear a familiar voice coming from a few groups away. "Where's Turney?" he says. "Where's Turney's desk?" John Straus has his sleeves rolled up, and his red tie sways as he strides toward me. Though he's still twenty feet or so from me, I can see he's holding a copy of *The Turney Tape*. I quickly turn back to my computer screen. I know he's heading for my desk. I grab one of my pens and start to roll it between my hands. I squint at the screen and pretend to be doing a complex math formula in my head. Then I hear his voice directly behind me. "Turney?" he asks. I turn around and say hey. I can feel hundreds of eyes on me, from all directions. "Have you ever considered doing something other than selling stocks and bonds?" he asks. For a moment I'm not sure if it's a compliment or an insult. I shrug and peer up at him, waiting for my fate. It's then that his face breaks into a huge smile. "This is great," he says. The expression on his face is better than any year-end bonus I've ever gotten.

The turnout for the party is huge. A resounding success. At one point, John Straus walks up and puts his arm around me. He gives me a hug. "So, Turney, where did you grow up?" he asks. I can see Stephanie smiling across the crowd from us. In this moment it comes to me. I just made my first power move.

4

TWO YEARS later, I'm still a sales assistant for Morgan with my
résumé burning in my hands. Some power move. It's been more than
five years since I first sat in the conference room listening to Stephanie
and I'm still working as an assistant.

"I can no longer work for my group," I tell Stephanie. "I have to do
something else." I've lost all hope of becoming a trader at Morgan. She
pulls me into her office and closes the door. There's nothing in Stephanie's office that indicates a life outside of it—no vacation photos or
pictures of family or husband. The picture of her and O.J. disappeared
after the car chase. She's spent twenty-five years at Morgan, and for
most of that time her whole world has been running the assistants'
program. I look into her eyes and can tell she's conflicted. In one sense,
she can't imagine why anyone would want to work anywhere else. But
there's another aspect as well. Though I have no evidence to prove this,
maybe what I see is a secret longing for an escape herself. She scribbles

something on a piece of paper and hands it to me. For a second, both of our hands hold the paper.

"Don't tell anyone I'm doing this for you," she says as she finally lets go. Although I don't know this for sure, I would bet that she has never done this for anyone. On the paper are the names of contacts on the Lehman Brothers and Merrill Lynch trading floors.

Both interviews go fine. But it's obvious they aren't hiring and are just doing a favor for Stephanie. I return to the floor in PCS after my second meeting. I set my file folder filled with my résumés on an empty desk. Stephanie has allowed me to return to floating to free up time to interview, but there's nowhere for me to float today. Then the phone rings. Only Stephanie and the receptionist know I'm at this desk. It must be a wrong number. I answer it with a hello like I'm at home. "Get your ass over here now," the female voice on the other end of the phone says. It has to be a wrong number. I'm just about to say something smart, or hang up, when I hear, "Turney, I'm serious, get over here right now," she says. I realize it's Keryn.

Keryn left Morgan a year ago to go to a start-up hedge fund called the Galleon Group. I haven't had much contact with her since. I heard through the grapevine she's doing really well. Dave Slaine helped her get the job and then went over there himself a few months later. Liz, who worked with all of us at Morgan and then got her big break with Lehman, saw me today at my interview. She called Keryn and told her I was looking for a job. I know nothing about Galleon, and very little about hedge funds. I don't even know what the job is. I ask her if I can come in tomorrow.

"Fine," she says. "Be here tomorrow around lunchtime." She gives me the address and tells me she'll call me tonight at home to go over everything I need to know for the interview.

I'm not sure why Keryn thought of me when the job opened at

Galleon. The last time I was with her was her last day at Morgan. She was saying goodbye to everyone when I walked over to her, smiled, and offered my congratulations. Then I thought I'd be a wise guy and offer to make out with her as a going-away present. She said sure. And right there, in front of forty Wall Street professionals, I felt my manhood shrink. I couldn't do it. Maybe that's why she liked me, why she called me about the job before anyone else. Wall Street is full of ego and bluster. In me she saw something a bit more authentic, like the guy who was too afraid to ask the pretty girl to the senior prom.

A few days after my Galleon interview, the phone rings in my apartment, a four-bedroom in a typical high-rise building on West Sixty-Seventh Street. I've lived here for a couple of years now. The phone rings again. It's Monday afternoon and nobody's home to answer it. The phone sits on a chair that looks like a giant hand with the palm for the seat and the fingers for the back. It keeps ringing. The chair is surrounded by contemporary furniture: a couch, chairs, tables, and lamps. There's a Foosball table and a homemade bar. The place is strewn with remnants left from the weekend—a few empty beer bottles and a pizza box. My roommates and I live in an Alpha Pottery Barn frat house. The ringing stops and the call goes into voice mail. "Nobody can come to the phone, but we'd like to know you called . . . For Turney, press one; for Jason, press two; if you want Jayme, press three; for Ethan, press four; and if you need Johnny, well . . . sorry, there are no voice mails left."

When I get home I check my messages. "Hey, Turney, this is Janine from the Galleon Group," the cheery voice says. "We'd like to offer you the trading position. Please call me back so we can set up a time for you to come in and sign the contract." Later, Janine would tell me she almost reconsidered the offer when she heard how many roommates I had. How could she take me seriously? "Welcome to the buy side," her voice mail says.

SO WHAT'S the buy side? I don't really know the difference between the sell side and the buy side, but I soon learn. Imagine the relationship in biblical terms. Old Testament. If you're on the buy side, you roll into the marketplace with a wagon filled with the pharaoh's gold, charged with buying the best products you can. The pharaoh will compensate you for good purchases. Now, though you have a proprietary relationship with the pharaoh's money, it's not your money, and the only thing you stand to lose is what you might gain. And you stand to gain a lot if your performance is good. Like, the next time you roll into the marketplace your wagon might have custom rims or built-in GPS. But you're not the only wagon of gold. So when you get there you have to be ready. The open market is buzzing. There are merchants everywhere. If you're on the sell side, you want the pharaoh's buyer as your customer. Every merchant wants to get the highest price he can for all of his goods, and they all want to rid themselves of the crap

in their inventory. They want the highest revenues. Competition between the merchants for your attention is great. They need you. Some
of them offer you boat rides down the Nile with a few "mistresses of
the house," or a tomb in the pyramids, or a weekend in Mesopotamia
with some really good lotus. Whatever. But a lot of them are phonies,
and if you end up buying the crap, or paying too much, maybe the
pharaoh doesn't let you drive the wagon next time. Or worse, you
have to go back to being a merchant. If I buy some livestock from the
guy who took me down the Nile on Thursday night and I can sell it
at a profit to the guy I went to Mesopotamia with on Friday, then I'm
going to do it. So in one sense, you need the sell side almost as much
as they need you. On Wall Street the buy side can buy or sell—they're
the customer. The sell side is selling information, research, and customer facilitation.

In the simplest terms, the buy side is the client. The sell side loves
clients.

RAJ RAJARATNAM, Gary Rosenbach, Krishen Sud, and a fourth guy named Ari Arjavalingam (who worked on the West Coast) started Galleon in 1997. They all came from Needham & Company, a small investment bank, where Raj's performance, especially in tech stocks, was making the firm a lot of money. He was also making a lot more money for himself—ten times the profits he made for Needham. When the partner, George Needham, found out, he told Raj, Gary, and the others that they could no longer trade in their personal accounts. It was then that the four of them bolted from Needham to launch the Galleon Group. Their timing was sublime. It coincided with both the technology boom and the emergence of hedge funds. Still, in the early years, they had to scratch and claw for every resource they got, but now, in 1999, Galleon's sails are aligned with the favorable financial wind.

On the day I sign my contract, I meet most of the management team at Galleon, including Krishen, Gary, and Raj, who is on the phone when I'm introduced to him again. I met him briefly when I was interviewing. A delightful bull of a man, with dark skin, thick glasses, and a mustache, he smiles and shakes my hand firmly while cradling the phone between his shoulder and ear. He has a gap between his front teeth, which gives him a friendly appearance. It makes me want to smile. But I also know that the seat of the person I'm taking over for is still warm. From what I was told, she was attractive, smart, and aggressive. There was one problem. She was accumulating losing trades and not booking them into the portfolio. In Galleon's code, this is tantamount to stealing. When she could no longer keep it a secret and the bosses found out, she was fired on the spot. No one lies to or steals from Raj.

Krishen runs the healthcare portfolio. It took me a year to figure out, but in many ways, Krishen is Raj's alter ego. While Raj is Sri Lankan, Krishen grew up in Mumbai, India. Thin, with pleasing features and cinnamon-colored skin, he has a gentle demeanor. Everyone seems to like Krishen, especially investors. Someone once said of his skills at raising capital that he's the type of guy who can walk into a third-grade classroom and leave with all the lunch money. He shakes my hand and with a distinguished smile tells me they're pleased to have me as part of their team. So far, so good. It seems everybody's nice and happy to have me here.

Then I'm reintroduced to Gary on the trading desk. About forty, with a brown receding hairline, he's got on a golf shirt and faded jeans that are a tad too tight. His most distinguishing characteristic is his nasally voice. He smiles and stands up to shake my hand. Welcome aboard, he says. Then he looks me up and down and smirks.

"A hundred and fifty k, huh?"

"I did," I say.

Rosenbach interviewed me, and one of the questions he asked was how much I was making at Morgan Stanley. I told him $150,000. I was only making about $35,000 because I had left my group in PCS and was floating again.

He laughs and tells me I'm a liar but he admires my guts. Either he knows the truth or he's bluffing. Regardless, Gary makes me uneasy. He then begins to give me my job description, words I'll hear over and over for the first six months of my time at Galleon: Never let a phone ring more than once. Take a report. Book the trade into the system. Answer the phones. Take a report. Book the trade into the system. Answer the phones. Take a report. Book the trade into the system. Again, again, again. Recap all the trades at the end of the day. Make sure you confirm, buy or sell, the share amount, price, commission, and the correct account. In the morning make sure there are no trade breaks. No mistakes. When he finally finishes he looks directly into my eyes. "Each day expect to be fired," he says. "If you're not, then you've had a good day."

The terror begins each morning in the shower. The frightening thoughts come one after the other like punches to my solar plexus. Did I book everything correctly yesterday? Did I remember to do everything Gary said last night? Each and every morning, I go to work with a knot in my stomach. It's the same every day.

I'm the first one in the office. The only illumination is from the computer screens that were left on and now radiate screen-saver patterns. I flick on the lights. The new office is huge. It feels as big as a car dealership. The entire floor is outlined with small offices for the analysts. Half of the spaces are empty, but I guess we're planning on expanding. (After my first summer we move to a lower floor with a lot more space. As our assets grow, so does everything else.) The trading desk is past all of the offices except Raj's. It's laid out like the letter T.

There's one long desk against the back wall, where Gary and Keryn sit. Then there's a wider desk that comes out from the middle of the other desk, with room for three traders on each side. I sit in the middle.

I take my seat and begin to check all of our trades from the previous day. I have to make sure there are no errors. I have a bad feeling, but it's the same every day. It's like I'm carrying around a twelve-pound bowling ball. My mom always told me it's okay to make mistakes, but she never worked at a hedge fund. Even though I'm stressed, this time of the morning is still the calmest part of my day. There's no chaos. And no bosses.

But I'm still nervous. Along with checking for trade errors, I have to order breakfast for the bosses and all the traders and have it on their desks by the time they arrive. Their thinking, I guess, is if I can't perfect a breakfast order, how am I going to handle million-dollar buys and sell orders? Getting someone's breakfast order wrong sometimes incurs more wrath than losing money. What they don't realize is, I might say "crispy bacon" when I place the order, but I don't actually cook the bacon. I've become tight with the Hispanic girl at the deli. I stop by now and then just to say hello. *"Cómo estás, mi nombre es Turney, me gusta esquiar."* She laughs at my enunciation. But I don't think she understands the gravity of my situation. The bacon isn't always right.

Twenty minutes later, everyone starts to arrive. Through the door they walk, the same order every day, with the traders leading the way. Keryn's first. Every day it's the same: she carries a cup of coffee, an unread newspaper, and some personal issue from the night before, like a pipe bursting in her apartment or an alien that tried to abduct her. I couldn't make up half of the things that happen to her, and, except perhaps for the alien, all of her stories ring true. Her life is crazy. Todd-o is next. Why they call him that I have no idea—his last name is Harrison. Handsome, with dark hair and eyes, he looks every inch the hotshot options trader he purports to be. Galleon poached him from Morgan Stanley. He sits to my left and the first words out of his mouth always are "Oh man!" I know what comes next. Each one of his stories begins in this manner. They always involve a limo, a chick who stuck her claws into him, and animal sex back at his apartment. I hope he gets laid half as much as he says he does. But I'm not sure why he tries to impress me.

Then comes Dave Slaine, my protector. He's arrived straight from the gym. If I didn't know any better, I'd guess he had shoulder pads underneath his golf shirt. He already knows everything happening in the market before he sits down. I feel safe with Dave sitting to my right. I know I could be fired at any minute, but in Dave I feel like I have at least one advocate. When Gary asks me a question I don't know, Dave usually whispers the answer to me.

And then there's Ruby, who's a Bruce Willis look-alike—the shaved-head version. His real name is Craig. He wears tight designer jeans and open-collar shirts. If Abercrombie and Fitch had a department for forty-year-olds, Ruby would be their best customer. The thing about Ruby is, I don't really know why he's here or what he does exactly. He sits on our trading desk, but he isn't an employee of the firm that I know of. He's a cross between a runaway teen we picked up at the bus stop and a kid from the Fresh Air Fund. He used to be a bouncer at some club like Odeon or Heartbreak, or one of the other eighties nightclubs out of *Bright Lights, Big City*. Some days it seems like he still thinks he's a bouncer or maybe a bodyguard, the way he assesses people who walk through the office door. He's still in bouncer shape. He's a gym rat just like Dave and Gary. But for all the time I work at Galleon, I never really figure Ruby out.

The penultimate arrival is Gary. Raj, the boss, is of course last. But his entrance, despite his hulking frame and swarthy skin, pales in comparison with Gary's. Raj is as sunny as a beauty queen in a homecoming float—rose petals seem to cover his path. When Gary walks in, apprehension fills the office. He's dressed in a Greenwich Country Club golf shirt and jeans. The first thing he does is turn down the thermostat. He likes the temperature a few degrees below comfortable. You never know what you're going to get from him. On this day, he says good morning to Keryn and asks why she didn't call him with where AMD is trading. The wheels start turning in his head a moment before his eyes snap open in the morning. I didn't see AMD on the tape so I didn't even know there was news out. I put my head down and hope to go unnoticed. And I pray that I got his breakfast order right.

But this day is going to be different. Gary's fruit cup and yogurt are fine, but on my terminal, Goldman Sachs is showing that we bought 100,000 shares of IBM yesterday. I booked a sell. This is a problem. A huge problem. I immediately hit the Goldman light and ask our sales trader John. He confirms it was a buy.

"Are you sure?"

Yes, he says. He traded with Gary. So now it means one of two things: either Gary accidentally told me it was a sell order when it was actually a buy, or he told me it was a buy order and I accidentally typed it in as a sell. Either way, it's going to turn out to be my fault. What makes the matter worse is Gary, Dave, and Raj have been basing their trading decisions on the wrong position. We began the day owning 100,000 shares of IBM. If I had booked the 100,000 that Gary said he bought, we should be long 200,000 shares. Instead, our portfolio reads that we're flat. IBM is trading around $130. My mistake, if I made it, is a risk to the firm of $26 million. Chances are, IBM isn't going to zero, but a major fluctuation in the stock could still cost Galleon a lot of money.

My desk is a few feet from Gary's desk, but I decide to get up and walk over. No need for everyone else on the desk to hear what I have to tell him. He's on the phone, and doing three other things, but I interrupt. He sees the expression of dread on my face and immediately knows something's wrong. He lets the phone drop to his shoulder and looks at me with disdain.

"What'd you fuck up this time?" Gary never misses an opportunity to crush me. He's the nine-year-old, and I'm the spider whose legs he relishes pulling off one by one.

I don't have a choice. I have to tell him about the error.

"I just need to know if you bought or sold IBM with Goldman yesterday." It's my last hope. Maybe Goldman fucked up the trade.

"I bought 'em," he says. "You know that, I yelled it over to you." Worry begins to churn in my stomach. This is not good.

"I'm sorry, I, I musta heard you wrong or, or I typed it in wrong," I say.

"So you're fucking telling me we are long a hundred IBM?"

"Actually, two hundred," I say. He looks at the futures to see how the market might open. Last I checked they were down small. He asks Keryn if IBM is trading. She types it into the computer quickly and gives me a sympathetic glance. The last two years she's been dealing with him, but for some reason she can control him better than most.

"There's only a few thousand on the tape," she says, "but I'm sure I can get someone to put me up at last night's close." In other words, she will just call a broker and tell them to put 200,000 shares of IBM on the tape and they will assume the risk. She's trying to help me, but Gary stays livid. He starts shouting about how incompetent I am. He screams over to Raj to tell him the IBM position is off, and then he screams over to Dave to tell him the same thing. He doesn't have to scream it again, but he likes to humiliate me. I start to walk back to my desk.

"Where the fuck are you going?" he asks. "Get back here." He throws what's left of his breakfast in the trash can. I don't know what else to say. I look at him, but I can't hold his stare.

"I'm sorry," I say finally, and start to walk back to my desk again.

"Oh no you don't," he screams. "Stand in the corner! Five minutes!"

I look at Gary and then the corner of the room. I think he's serious. Dave starts to laugh and Keryn and Todd-o are trying not to. Even Gary and Raj are smiling. Gary goes straight-faced again and points to the corner at the other end of the trading desk. I'm not sure what to do. I walk over to the corner. I don't say a word. I face away from the desk about two inches from where the walls connect. I'm almost thirty years old and I'm stuck in the corner like a first grader. I close my eyes. I hear chuckling behind me. I think they're grabbing analysts and assistants from other parts of the office to have them look at me. Maybe Gary did say "buy," but why would I type "sell"? I want to laugh. The idea of an adult professional having to stand in the corner is comical, even if the adult professional is me. Now I have to try to stifle the laugh and pretend I've been humiliated or Gary will think up some other punishment. After two minutes, Dave yells over and tells me he needs me for something. I know he's making up an excuse and I'm thankful. I run back to my desk. He tells me I can't make mistakes. Fifteen minutes later Gary's on the phone belittling a sales trader from Herzog.

I have a better chance of predicting the market than I do Gary's moods. He doles out punishment just for the sake of punishment. It really has nothing to do with my performance or lack thereof. In fact, only a few short weeks after the corner incident, Gary tells me he wants me to start trading on my own. "Trade fives and tens," he says in between bites of perfectly buttered bagel. "And make money." It's that simple. In comparison with the share amounts Galleon is doing, 5,000- and 10,000-share lots are insignificant. Yet, for me, it's a defining moment.

That morning, I wait until ten a.m., when things have slowed down a little. The last message I want to send to the bosses is that I'm too busy trading my 5k lots to perform my daily responsibilities. I decide to buy 5k shares of Microsoft (MSFT). It's liquid, so I can get in and out without any hassle. I have no basis for my buy other than it seems like the other traders on the desk are buying tech stocks today. The market is up small and if techs take off maybe MSFT will too. I book the buy into the system. The stock trades up a quick dime. My chair is adjusted so both of my feet are firmly on the ground. I'm rolled up so close to my desk, it pushes against my stomach. I focus on only MSFT on my computer screen. Each tick upward vibrates in me like the bass beats from a sound system in a club. I want my first trade to be a profit. I'm not sure what to do. It keeps ticking up: .11, .12, .13, .14 . . . I hit the Lazard light and tell Langel, our sales trader, to sell 5k MSFT. "Sold, 5k MSFT forty-five point fourteen," he says. I scalped my first trade. I book the sell order into our system. I made .14 on 5,000 shares! But I paid .06 commission on both sides, on the buy and the sell, so my profit is only .02. The reason we pay brokers .06 a share is for their research, resources, and facilitation. In order to get the kind of service Galleon wants, we have to pay brokers millions of dollars a year. For my personal trades I can't afford to lose so much on commission. I look at our performance screen. I see symbol MSFT— shares 0—profit/loss +$100.00. Woo hoo! A hundred bucks! But it's better than a loss, and now I'm ready for my next trade.

I want to buy QCOM (Qualcomm). I lost all of my profits on

commissions, so I'm going to buy it on the Instinet machine so I only have to pay a .01 commission. I click on the buy button, type "QCOM" on my keyboard, type "10,000," and hit send. I look at my screen; I bought ten, thirteen, twenty, thirty thousand shares. *What's happening?* I keep buying more shares. Up, up, and up. I can't stop it. I look at my 0 button and it's stuck in the down position. The keyboard they gave me was the oldest, crustiest one they had. Oh my god, I just bought 100,000 shares of QCOM. I'm not sure what to do, and then I hear Dave scream, "QCOM being downgraded by Merrill!" He has no idea I bought the stock or that I bought 100k shares of it. The stock is down four points before I even realize what's happening. In a matter of minutes I've lost $400,000. I have no idea what to do. Dave stands up and leans over to my computer screen. "Jesus Christ," he says. He hits the J. P. Morgan direct wire and tells him to sell 100,000 shares of QCOM, on the wire. Meaning it will be done before he hangs up the phone. And as he does he says to me, "You're welcome." The stock is in a free fall. QCOM is down another six quick points, but now the broker is on the hook for the extra $600,000, not us.

Dave calls the broker later to thank him and tell him we owe him one. "You owe me ten," the broker responds. No one says a word to me the rest of the day, but I don't have to stand in the corner, either.

My days at Galleon are difficult. I have no confidence. I'm always looking over my shoulder waiting for a kick to the face for not booking a trade right or not picking up the phones fast enough. When I scope out the room I see brash, overconfident traders who push around anyone on the other end of the phone. Outside the office they appear like everyone else in Midtown, but in the office they have swagger. This seems to be a prerequisite for all buy side traders. I don't think you have to be a bully to succeed in trading, but it sure helps. And on a trading desk filled mostly with bad cops, it's only natural for me to assume the role of good cop. I bend over backwards to help the sales-men who cover us. They're ecstatic when I pick up the phone. It means they aren't going to get a tongue-lashing for whatever trading sin they might have violated, or for merely being born. They always want to take me out to dinner or meet for a drink. Sometimes they even offer to take me to a game or a concert. I get asked at least three to four times a day. I never want to say yes. I'm afraid they'll ask me ques-tions about the market. Questions I can't intelligently answer. They'll realize I'm a fraud and don't belong.

One day Gary tells Keryn, Todd-o, and me to meet him in the conference room after the closing bell. Todd-o appears bored, Keryn is texting someone, and I feel like I might puke. I'm not sure why he wants to talk to us. We wait. Gary saunters in and pulls out the seat at the head of the table. Todd-o is now alert, Keryn's phone is put away, and I can't stand not knowing what the meeting is for. I focus on Gary's lips. I want to anticipate what he might say. "Who've you been out with this month?" Gary asks, primarily looking at Todd-o and Keryn. They respond with a couple of business dinners they've been to. It sounds to me like Keryn is exaggerating, but I know Todd-o goes on some dinners. Then Gary looks at me. The only people I've been out with are Ethan, Jason, and Jayme, and we crushed it at Red Rock West on Saturday. I almost lost an eyebrow from the bartender's fire-breathing stunt, but I know that's not what he's talking about.

"No one," I respond.

He mimics "No one" like a five-year-old. "Play the game," he barks. "Get information." He knocks his hand on the desk a few times as if we were sleeping. "If you guys want to continue working here," he says while wiping the scuffs from his dress shoes, "then you need to start getting some calls." Keryn and Todd-o nod. "I don't mean the great calls we're already getting—I mean new ones." He stands up and adjusts his shirt into his pants and turns for the door. "We have a new requirement here: you have to go on at least two business dinners a week. I want you to write up who you went out with, what you discussed, and how you improved the relationship," he says. Then he leaves. Todd-o follows Gary out of the room; Keryn reaches for her phone to finish texting. I don't want to go out with the sell side.

I guess the reason I agree to grab dinner with John first is because he rarely discusses business. Skinny with a beer belly and goofy, he's not your typical Goldman Sachs employee. He's more like a cartoon character. Whenever he picks up the phone he's usually giggling about a prank he pulled on his desk-mates or telling a fart joke. He cares more about trying to make us laugh than being a sales trader. John is a few years older than I am, but it seems like he's been in the business forever. He's at the bar of the Upper West Side location I picked when I enter. He told me I could pick any restaurant in the city. I want to be close to my apartment. If things go bad I can just run out of the place and go home. Halfway through the first cocktail, I realize he just wants to get to know me. He likes me; he wants to be my friend. He's fun. We order food at the bar. He asks me tons of questions about the guys I work for. He wants the dirt. I'm scared to tell the truth. By the third or fourth cocktail I'm feeling more comfortable and am willing to speak more freely about Galleon. "If I make a mistake," I say, then take a sip of my drink. "Regardless if it cost the firm money or not, they get medieval on my ass."

"That's standard operating procedure," he says as he lights up a cigarette. "Do they hit you?"

I think he's joking. "No." I point at his cigarettes and ask for one with my facial expression. It's not my first one ever, but close.

"Look," he says. "Are they paying you well?"

"Yeah," I say. "I'm not sure what my bonus is going to be, but we're making hundreds of millions of dollars, so I'm hopeful."

"Then don't worry about it," he says.

"I guess," I say. I want to say more. I want to defend my point, but he makes a valid one too. If they're going to pay me a lot of money, they can do whatever they want to me.

"You wanna hit a strip club?" he asks as he takes his last bite of steak.

"No thanks." I stand up and put on my coat. The strip club fascination is lost on me. I'd rather talk to normal girls.

After he pays the check he tells me there's a car for me outside. I live just ten blocks away and tell him I can walk it. "What are you, Mexican?" he asks. I'm not exactly sure what being Mexican and walking have to do with each other, but I just smile and tell him I can hoof it. "No," he insists, "take the car." It doesn't make any sense, but I open the car door and thank him again for the night. "We can do it every week if you want," he says. The car is all black; the backseat feels more comfortable than my couch. I ride the ten blocks home in silence. The driver must think I'm an asshole. I feel like I should tip him or something, but I'm not sure exactly how this works. I watch the city blocks pass me. I feel like I'm in a movie. I could get used to this. When we get to my apartment the driver smiles and tells me to have a good night.

It gets easier. Twice a week I go out with sales traders. Every time I pick the restaurant or bar we go to, and each time I get a ride home by car service. I start to enjoy these nights. I'm the client. There's very little I can do wrong. At first I don't understand it. Why are these guys tripping all over themselves to be my friend? Much later I realize that people on the sell side buy call options on people just like stocks.

Today I might not be the head of the desk or control most of Galleon's order flow, but it's in their best interest to befriend me early in my career. Take care of me now, and I'll remember you later.

In December 1999 I attend my first Galleon holiday party. It's held at a brightly lit restaurant in Midtown. The décor and tables are a few decades old. This place might have been cool twenty years ago. The staff looks like the cast from the movie *Cocoon*. "I'm gonna get fired," Janine says. She planned the party and booked the talent: a mentalist. I wonder if he can read the lack of excitement in everyone's mind. I'm sitting at a back table with Janine and Sally, Janine's assistant, a spunky free spirit. I really like Janine and Sally. We could sit and bullshit all night. Gary approaches our table and my stomach sinks. Some people on the Street call him Rosy, for Rosenbach, but I see nothing bright or cheerful about him. He starts asking me questions: Where'd the market close today? How did Microsoft trade after the bell? How many points are the Giants giving? He doesn't give me a chance to answer, just shouts the questions out in his high-pitched, whiny voice. He already knows all of the answers. I shift in my seat. Janine and Sally roll their eyes when he's not looking.

"Let's do tequila shots," he says. He points his finger at the waitress. "Eight," he barks. There are only four of us at the table. He levels me with a stare. "I'll give you eight hundred dollars if you can drink all eight shots," he says. At first I don't know whether or not he's kidding. I sit upright and feign confidence. "I'm serious," he says. "Eight shots. Eight hundred. But if you puke, you lose." The waitress places the tray with eight shot glasses filled with Patrón tequila on the table, and eight sliced lemons. "We don't need lemons," he says. I feel backed into a corner, like I can't say no. It's just shots, and I can use eight hundred dollars. "Everybody gather round," Gary yells.

Here I go. One shot, two shots, three, four, and five. Six fills my eyes with tears and seven makes me gag. I feel my body temperature rising. As I pick up the eighth shot, tequila drools from my lips. The crowd begins to chant—it sounds like a Rangers game. I stand and the floor moves. I steady myself and bring the shot glass to my mouth. When I fire it down, I fall back on the settee with a thud and the room erupts in laughter. Rosenbach peels off eight hundred-dollar bills from a huge wad and drops them on the floor at my feet. On my knees I gather the bills. I'm drunk.

The next morning I'm bloodshot, battered, and humiliated. I make my way to the desk. No one seems hungover except me. I need coffee. Rosenbach sits in the kitchen. On the counter in front of him are boxes of jelly doughnuts, compliments of some broker. He rips one down the middle and stuffs half of it in his mouth and says: "I'll give you eight hundred if you eat eight doughnuts in three minutes."

7

AN EARLY evening a few months later, the office is empty except for Gary and me. I'm on the Internet trying to see how the Cleveland Indians' spring training is going. I need to kill some time before my business dinner with CIBC. It's at Mr. Chow's, a trendy hangout for fashionistas, celebrities, socialites, and international food groupies, where waiters in white tuxedo jackets serve you your Peking duck. Chow's is close to the office, so it doesn't make sense to go home. I'm not sure why Gary is here; his limo usually picks him up right after the market closes. He calls me over to his desk and tells me to take a seat in Keryn's chair. All of the usual tension is gone from his face. He looks almost soft. "You've been doing a good job lately," he says. Getting a compliment from Gary is like having a lion say you taste good. "You know, since the Qualcomm trade," he adds. When "the" is said before the mention of a trade, it's either a really, really good thing or, in my case, a really, really bad thing. We've been so busy lately, I didn't think he noticed how I was doing.

"Tomorrow I want you to trade with First Boston and Goldman," he says. "I want you to trade names in and out." He's reading an email on his computer as he talks. I don't say anything. "Pick names that are liquid—you know, like Mister Softee, Intel, SunMicro." I just recently figured out Mister Softee is Microsoft. "I want you to trade as much as you can," he says. He starts typing an email to someone. "Try and lose as little as possible."

"You don't want me to make money?" I ask.

"Not the point," he says as he clicks send. "I want you in and out of these names all day. Buy a hundred Intel with First Boston, wait five minutes, and then sell it with Goldman." His cell phone rings. "Just trade back and forth all day," he says. He clicks the talk button and tells his driver he'll be right down. "Stick with me, Turney. I'll make you a star." I watch as he gets up and leaves. The whole conversation is weird: what he wants me to do, and how nice he was in telling me.

Undoubtedly, part of Gary's good humor is because of the business Galleon is doing. By 2000, our reputation on the Street is vicious. That happens when some of your funds have triple-digit returns. We no longer talk in millions; we talk in billions. Investors can't give us money fast enough. If a salesman or trader won't do what we want, there are ninety-nine other guys standing in line to service us. Each day a new analyst shows up and occupies one of the vacant offices. We've picked off another senior trader from Morgan Stanley, and the bosses have promised to hire a couple of younger guys to take over my grunt work.

But there's also something about Gary's directions that makes me suspicious. Coinciding with the firm's insane growth is an ever-thickening atmosphere of intraoffice distrust and competition that flows down from the top. Raj is notorious for taking two analysts who are equal in status and manipulating a rivalry between them. I call it the Raj cockfight model. He whispers something to one analyst and then the other, and then likes to sit back and watch them scratch each other's eyes out. It's survival of the fittest. The one who wins the fight gets to keep his job; the pile of bloody feathers gets swept out the door. He tried to do it with Keryn and me, but he didn't take into account, or didn't know, how close we were and that we talked all the time out of the office.

On top of that, a rivalry is developing between the two funds under the Galleon umbrella. Raj, Gary, and Keryn attend the tech fund, while Krishen, Slaine, and I focus on healthcare. When I first started at Galleon, the healthcare fund made up only about 10 percent of Galleon's assets under management. But in the short time I've been with the firm, healthcare has ballooned to over a billion-dollar fund. Though only a third the size of tech, it's become wildly successful by any measure. Much of its growth is due to the bull market streaking upward, but some of the credit has to go to Slaine, the head trader. Though Gary and Slaine are friendly, go to the gym every morning together, and even pal around some, their competitive natures simmer just under the surface. So, even though Gary is my de facto boss, he's crossing a not-so-invisible line by giving me the opportunity and telling me he'll make me a star. But all I know is, I'm about to start trading in earnest—and that's a lot better than ordering breakfast.

The next morning I'm back at my desk. I get through my routine and the morning meeting unscathed. When the market opens, it's go time. I decide to buy my first hundred thousand shares of INTC with

First Boston. I sell it two minutes later with Goldman. I make two cents but lose twelve cents on my commissions. A loss of a dime. I do it again. Lather, rinse, and repeat. I decide to buy two hundred SUNW, sell it a few minutes later. Again, again, again. It's not even lunchtime and I've traded a couple of million shares. I've lost a total of $75,000, but we've paid Goldman and First Boston $60,000 each in commission. And that's the point, Gary tells me at lunch. "Good job," he says. It doesn't feel very good, but if he's happy, then I'm happy. Though it still doesn't make sense to me, it's fun. And, both my Goldman and First Boston sales traders are thrilled.

It makes more sense the next day. First Boston prices an IPO, Selectica Inc., symbol SLTC, putting four million shares on offer this morning. I have no idea what the company does, but its IPO is about a hundred times oversubscribed. Every client of First Boston is trying to get an allocation. This is what everyone refers to as a hot deal. We put in for a million shares last week just like everyone else on the street. First Boston calls and I pick up the phone. My sales trader tells me we got 100,000 shares and the deal is priced at $30. He says we got one of the highest allocations on the Street, which is probably true. Most of his clients got shut out or received an allocation of five, ten, or twenty-five thousand shares, he says. I tell Gary and then Raj. Then, like I always do, I type it into our system so the portfolio reflects the position. Gary sees the trade pop up on his screen and calls over to me: "Nah-nah-nah-nah-no," he says in his nasally whine. "Book it in the admiral's account."

The admiral's account is a private fund made up mostly of Gary and Raj's money. I don't know how much they have in there, but it's substantial. Employees are also allowed to invest through the admiral's account. When I first started at the firm it was strongly suggested that I do so. "Trust us," they said. "Put your money in there." I did.

I had my IRA, which was about fifty grand (I had rolled it over from Morgan), and maybe five or ten thousand more.

I highlight the SLTC trade, double-click on it, and change it from the main fund to the admiral's account: *Buy 100,000 SLTC $30.* After the market opens, our First Boston guy calls again and tells me SLTC will open around ten a.m. I yell it out to the desk so everyone hears me. At about ten minutes to ten he calls again. "Looks like it might open at forty," he says. Five minutes later, our First Boston light is glowing again. "Looks like sixty-two!" Three minutes go by and First Boston is lit again. "Eighty, maybe higher!" he says, his voice electric with excitement.

When the stock opens, the office erupts in a joyous scream. "Free money, baby," Gary yells. I look at my computer screen and see SLTC just opened at $94. It's trading hundreds of thousands of shares a second. The last sale on my screen is trading so fast, the figure is literally dancing. It's already through $100.

It becomes clear to me then how the game is played, and why Gary wanted me to trade in and out and didn't care if I made money for the firm. It's quid pro quo: the bigger the commissions we pay the sell side, the better information and allocation we receive in return. The seventy-five grand I lost for the firm the day before is just part of a business model that generates huge profits. With the stock now at $110, we make eight million bucks. It's like they just handed it to us. And there's nothing wrong with it from a legal standpoint, I guess. Wow. What a business.

But then Gary calls over to me: "Turney," he says, "call Baby Arm." Baby Arm works directly on the floor for himself. With his nighttime open-collared silk shirts that reveal a chest filled with curly black hair, and his fondness for gaudy jewelry, he looks like he's right out of the cast of *The Sopranos.* If he went to college, he's never mentioned it. He's a big guy—supposedly *all* his body parts are big, hence his nickname. Whenever we need tickets, a favor, or anything, he's available. He's in the favor business, like a concierge service that also trades stocks. "Tell him to cross a hundred thousand SLTC," Gary says. In simple terms, crossing stock is a transaction with one buyer and one seller. Typically, you only cross stock with another client or broker. But what Gary wants me to do, using Baby Arm as the facilitator, is cross the stock with ourselves. We'll buy and sell the same stock—I'm not even sure this is legal. Though I don't understand why he wants me to do this, I do as I'm told. There's a lot, I realize, that I have to learn about Galleon. Baby Arm, when I get him on the phone, has no problem with buying and selling the stock—he stands to make six cents' commission on both sides. A hundred thousand shares of SLTC at the same price, one trade, two sides, make him a quick twelve grand. That's a lot of silk shirts.

It is later, maybe that night or soon after, that I realize what I've become a part of. The new deal was priced at $30, and I booked the buy of 100,000 shares at $30 in the admiral's account. Our money. When the stock reached $110, I called Baby Arm on the floor and asked him to buy and sell 100,000 shares for me at the same price. I booked the sale of 100,000 shares out of the admiral's account and booked the buy in the main fund, where investors have their money. The only trace of the trade left in the admiral's account is the $8 million profit.

This same scenario, albeit with different stocks and banks, happens with regularity at Galleon. We buy a stock in the morning and, depending on how it performs, decide in the afternoon which account it should go in. It's never an issue with investors because the performance in the main fund is always good. If investors saw the performance of the admiral's fund, believe me, they would start asking lots of questions. But they haven't.

I know what we're doing isn't right. There must be some fiduciary responsibility. But the way the money begins piling up is intoxicating. There are times that I take out my calculator to figure out how much I'm making. On good days I might make five grand. If I had the money, I could make more from investing in the admiral's account than from what Galleon is paying me.

A FEW weeks later, I'm in the office and it's slow. Gary is out at a charity golf event, Raj is at an outside meeting, and Slaine is in the conference room on a call. I'm working on a spreadsheet, a guest list for a party Galleon is planning. I begin to call our sales traders to find out if they plan to attend and if they'll be bringing anyone. I can also add five names of my own, I'm told—but only those people who supply good information. I guess that leaves out my roommates. Then I notice one of our outside lights ringing. "Galleon," I say after one ring. The voice on the line is muffled, like they're whispering something to me. Again I say "Galleon," and this time I can barely make it out: "Is Gary there?"

"No," I say. "He's out of the office." A few silent moments go by.

I'm just about to hang up when I hear the whisperer's voice again: "Is Raj there?"

"Sorry," I say. "He's off the desk—can I help?" I can hear him breathing. His voice makes me imagine a trench coat and a phone booth. Very mysterious.

Finally, Mr. Whisper's voice is a bit more intelligible. "Jefferies is going to upgrade Amazon in six minutes," it says. Then I hear a click, and just like that he's gone. I have no name, no phone number, and no idea if the information is correct. I glance at the clock on my computer. It's 12:59 p.m. I don't know who to tell or even if I should tell anyone. Mr. Whisper could be some kind of whack-job, or maybe this is one of Gary's sick jokes. As crazy as it sounds, Rosenbach is capable of pulling a stunt that would cost the firm money just to get a laugh at my expense. I look back at the clock. It's one sharp. Thoughts start to swirl in my head. Maybe I'll just buy some AMZN and see if it's upgraded. But then, just as quickly, I decide not to. This doesn't make sense. Who calls in the middle of the day and talks like he's a character in some Bond movie? The minutes on my computer clock are moving like seconds: its 1:02. But if I don't buy any AMZN and he's right, will Mr. Whisper call Raj or Gary later expecting a pat on the back? *Fuck.* It's 1:03. I have two minutes to decide. I catch Keryn's eye and give her a quick recap. "Who was he?" she asks. I have no idea, I say. She shrugs and goes back to work. It's 1:04. Screw it, I say to myself. I buy 100,000 shares of Amazon and push back in my chair. I hope Mr. Whisper knows what he's doing.

Exactly at 1:05 p.m., AMZN stock starts to move up. At first it's a quick fifty cents and then, seconds later, it's up two dollars. The Jefferies light starts to ring and I pick it up. He tells me they're upgrading AMZN. I want to say I know, but I thank him and hang up. As I watch the stock go up the idea that I might have done something illegal seeps into my thoughts but lasts only for the briefest of moments. This is how it's done, I reassure myself. Every day, Gary and Raj pound it into my head that I need to get an edge. This is what they're talking about. Every time the outside wire rings I'm going to pick it up. I want to talk to Mr. Whisper.

The stock is up almost five dollars when Raj walks through the front door. I wait until he gets into his office. There I tell him about the call from Mr. Whisper and that I bought 100,000 shares. Our P&L shows a profit of $500k. He looks down at his computer screen and begins to giggle. Raj is a big giggler, especially when things break his way. I ask him if he wants me to sell the stock or hold on to it. "I got it," he says, smiling. For the first time in my Galleon career, I feel less like a clerk and more like a trader. After the Amazon trade, I realize that nothing in the world of hedge funds happens by accident. It's all about getting information the fastest, and however you can. If I'm going to make money, real money, buy side money, then I need to find some way of creating my own edge.

In the weeks leading up to the party, the hype has the office, and those jockeying for an invite, worked into a lather. One thing's for sure: it isn't going to be your average Wall Street social. That a buy side firm is entertaining the sell side is, by itself, unique. It's always the other way around. But Raj doesn't want to just entertain them; he wants the party to be remembered. The firm has rented a massive dance space—it can accommodate a thousand—in Midtown called the Supper Club. Though the party is the hottest ticket on the Street, the guest list isn't exactly restrictive. If you cover us, back us up, or can help us in any way, you get an invite.

One morning, the guy Raj hired to plan the party and arrange for the talent, which includes the headliner Donna Summer, walks in the door. There's something about him, a hip-looking, tall dude with shaggy blond hair, that I like immediately. Maybe it's his entrepreneurial manner, or that his company seems ultracreative—along with having him plan the whole party, Raj has also commissioned him to write a rap theme song for Galleon—or maybe he represents a non–Wall Street part of me I've almost completely forgotten. He introduces himself as Jesse Itzler, and then I realize he also goes by the rap name Jesse Jaymes.

"Hey, Jesse," one of my desk-mates yells out. "Turney here is a rapper." I turn a baby girl's nursery shade of pink. "That so," he says, nodding his head in approval. "What's your rap name?"

I contemplate choking on a pen cap so I don't have to tell him. I remember in 1991 watching *Yo! MTV Raps* and seeing his videos "Shake It Like a White Girl" and "College Girls Are Easy." I know he's won an Emmy for "I Love This Game," a rap song he wrote for the NBA, and he also wrote the New York Knicks theme song, "Go New York Go."

"Cleveland D," I say, finally.

"Nice," he says.

Now, calling me a rapper is, to say the least, a bit of a stretch. It's true, I love hip-hop. And it's also true that in 1988 I formed a rap group called Maximum Intensity with my best friend, Nathaniel, who called himself Live T. Most of our other friends hated rap music. But we were in high school in Kennebunk, certainly one of the most un-hip-hop places on earth, and we mostly performed in Nathaniel's barn to an audience of zero.

A couple of days later, the phone rings at the desk and it's Jesse. He wants to know if I'll help him with the lyrics for the Galleon theme song. "Really?!" I say, in an embarrassingly high-pitched voice. But I follow up with a very manly "Sure, love to." After all, though it might be a big jump from Nathaniel's barn, when will another opportunity like this come along?

I meet Jesse at the studio a week before the party. It's on the Upper West Side in the basement of a building. I'm not sure I'm in the right place until I find the buzzer, above which a small tag reads MILL-ROSE MUSIC. I walk down the rickety staircase. The carpet is dark, the walls are dingy, and the whole place smells musty, but the studio looks professional. There's a couple of recording booths, with the engineer's table in the middle and a couch and chairs in the back. The engineer sees me and says, " 'Sup?"

With only a week to write, record, and produce the song, I don't understand how he's going to get it done in time. I prepared for our meeting for a week—or rather, I *worried* about our meeting for a week. I wanted to prepare, but I didn't know where to start. I've come up with one idea for the hook, but it seems foolish now. I sit on the couch and Jesse sits on a chair across from me and begins asking me questions about Galleon: what it's like to work there, what's Wall Street's perception of the firm. I tell him one of the names the Street calls Galleon is "the good ship." And that's when my one idea pops out of my mouth. Why don't we sample the song "On the Good Ship Lollipop" but change the lyrics to "On the Good Ship Galleon"?

His face breaks into a smile. "Cleveland D!" he belts, his head pumping up and down. I breathe a sigh of relief.

I start to relax and the lyrics began to flow: "It's the Good Ship Galleon . . . When Wall Street has a rally on . . . When traders trade . . . Everybody in the place gets paid . . ." Shirley Temple would be proud. Jesse has a female vocalist lay down the chorus. Then, with all of my notes and suggestions, he gets into the booth and starts to rap. I'm in awe. In less than twenty minutes, he's done. "Your turn," he says. Jesse had suggested I rap a few lines, or in his words, eight bars. At first I was excited, but now I'm nervous. I think about Nathaniel and all those afternoons and evenings we spent practicing, mimicking the latest hit or coming up with our own rhymes. I need to do this.

The engineer plays the track of Jesse's last line so I'll know where to jump in. I have to finish his line and rhyme it with "CNBC." Here's what I do: "And me, Cleveland D . . . ," I begin. "Hit me, bid me, I need liquidity . . . Stopped me on five? Stupidity . . . I'm at Galleon where it all connects, trading healthcare and biotech . . ." When I finish, the producer looks at me with an "Are you serious?" expression. He plays it back and I sound awful, like a tone-deaf robot. I might have to change my rap name to Tone Duff. I try it again with little improvement. Nine more times we lay it down. And nine more times the producer shakes his head back and forth. Finally, on the eleventh try, he shrugs and my first (and only, to this point) rap recording is born. So I don't sound like Chuck D or Jay Z or even Vanilla Ice—I still have a CD I can send home to Nathaniel, which he can play as loud as he wants, silencing all the haters in Maine.

The night of the Galleon party, I'm at a bar across the street from the Supper Club. Baby Arm asked me to meet him beforehand. He said he had a present for me. He walks in after I get my first beer. Shockingly, he's wearing a sport coat: black, expensive, Armani maybe. But when he turns his back I see the coat is embroidered with a white Chinese dragon. "Turney Motherfucking Duff," he says. He grabs me by the shoulders and forces me to hug him. He's either unaware or doesn't care about the beer I spill on him. Baby Arm orders a Heineken and some shots and then tells me to hold out my hand. He slaps something into my palm. I look down and it's a tiny two-inch ziplock bag with white stuff packed into it. "Go nuts," he says. I'm not quite sure what to do. I put it into my pocket and ask him how his day was. After we complete most of our small talk, he asks, "Are you gonna hit that in the bathroom or what?" I smile and set my beer down. I enter a private stall, lock the door, and reach into my pocket. I've never seen coke before. All I know is, when I was in high school, Len Bias, the college basketball star, used it and his heart stopped working, and also if you had a suitcase full of it, it was pretty much guaranteed that Don Johnson was going to knock down your door and blast a few bullet holes into your chest. I'm not even sure how to use it. Should I pour it out? Is he going to ask for it back? Will he know how much I did? I have to do something with it. Am I supposed to do the whole thing? I touch it with my finger and put a tiny bit on my tongue. My entire mouth goes numb. I close the bag and stuff it back into my pocket. I head back to the bar. Baby Arm waits a few moments and asks for it back. "Let's hit this party," he says. We leave our half-full beers on the bar. I hope he doesn't realize I didn't take any of the cocaine.

The party's insane. Seven hours later I'm standing outside. I see Baby Arm getting into his car. He stops when he sees me and walks over. "You need any more?" he says, pointing to his pocket.

"No thanks," I say.

"Hell of a party, man," he says. "Fucking epic." He holds up his copy of the CD and shakes it like it's hot. "The Good Ship Galleon" is a hit. Everyone receives a copy, and I hear people singing the catchy chorus: ". . . put your money on Galleon."

Baby Arm seats himself in the back of his town car but leaves the door open.

"A hedge fund with a rap song can only mean one thing," he says.

"What's that?"

"Party's over."

As great as the night has been, as unlimited as Wall Street's ceiling seems, something feels prescient about Baby Arm's words. All I can think of, though, is that for me, the party *isn't* over. It's just about to begin. As the sell side streams out into the street, I hear some of them call my name. "Great tune, Turney," they say. And, all of a sudden, I feel my edge beginning to form.

9

THERE'S A saying on Wall Street that being late is the same thing as being wrong. Technology stocks are like a nine-year-old boy with a wad of Bazooka in his mouth. The bubble he blows is so disproportionate, stretched so thin, that it has to snap. When it does, his face will be covered with a gooey, sticky mess. Betting on tech stocks is Raj's forte, the reason he rocketed to the top of hedge fund earners. It's against his very nature to have a negative view on the market. But it's also against his nature to be late.

I'm at my desk and the market is ripping. There isn't a red symbol on my screen—it's green everywhere. "Toe tags and body bags," someone yells across the desk. "Anyone shorting this market is getting carried out." And then the phone rings in Raj's office.

"Raj on the hop," one of the assistants yells out. Raj walks past the trading desk and enters a small conference room with one of our analysts. He shuts the wooden door, but we can see through the glass window. He almost never shuts the door. Like a herd of deer that hears a shot in the distance, everyone's ears are up. The traders exchange looks, wondering if the others know what's going on. Raj and the analyst are talking to someone on the phone. This looks serious.

Twenty minutes later Raj calls Gary and Dave into his office. The rest of us sit and wait. Just moments later, Dave strides out and throws a stack of sell tickets at me. All of the orders are tech stocks. I'm routinely given orders to execute, usually healthcare stocks. But normally it's one or two at a time. Today, though, the stack is really big. "Sell these—don't fuck around," he says. "Get them done, *now!*" Every trader on the desk has forty sell orders. We're having a garage sale—everything must go. Either we know something or we're going out of business. Raj steps out of his office. He cups his left hand on the side of his mouth as if he's about to whisper something, but instead yells over to an analyst: "Send me an email with fundamental reasons to sell Nortel," he says. "Make sure you put something in it about them canceling from the Robertson Stephens conference." Robertson Stephens is a boutique investment firm based in San Francisco. Once a year, it hosts a technology conference where all the big players and investors gather to press flesh and talk about the industry and the future. That Nortel, one of the biggest players, pulls out at the last minute doesn't necessarily mean it has bad news. But it could certainly be construed that way.

Meanwhile, we hit the phones. I give out four or five orders at a time.

"Go to the market," we say to brokers. "Just get 'em done."

Our phones light up like a QVC switchboard during a gemstone jewelry clearance. I take report after report, trying not to make any mistakes. I still haven't given out all of my orders yet. The stack on my desk remains big. Everyone is yelling at everyone. I don't know who is saying what. *Slaine, Morgan needs you! Gary, you sold 250,000 CSCO. Ruby, don't fucking touch the phones. Gary, call Merrill's option desk. Goldman needs you, Keryn. Pick 'em up, pick 'em up. Turney, Piper only sold a hundred-k CTRX, whaddya wanna do?! Slaine, Morgan on the hop! Turney, J. P. Morgan has reports. Pick it up now! Fuck! Pick it up!*

It's utter chaos. I'm trying to give out my entire stack of sell orders, take reports for everyone on the desk, and book them in our system. A normal busy day for Galleon is a total of one hundred orders, but that's for the whole day. We're in the midst of more than twice that in an hour. I pray I'm not making any mistakes. After an hour of complete bedlam, the room quiets. We did it. We sold more than two hundred positions. Now we're flat; we don't own any stocks. Unbelievable!

While everyone else on the Street was buying, Galleon was selling. Earlier in the day, it looked like the market was going to be up big, but now, with all of our sell orders, it's struggling to stay positive. I push away from the desk and finally exhale. I'm just glad it's over. But it's just then that Raj calls in Gary and Dave again. Now what?

It's like *Groundhog Day*. Dave comes back and throws forty new tickets on my desk, but now we're shorting all of the names we used to own. Shorting is the same thing as selling, but without owning the stock. You sell first and hope to buy it back cheaper. Not only did we sell all of our stocks, but now we're betting against them. Chaos again, but even worse this time because we're racing against the closing bell, which is in thirty minutes. Traders screaming, phones ringing, Raj asking if we're done. I can't keep things straight. I don't have time to think. At all times a phone is on my ear, I'm listening with my other ear to my desk-mates, and I'm trying to book trades. When the closing bell finally rings, Galleon is 100 percent short. Two hours ago we owned almost every technology stock, and now we're short them all. This is uncharted territory, exposure this hedge fund has never had before.

A hush holds the room. Raj stands behind Gary's desk; they're watching the news scroll across the tape. Two minutes after the bell, Nortel Networks reports terrible earnings, and their future earnings forecast is even worse. At the height of the tech bubble, the company grew faster than its expertise. Now their stock is being halted. This is not only bad for Nortel, but bad for the whole market. The aftermarket futures are getting killed, down huge. The bubble is about to burst and we're going to make a boatload of money tomorrow. "Holy shit," I whisper.

Then Gary instructs me to book 10,000 Nortel puts (1 million shares) at $.25 per share commission to the broker—that's ten times the normal commission. I start to feel like I've wandered into a heist and Gary just handed me a mask. If we didn't have prior information, why are we paying extra commissions? It has to be hush money. I book the trade because Gary tells me to. But I can't help thinking how thin that reason would be as a legal defense. When I show Dave the ticket, he tells Raj we're all going to jail. "I didn't authorize the trade," Raj answers. "It's Gary's and Gary's alone." *Oh my.*

Over the next few weeks, the atmosphere in the office is tense and suspicious. A couple of my fellow traders talk about lawyering up. Dave tells me the SEC called Raj and wanted to know why he sold all of his tech stocks. Raj told them he did it because Nortel was pulling out of the Robertson Stephens conference. In that moment, I remember Raj screaming to the analyst to include in his email the information about the tech firm backing out of the conference, and I realize Raj was creating a paper trail to support his alibi. And it worked. Raj's excuse was good enough for the SEC. They probably even told him to have a great day before they hung up.

In the office, there are internal meetings with the partners. Everybody wants to have their stories straight. I realize Raj has his alibi, the email from the analyst listing the reasons to sell the stock. And I'm told to keep my mouth shut. But far too many people on the Street know about the trade—"the Nortel trade," they call it—and their reaction ranges from jealousy to awe. Galleon has just pulled off a billion-dollar flip.

10

BY THE fall of 2000, we have hired two young guys. Rob and Chad, twenty-somethings who have even more to learn than I did, including trade breaks and making sure everything is recapped correctly. I can see the worry in their eyes every morning when they arrive. The market has spent all summer trying to rally from the burst bubble. Galleon is holding serve. We aren't going to be up triple digits like we were, not even close. But we now manage billions, so we don't have to be.

But though I've come a long way in the short time I've been with Galleon, I still haven't broken through with a big trade, or secured a steady flow of information. Then one day the Leerink Swann light rings. They're a tiny brokerage firm in Boston, focusing on healthcare. I'm the only one who answers their line because everyone else thinks they're useless. I'm starting to think the same thing. There is shorthand we use on the desk. Brokers who call are either an MG or a YG, "my guy" or "your guy." By default all of my MGs are the people no one else wants to talk to—the Island of Misfit Sales Traders. I'm still the low man on the trading desk besides Rob and Chad, who don't talk to anyone. Funny thing about Misfit Island, though. Every once in a while you find a Cabbage Patch doll in the mix.

Besides, the girl who covers us from Leerink is fun. She can trade locker room stories with the best. Whenever she's in town we go out. I pick up the phone on the second ring. She's in a complete panic. She says something about Eli Lilly, but I'm not exactly sure what she's rambling about. After I hang up, I can't stop thinking about her call. It's not so much what she said but how she said it. My gut tells me to call her back. I do and she's just as breathless as the first time. Tell me again, but slowly this time, I say. "Eli Lilly is on the tape," she says, her words finally catching up with her excitement. "They're discontinuing generic Prozac."

"Okay," I say. I'm hoping for more. So what if Eli Lilly is discontinuing a brand? They do that all the time. Generic Prozac is lunch money to them.

"You're not getting it," she says. "Sepracor had sales of twenty-two point seven million last year and had expected to earn fifty to one hundred million in royalties from generic Prozac by 2003." Now I'm really lost. "Wait," I say. "Is Eli Lilly the trade, or is it Sepracor?" "It's Sepracor," she says. "They're partners with Lilly developing generic Prozac. Sepracor is fucked."

Now it clicks. Sepracor is partners with Eli Lilly, which is pulling the plug. Sepracor basically has nothing. The share price of Sepracor should go down huge. I call my Citigroup trader and buy 500 puts in SEPR (Sepracor), the equivalent of shorting 50,000 shares. The stock started the day around $120 and is now trading right around $105. Already down over 10 percent. Sell side healthcare traders start calling me to ask why SEPR is getting killed. "I'm not sure," I say. I buy 500 more puts; it's down another five dollars. I buy 500 more. The stock is now trading around $99. I have no idea how much the stock should be down, but if they were expecting $50 to $100 million in royalties and the number is now zero, the stock should be down much more. I buy another 500 puts. Now I'm short the equivalent of 200,000 shares at an average of $99 and the stock is at $98 . . . $97 . . . $96 . . . Sellers in the market start to panic. Several brokerage firms have begun making a negative call on SEPR. I call my girl at Leerink and ask what SEPR's value should be. She yells over to her analyst. Ninety is the right price, he tells her.

I call back my Citigroup trader and tell him to sell my 2,000 puts. Selling a put is like buying the stock. "Sell them right now, get it done," I say. He calls me back with a report a few minutes later and the stock is at $94. I just made 5 points in ten minutes on 200,000 shares. A million dollars. "Nice trade, dude," my Citigroup trader says. I was guessing. A guess that when everyone else figured out what was going on it would turn into a massive move downward in the stock. Who needs research? I look around because I want to high-five someone. I fight an urge to yell "How ya like me now, bitches!" But I don't. It won't fall on the right ears anyhow. Raj and Gary are both out this morning and Dave and Krishen are back in a conference room. When they return to the desk, I casually mention I made some money. When they look at the P&L on their screens they'll see.

When they do see the trade, they ask me how I did it. I think about my girl at Leerink, and then Mr. Whisper. "I saw the news come across on Eli Lilly and I just put the two together," I say. Although Dave and Krishen seem proud and happy for me, I can tell Gary and Raj especially are wondering what else I knew about the trade. But they won't get that information from me. I own the Leerink light now.

11

THE FIRST six weeks of 2001 have been difficult. We chased a rally in January, but missed it. Now the market is selling off again. We're losing money. Let me repeat that—we're *losing money*. It's a time when all hedge funds must navigate to survive. Well, except for maybe Madoff. For a hedge fund, a long stretch of bad luck or poor decision making will lead to negative returns, causing binary consequences. The first is hindsight: The Friday you took off last week means you're lazy. The stocks you could have sold last month at a profit and didn't now symbolize your stupidity and worthless view of the market. Every employee is under review. Every trade, thought, or mistake from your recent past gets highlighted and double underlined. The second consequence is a bit harder to describe. Think of it as "looming clouds." It's like how dogs behave, barking and crawling under a table an hour or two before a massive storm hits. It might be because of the change in barometric pressure or the buildup in electricity. It could be because of their heightened hearing and sensory capacities. Or maybe it's just because they pay attention. Regardless, in early 2001, if Galleon had an office dog, it would have been barking loudly and seeking shelter beneath the trading desk.

It's under these looming clouds that I enter the office on Valentine's Day. A handful of KISS ME candy hearts sit on my desk. I don't hate Valentine's Day, because that would suggest I care. I'm a single, thirty-one-year-old trader on the buy side. And though I get verbally abused sometimes in the office for not having a serious girlfriend, my life is moving far too fast to fall in love. Besides, I'm having too much fun. I spend money without worry. I hang out with my roommates whenever I want. I'm not ready for a girlfriend.

I flip on my computers and pop a pink heart into my mouth. I check my emails. When I look up, Gary is sitting at his desk. I didn't even hear him come in. He has a welt above his eye. The gash is fresh and glistens with bacitracin in the fluorescent lighting. His head is bowed, the posture of a beaten man. He picks up the phone.

"Gary," I shout over. He slowly rolls his eyes up to meet mine. He's lost a shade of skin tone: he looks ill. He looks like he didn't sleep last night. The obvious question is on the tip of my tongue, but then I hear a voice inside say, *Don't ask, don't ask.* I quickly turn back to my email and say, "Never mind, I figured it out."

One by one, the rest of my coworkers enter the office. Each sees the welt over Gary's eye, his dour expression, and turns quickly away. Some of them already know what's happened. Cell phones were buzzing right after the incident. Gary, no doubt, called Keryn; Slaine had probably already spoken with Ruby, since he was with them. It's ironic: I was first in the office but am last to know. And although cellular connections burned with gossip, the office is enveloped by an eerie silence. Slaine lumbers in last, a half hour later than usual, and sits down next to me. He doesn't look at me. I glance his way to try to get his attention. He rubs his phone with a disinfectant wipe the way he does every morning. I keep trying to make eye contact, but to no avail. He knows I'm looking at him. He finally turns his head toward me and leans in close. "I bitch-slapped him," he whispers to me. I shove four candy hearts into my mouth.

Of course, in this moment, I have no idea of how dramatically those four words will affect my career. All I know is, I'm consumed with a mix of emotions and curiosity. No matter the reasons that pre-cipitated the event, Gary had it coming. No one knew this more than me. *But why now? And why Slaine?* These are the questions dancing tantalizingly in my brain. Then it strikes me. It was just a few days earlier that Raj had started needling Slaine. "Why do you take shit from Gary?" Raj had said. Though Raj often pits one employee against another—his cockfight model—he hadn't up to that point done so at this level of management, at least that I knew of. But this is an ex-traordinary time. We aren't making money, and Raj isn't used to that. Maybe he thinks a small internal war will stir things up. He likes that Slaine and Gary compete for his attention. He gets off on it, like a hot cheerleader might get off on fielding several suitors. But I doubt Raj expected his little manipulation to escalate as far as it did.

Rosenbach and Slaine went to the Reebok gym together to work out. It was six o'clock in the morning. After the workout, they ended up together in the steam room, although not alone. There were two other men in there with them. What happened next has been told many times and in varying ways. Naked and holding his towel, sweat dripping from his face, Gary started riling Dave about being bullish this year. "We're losing money 'cause of you," he said. Slaine, with his muscles glimmering in the steam, warned Gary to stop, not once or twice, but three times. But Gary didn't stop. Gary doesn't know what "stop" means when it comes to belittling people. Slaine even told Gary, like Babe Ruth calling his shot, what he was going to do if Gary continued. But Gary, his voice high-pitched and whiny like a dentist's drill, continued. And that's when it happened, an open-handed slap. Apparently the gash was a result of Dave's thumbnail catching Gary above the eye. For a moment, standing completely naked, enveloped by steam, Gary stood stunned, glaring at Slaine. "Twenty years of friendship," he said. "Down the drain." Then he turned and stormed out of the steam room.

All that day I sit between them and not a word from one to the other crosses my space. I begin to feel like the Berlin Wall. At one point, Raj pulls Dave aside (but within earshot) and tells him he has to figure out a way to work with Gary. "It didn't happen on campus," Raj says. "It's not my problem." The next day is the same, then a whole week of absolute silence between them. But the rest of the office buzzes behind their backs. Word comes that Gary's wife has called Raj to tell him he has to fire Dave. She says Gary is afraid to come to the office. He fears for his safety. The rest of us think it's comical, but we know it's just a ploy to make Raj choose between the two. The hostility is exacerbated, if that's even possible, by the lackluster market. I wonder if the bitch-slap would have happened at all if we were making money. Of course, everyone on the Street knows of the incident. But when I'm asked about it, which I am all the time, I just shrug and say something about verbal abuse being just as bad as physical, a thinly veiled reference to Gary's rudeness in the office. A month later, the relationship between Gary and Slaine is so fragile that something has to break. And it does.

One morning Slaine tells me to follow him into a conference room. He sits across the table from me. The material of his Izod shirt stretches to its limit across his chest. "This morning I'm telling Raj and

Krishen I'm resigning," he says. "I'm starting my own hedge fund with two other guys." His tone is matter-of-fact, but friendly. "I wanted you to know first." It's not as if I'm shocked. I knew something had to happen, and I also knew the chance of Gary's leaving the firm was slim. Gary's a founding partner, knows Raj all the way back to Needham. I wonder how I'm going to deal with Gary all by myself. "I think you should stay, see how they treat you," Slaine continues, as if he's reading my thoughts. "If they don't treat you well, come work for me." After all his help, Slaine is now giving me my greatest defense against Gary. If Rosenbach gives me any more shit, I'll follow Dave right out the door. The thought gives me comfort. And with comfort comes clarity. It dawns on me that this could really turn out well. With Slaine gone, Galleon needs me.

And just like that, in David's still warm seat, I'm the sole trader responsible for the billion-dollar healthcare portfolio. I think the firm is looking outside the office to add a trader for the healthcare team, but until they do, it's all mine. I start getting to the office at six a.m. I need to know everything there is about healthcare. I stay after work to ask Krishen about all of the different sectors. I plan three business dinners a week. I seek out the smartest healthcare guys in the business. The sell side sees me as the new golden ticket. I'm in charge of distributing the commissions. The first month is a hard adjustment, but by the second, I think I might be able to pull this off. The third month, I'm starting to believe they aren't going to hire anyone else. I don't make any mistakes; I handle all of the order flow. I know everything happening in our sectors, and Krishen leans on me for insight. Even Gary treats me like a trader. And Raj asks me questions about the market. This is really happening.

The rumors and fears in the office about the Nortel trade died down after a few months but haven't completely gone away. Every now and then at business dinners someone brings up what happened, but it's usually in the context of overall admiration. Ultimately, on Wall Street, it doesn't matter how you make the money, only how *much* you make. And, despite the downturn in the market, Galleon's reputation as a moneymaker continues to grow—our assets under management are close to $5 billion. We're one of the largest hedge funds on the Street that I know of. And certainly among the most active—we trade all day and every day.

Though the shock of David's leaving subsides, it leaves a scar. For one thing, it drives a wedge between Raj and Gary. Slaine had been Gary's best friend—the best man at his wedding. After the steam room incident, Gary, at least as far as I know, never talked to Dave again. But Raj, always the businessman, kept his relationship with Slaine—at least, that's what he led Gary to believe.

It's during those first three months as Galleon's head healthcare trader that my relationship with Krishen grows. Among all the people and characters on Wall Street I've come to know, Krishen is one of the good guys. Honest, fair, and hardworking, he doesn't fit the mold of an evil portfolio manager. Every night he goes home to Greenwich to be with his family, which includes two young boys. Their artwork adorns his desk. Krishen is passionate about politics and issues outside of Wall Street, such as the environment. I admire the way he lives his life.

Not that I'm ready to live the way *he* does. Aside from my new position and the abundance of business dinners, my life at first doesn't change much. Even though I go out often with sales traders, I don't care for the fancy restaurants that are populated by buy side guys and other Wall Street big shots. I like wearing jeans and T-shirts and going to Mexican places on the Upper West Side, like Rancho and Santa Fe.

One night I'm with a sales trader at Santa Fe and when the bill comes he says, "I'm going to get in trouble for this. This check is too small."

My dinners take on a whole new purpose and agenda. When John from Goldman offers to meet me for a drink, I jump at the chance. Though I know on which side of the table he sits, I enjoy being with him and think of him as a friend. Plus, I think he can help me navigate the uncharted waters I'm swimming in. We meet at the same bar we had the first time, on the Upper West Side. This time I'm there before him. He walks in wearing a huge smile. His thinning, brownish-blond hair is a mess on top. He holds out his arms to hug me. I stand and he squeezes me hard. "Turney, baby," he says. He releases me and takes a step back. "Look at you, all growns up." He pretends to wipe away a tear from his eye. "I'm just so proud," he chortles. "Have they interviewed anyone for Slaine's spot?"

"Not that I know of," I say.

"This is good, really good," he says, taking a sip of Jack Daniel's. "I want you to call me first thing every morning. I'm going to put my pharma trader and biotech traders on the phone with you." This is the very first time I've seen John talk seriously about business. He stares right into my eyes. His face shows little expression. "I'm gonna have them give you a rundown of everything happening in healthcare." Though I believe he's trying to help me, I can also tell he's trying to help himself. We order another drink and toast to my promotion. I tell him again this might only be temporary. I don't really feel that way, and neither does John. I don't see myself going in reverse, and neither does he. I drain my drink, push the empty glass across the bar, and stand. "Where you going?" he asks.

"Dinner, I told you."

"You double booker, you," he says, feigning injury. "Now that you're a big-shot hedge-fund trader, you don't have time for the little guy?" I give him my best *Come on* face and shrug, and he finally breaks into a smile. I go into my pocket to pull out some cash. "Please don't embarrass me," he says. I smile, stuff the bills back into my jeans, turn, and start for the door. "I'll have my guys call you in the mornin'," he hollers after me. I wave back at him without turning around, step into the night, and flag a cab for downtown.

Though by definition buy siders have strong personalities, at Galleon there's never been any doubt on whose head sits the crown, and until recently not even Krishen would think of challenging Raj's leadership. Though Krishen is friendly with his partner and the two men take their wives along on social events together, Krishen seems happy to be in service of the king. Or at least he was. Now it seems those roles have been turned upside down. The idea of a mutiny on the "good ship Galleon" is unthinkable, and yet that's exactly what begins to occur.

On a Friday I hear shouting coming from Krishen's office. He never raises his voice to anyone, let alone to Raj. Some minutes later, Krishen storms out of his office. He holds a stack of files as if he's a fullback on a one-yard plunge. Fronting Krishen are three of our top healthcare analysts, like a flying wedge. They plow through the room and out the front door. They leave a vacuum in their wake. Whispers and shrugs are exchanged. With the exception of Raj and the four who just left, no one knows what's going on. But everyone knows something big just happened.

The weekend goes by like it's the last period in grammar school. Finally, Sunday afternoon, the phone rings and I hear Krishen's soft, singsong inflections. He tells me he's starting up his own healthcare hedge fund and that he'd like me to work with him. He gives me the address of a temporary office space he's taken and tells me to come in the following day, Monday, to talk.

That night I can't stop thinking about the events that are unfolding. Just a few days ago, the thought of Krishen's quitting the firm was absurd. Along with being devoted to Raj, he also made an absolute fortune working at Galleon. In 2000, both Raj and Krishen made top ten lists of highest earners among hedge fund managers. And according to one list, Krishen's $48 million made that year was nearly twice what Raj was compensated, but I'm sure it didn't include the money Raj made in the admiral's account. Why would Krishen jeopardize that kind of money, I wonder, unless he's convinced he's heading to an insanely lucrative situation? All of this contemplation makes for a fitful night's sleep as I summon visions of life-changing opportunity and a once-in-a-career move. What's he going to offer me? Head trader? Partner? Founding partner? Traders at this level get a percentage of the profits. I'll ask for ten, but settle for five. I need to fall asleep.

First thing Monday morning, I call the desk at Galleon and tell them I have a dentist appointment. I make it sound like Krishen knew about it so Gary won't be suspicious. I doubt it'll work, but I don't have another idea. I dress in khakis and a blue button-down and head out the door. It's a beautiful early June day. The temporary office is at Fiftieth Street and Sixth Avenue. I walk there.

Sitting in the conference room are Krishen and the three analysts who followed him out Raj's front door: Nate, Angeli, and Zandy. Nate is maybe forty. His hair is perfectly coiffed in a square-back, Brylcreem, Republican sort of way. Angeli is also fortyish, and has one defiant white streak in her short black hair. Zandy is younger than I am. She worked in a lab somewhere in the U.K. My guess is her parents were hippies and they probably think she's still in a lab trying to cure diseases. Krishen begins by apologizing about the scene he caused on Friday. He tells me a little more about what happened. He approached Raj with the idea of spinning off a new healthcare hedge fund. Krishen hoped to get his blessing for the project. Although he doesn't tell me the more intricate details, Krishen makes it seem that Raj would have had some type of role in the new venture, as an investor. At first Raj was receptive, a handshake. But when Krishen returned from lunch, Raj had already offered his job to Angeli. He was trying to push Krishen out and not let him take his own analyst with him. It was Raj's way of telling Krishen to go fuck himself.

But given the disruptive events on Friday, Krishen seems just fine. In fact, the positive aura he emits is contagious. I feel like this might be an amazing opportunity. Everyone on Wall Street talks about their "number." It's usually a single or double digit, at least in the strata in which I exist, something like "five" or "ten." Those numbers are the millions you need in the bank to leave Wall Street. The longer you stick around, the more children you have, the better the schools they go to, the more ex-wives and bad investments you collect, the more the number rises. I've never seen anyone hit their number and leave.

I was told in my first year working at Morgan that if I stayed on Wall Street longer than five years I'd never leave. They called it the Golden Handcuffs. "Maybe for *you*," I said back to them, "but I'm different." I wasn't about to let money dictate how I lived my life. That attitude has served me well. I've now been on Wall Street seven years. I'm not really sure what my number is, but five might be enough. As I sit in Krishen's office, that number is dancing right in front of me. On top of a salary of $150,000, Krishen offers me 3 percent of the business. I tell him I want 10. We settle at 5.

Now the only thing left for me to do is resign. Back in Galleon's office, it's as if someone turned up the heat. The collar of my shirt is soaked in sweat. I don't know why I'm so worried. All of sudden I feel like a kid walking to meet the bully behind the school. I ask Gary and

Raj for a minute of their time. I can tell by their expressions that they know what's happening. We enter a small empty office.

I have the speech all prepared. I heard myself say it in my head thirty times on the way over. Somehow the words don't sound as forceful coming out of my mouth as they did in my thoughts. "I'd like to thank you for the opportunity and everything you've done for me . . ." I try to keep eye contact, but it's difficult. I see the wheels beginning to turn behind Raj's eyes before I'm halfway through. He nods his big brown head slightly. His usual happy-looking countenance is now hard and unfriendly. When I'm done he tells me he needs to speak to Gary alone for a minute. I stand by my desk and wait. All the traders are looking at me, dying to ask me what's going on. They have a good idea but they want the details.

When Raj comes out of the office just a few minutes later, he looks like a bull about to charge. But his words are measured. "We'll give you three hundred grand to stay," he says. Just like that. $300k. "And we'll wire it into your bank today." I don't know whether he thinks I'm too valuable to lose or he just doesn't want Krishen to have me— probably the latter. For a moment, I consider the offer. But I've called my Uncle Tucker and told him about my situation. He's given me sound advice throughout my career, but none better than in my most recent conversation: "When you make up your mind, stick with your decision," he said. "And if you do decide to resign, don't let them talk you out of it, because they'll never forget."

I knew he was right. Raj and Gary would never forget the day I took $300k from them. Someday, somehow, some way, they would get their money back. I look at the big man in front of me. His eyes shimmer with anger. "Thanks," I say, "but I've already given my word." I turn my back and walk out of Galleon for the last time.

In the summer of 2001, Argus Partners is formed. My first order of business is to start making calls to my sales traders, those who covered me when I was at Galleon. At first I'm surprised at the icy reception I receive. Then I realize, a cutthroat outfit like Galleon isn't going to just sit idly by while Argus builds itself into a competitor. Gary tells all of Galleon's coverage that if they do business with me, they can't do business with him. And that means millions and millions in commissions.

I arrange face-to-face meetings with every brokerage firm on the Street. Gary might be able to bully my old sales traders into not covering me, but he can't stop me from meeting new ones. I really believe Argus Partners is a bullet train, and if they don't want to be left at the station, they'd better hop aboard. To signify confidence, I decide to invest in my image and buy a new suit or two.

I walk into Barneys wearing baggy shorts, a T-shirt, and flip-flops. The casual outfit aside, I think I have a decent sense of fashion. But I also have a tattoo of Chief Wahoo, the Cleveland Indians' mascot, on my ankle, so I'm not exactly Isaac Mizrahi. A salesman sees me wandering aimlessly and asks if he can help.

I tell him I work at a hedge fund and need some new suits. Immediately I'm led to a private dressing room where I'm cross-examined by two fashionistas named Peter and Kevin: How would I describe my style?

"Old Hollywood," I say. "Think Clark Gable or Bogart." I'm full of shit, but I figure I'll just wing it.

"Colors?"

"Blues and blacks," I say.

"Shoes?"

"Ones that fit," I say. Peter looks down at my flip-flops and almost pulls a muscle trying to not be judgmental. When he asks me what my social life is like, I smile.

"Cocktail parties? Charity events? Clubs?"

"Yes. Yes. Yes," I say.

"Do you have a girlfriend?" he asks.

"Several," I say. I don't.

Peter tells me to strip down to my underwear. The changing room doesn't have a door. Awkward. I guess this is normal. Nearly naked, I stand in the dressing room and wait. Someone new brings in a worn pair of dress shoes and a pair of socks. Smiling, I give him a short-armed wave and say hi.

Over the next two hours, suits are whisked into the room. I have a "yes" rack and a "no" rack, both of which fill quickly. I feel like I'm in the movie *Pretty Woman,* but I'm unsure if I'm Julia Roberts or Richard Gere. I look in the mirror at myself draped in Dolce & Gabbana, Gucci, and Prada. With each suit I try on I feel more powerful. "Hi there, buddy," I say to my reflection clad in the navy blue Prada. Peter is confused by my Gordon Gekko portrayal. "Sandbagged me on Bluestar, huh? I guess you think you taught the teacher a lesson that the tail can wag the dog, huh? Well, let me clue you in, pal. The ice is melting right underneath your feet." Kevin, who has seen the movie, laughs at my performance.

I end up buying five suits, two pairs of shoes, and a bunch of shirts. I don't even look at the amount on the American Express receipt. I just sign it and shove it into my shorts pocket. "It'll take a couple of days to do the alterations," Peter says. That's fine, I think to myself, as long as I have them next week. That's the first meeting of my brokers tour.

When I finally work up the courage to look at the receipt, it's for over twenty-one grand, just a few grand less than what I made my first year on Wall Street. But as it turns out, my shopping spree at Barneys is worth every penny. I get the red carpet treatment from each of the brokers I visit. In all of my meetings I'm introduced to my new sales traders. The managers at these firms must have done their homework, because almost every person I get paired up with is a young single guy who loves to entertain, which is now fine with me. I like exclusive clubs, sporting events, concerts, and fun dinners. I salvage only a few of my old salesmen from my Galleon days. Now I know twice as many people on the Street. *Thanks, Gary.*

12

MAYBE IT'S the suit, or the confidence I gain wearing it, but my meeting with Goldman Sachs goes so well that they ask if I'll speak to their new class of summer associates. When the day comes, I stand in the bar area of Bottino, an eclectic Tuscan Italian restaurant trying to be swanky. It's just up the street from Red Rock West. I peek into the private dining room to assess my audience. Gathered around the tables are thirty or so MBA students. There isn't a more sought-after internship than the one at Goldman Sachs, and every big business school in the country, from Harvard to Stanford to Duke to Wharton, is represented. I run back to the bar and order two shots of tequila. I want to steady my nerves. I didn't think to prepare anything to say. "Just keep it clean," says the guy from Goldman who asked me to speak. "You know how the Ivy Leaguers are."

I look out into this small sea of blue shirts and red ties, with a few professional females mixed in. I hold a microphone. Thirty sets of expectant eyes look back. I clear my throat. Just then the tequila hits my cerebral cortex, setting off an explosion of warmth that spreads through my entire body. I don't even know why I was nervous. I bring them through my early days at Morgan Stanley and then my time at Galleon. I pepper my talk with hedge fund jargon and insider statistics, and I keep my manner folksy. "It's like anything else," I say to my rapt audience. "Just be human." Heads bob in appreciation. I look over at my Goldman contact, an Ivy Leaguer himself, who smiles proudly back.

Then I notice a raised white and skinny hand in the back of the room. The question comes from a young man wearing glasses. "If I'm your broker and I want to increase my business with your hedge fund, what's the best thing for me to do?"

"Well," I say, "you can start by taking me to Vegas."

13

I'M ON the roof of the Thompson Hotel. With small tables lit by candlelight, potted trees, and a view of the Empire State Building, it has a look that some might call chic. It's not exactly easy to gain entrance here. The booze is flowing, beautiful women surround me, and wealth is everywhere I look. I'm here to meet two new guys, Randy and James. They work at different firms but they're roommates. And as fortune would have it, they're both now covering me. Randy is tall with dark wavy hair, and he wears a sharp suit. He played lacrosse in college, and owns an athlete's confidence. James is his sidekick. He has dirty blond hair and is a little rough around the edges, the kind of guy you want to stay a couple feet away from for fear of rogue saliva projectiles. Randy works for a big firm. I think he understands the business. He doesn't jump right into trader talk. He wants to get to know me. I like Randy immediately. James seems like he can only talk about booze and girls—I'm not sure about him yet. They're with a few other Wall Street guys, who form a small semicircle around me. I'm the only one on the buy side here. I never have an empty glass. I don't even notice my new friends ordering me drinks, but I do notice Randy banging my arm with his fist. And this time I'm ready.

Randy holds his fist in front of me, as though he wants to play a game of one potato, two potato. I hold out my hand and he drops a bag of cocaine into my palm. A warm breeze flutters across the rooftop. I'm six cocktails deep and everything is wonderfully gauzy. I follow him to the bathroom and we enter separate stalls. I hold the tiny bag for a moment; a lot has changed since the last time I was holding cocaine, primarily my bank account and social status. The white stuff doesn't look so menacing this time. There are no alarming thoughts about Len Bias. It makes sense now. It's part of the culture. I might as well see what all the fuss is about. It's not really a big deal. I should just try it once. I dig my pinky deep into the bag and pull out a hefty amount and jam it up my nose and snort as hard as I can.

The high is immediate: a rush of energy like someone pushed a reset button. Gone is the gauze from the alcohol, and in its place every one of my senses is heightened. I feel invincible. When we return to the roof, I can't stop smiling. I take in the whole scene with a glance. There's a guy twenty feet away from me trying to hit on the girl at the bar. He's going to fail. Three girls are sitting at a table across the roof; they're looking at me and talking about me. They like me. As the cocktail waitress hands me my tequila, I look into her eyes and her whole backstory unfolds. She is from the Midwest, wants to model, but has low self-esteem. "Where you from?" I ask. "Ohio," she says, as though she's embarrassed by it. I'm Michael Jordan in the fourth quarter. I can't miss. And all I want to do is fuck someone. I can have any girl I want, and I'd be doing them a favor. I never want this feeling to end.

"You should come over to our place next week," Randy says.

"Yeah, dude, its fuckin' tendy," James adds.

"Tendy," I say, laughing. It must mean something good.

14

ONE BROKEN leg, 2 prescriptions of Vicodin, 4 planes hijacked, 7 escorts called, 10 percent loss in the market, 12 nights of cocaine, 16 weeks of mono, 19 terrorists, 24 one-night stands, 30 cartons of cigarettes, 75 new sales traders, 100 miles to the summer house, 150 business dinners, 250 nights out, $300 million in capital, 365 days later . . .

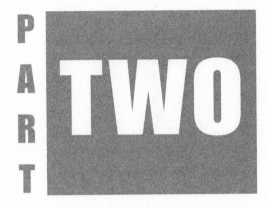

PART TWO

SUMMER 2002

I CAN smell the tequila I drank last night. It oozes from my pores. I'm still wearing my blue Prada suit from yesterday. It looks like I've just pulled it out of a gym bag. I have ten clean ones just like it hanging in my closet, but I woke up late again. I wonder what my personal shoppers at Barneys would think if they saw me right now. I reek of cigarettes too. It feels like my teeth are wearing little wool sweaters.

The trading desk is surrounded by glass. I work in a fish bowl. I'm in the middle of a newly renovated office on Park Avenue. New everything. Thank god Krishen isn't in today, or anybody else for that matter. My elbows are on my desk. I slowly raise my head and check the clock. As the opening bell rings every muscle in my body clenches. I sit upright and try to focus on the eight computer screens in front of me. There are twenty-five orders on my desk, each from five to ten million dollars and involving some sort of investment decision. My head throbs.

If I can just make it to lunch, I tell myself. A cheeseburger with a fried egg will help. I try to see how many minutes I can go without looking at the clock—sixteen is the record for the day. I can't keep my eyes open. I just need to make it to the closing bell.

2:55 p.m. . . . 3:17 p.m. . . . 3:58 p.m. . . .

I count down the final minute like a Canadian in Times Square on New Year's Eve.

I'm free.

Forty-five minutes later: There's an ounce of cocaine piled in the microwave. An additional few thousand dollars' worth of blow sits on a single plate in the kitchen. The place is littered with Grey Goose bottles, ice, cups, and straws for snorting. We call this East Side apartment the White House for obvious reasons, but it's more like a Wall Street crack house. Randy and James live here. I'm not sure what they do when their parents come to town. Everything is provided and paid for, compliments of the sell side. I never did tell Randy and James that the first time I tried cocaine was a year ago when I was with them at the Thompson Hotel. I guess I was embarrassed. I only come about once a month, but they treat me like a regular. They like to please all of their clients. Tonight they were kind enough to order in: Chinese and Mexican escorts.

I watch as two American Express black cards fly through the air across the kitchen. They land right on top of the blow. James uses the cards to chop the cocaine as twelve guys roll up their shirtsleeves. One of the hookers, Adelina, a large-breasted firecracker, drags a finger across my chest. Two traders who work for a hedge fund in Connecticut—and raced here by car service—grab the Asian twins and head to the bedroom. Dr. Fish, a three-hundred-pound sales trader who grew up in the Florida Keys, lays claim to Adelina and escorts her to the other back bedroom.

As I watch Adelina disappear behind the wall of Fish's girth, a guy approaches me and introduces himself as Gus. He's in his late twenties, with short dark hair. He wears a blue dress shirt that's open at the collar. He lives in New Jersey. He hands me a straw. All the other faces in the apartment are familiar; it's like a gang meeting with one inductee. I'm not sure who invited him. "So you're *the* Turney Duff," Gus says to me. I smile and pass the plate of cocaine. An internal warning light begins to flash.

"It's Gus, right?" I ask.

"Yeah, but everyone calls me Turbo," he says. " 'Cuz of how I snort the *'caine*."

He's smiling way too much for someone who hasn't snorted their first line of the night yet. The nickname's bad enough, but then he has to explain it? This guy is trying too hard. Strike one, I say to myself. "It's a pleasure to meet someone from the Healthcare Mafia," he says.

I roll my eyes. I want to turn my back. I wish he'd just leave, but he's holding the plate.

"That's really more of an urban legend than anything else," I say. Except it's not a legend. A trader at Fidelity in Boston named Tom Bruderman first coined the name. One day Bruderman—who owns a permanent place in Wall Street lore for an outsize bachelor party that included several rounds of dwarf tossing—was making a large buy of a biotech stock. Amgen, I think. "Don't tell the Healthcare Mafia," he told the broker. He was talking about a select group of hedge funds, including me at Argus. Though we wore the moniker with pride, it might have been more accurate to compare us to the team in *Ocean's Eleven*. While huge firms like Fidelity have a bureaucratic process to make investment decisions, hedge funds are much quicker. As head trader, as soon as I get the info, I can pull the trigger on a trade. Plus, we run in a pack, sharing information. So if we knew that Bruderman was buying, say, seven million shares of Amgen, we could front run his trade, buying the stock ahead of Fidelity. The Fidelity trade would push the price of the stock up, and we'd reap the profits. Front running is illegal, but extremely hard to prove. Still, the nimbleness and information sharing among "Mafia members" is something I use to my advantage.

But I'm not going to get into a conversation with Gus about it. Whether I belong to a mafia or play the role of Danny Ocean, we have a code of silence, *omerta*. I grab back the plate of cocaine and inhale a rope-size line. I snap my head back and wipe my nose. Gus is still talking.

"I've heard so much about you," he says.

"What'd you hear?"

"That if we ever met, we'd end up dead in a Vegas hotel room together," he laughs.

I laugh too. I picture a sleazy motel off the strip with two chalk outlines of guys holding BlackBerries and rolled-up dollar bills.

I always thought moans sounded the same in every language, but Adelina's are Spanish-accented. Even in the kitchen, it's clear how well things are going in the back bedroom. Fifteen minutes later, the guys from Connecticut emerge and shortly thereafter so does Dr. Fish. The three guys bump fists with three other guys, who head back to the bedroom—like tag-team wrestling. Fish and company gladly divulge the most intimate details of their conquests: nipple shapes and colors, bushes or lack thereof, positions. In no time we can hear the moans again. They sound exactly the same as before. After the second round of guys, the girls have reached their limit. Now they're in the kitchen with the twelve of us: six of whom have fucked them and six of whom haven't. The guys who had sex try not to act awkward. I guess they feel like they're standing in a police lineup, but nude—and the guys who didn't don't know exactly what to say.

"You girls can stay here and party," Randy says. The girls politely decline.

By eight p.m. the last of the guys are putting on their coats. They have wives, girlfriends, and children to go home to. I try not to judge, but I tell myself that when I'm married and have kids I won't carry on like I do now. I'm left standing with Gus, Randy, and James. I've started to do a lot of business with Randy. We might pay his firm a million dollars this year. I do business with James also, but not nearly as much. I don't know Gus at all, but I know his kind. The four of us head out for the night.

The Wetbar in the W Hotel is easy. James and Randy are regulars, and we're afforded full access. Several female bartenders in tight black shirts and skirts work the long bar that runs along the Lexington Avenue side of the lounge. The place is dark and sexy. Candlelight is the primary form of illumination. Hotel guests camp out on the back wall, but the Street owns the middle, and that's where the action is—if you want to call girls looking for a husband "action." The four of us sit in the corner booth. Before we left the apartment, we each took a spoonful of blow and dumped it into our cocaine doggy bags. When Desirre, our waitress, takes our order, Gus insists on paying. He puts his credit card on the table. Desirre, an attractive girl with dark hair and eyes, knows Randy and James well and asks if they want their usual. I order Patrón Silver on the rocks with three limes. "That sounds good," Gus says, and orders one too.

No, it doesn't, I think to myself. I don't love the taste of tequila; I love what it *does* to me.

We sip our fifteen-dollar drinks and take turns going into the bathroom to snort key bumps of cocaine. After a few big nights, sometimes it takes a couple of minutes to insert my apartment key into the lock because of the crusted powder on it. The bathroom is not the most conducive for illegal activity. Its unsuitability gives me an idea. I'm going to start keeping copious notes of bathrooms in New York. I'll call it a Zippets guide for snorting. The best bathrooms (five Zips) have a single lock, with no attendant. A mirror inside with a sink for cleaning up is preferred. It also helps when the bathroom is off of a hallway, away from the crowds. The Wetbar's bathroom garners only two Zips. There's no attendant, but there are four stalls, and it's a stressful walk from the stall over to the sink and mirror to check your nose. Randy and James are friendly with the general manager, who told them there's a hidden camera in the bathroom. To snort blow, you have to use the fourth stall and face sideways. When I hear that, I downgrade the bathroom to one Zip. Hidden cameras? In the bathroom? Sounds ridiculous, but ten minutes later I'm in the fourth stall, standing sideways, snorting away.

Gus digs in his pocket and surprises us with a few ecstasy pills and some weed. We traders on Wall Street pride ourselves on being the ultimate alchemists. Drugs, alcohol, money, and sex are all ingredients in the elixir of power. I grab two pills and pop them immediately. James and Randy both take one and Gus puts the remaining pill in his pocket, saving it for later, I guess.

One of the bartenders catches my eye. She's tiny, but busty. Exactly my type, pure and purely sexy. Her hair is auburn brown with a perfect Jennifer Aniston wave. I try to make eye contact, but I'm twenty feet away and she's busy filling glasses with ice and bourbon. After a few moments, I tell Randy to investigate. He knows most of the girls working here and enjoys doing me the favor. He also likes making his own moves. Randy runs his fingers through his wavy hair. The girls love him. It must be the ex-lacrosse thing—even the twenty pounds he's put on since his playing days don't diminish his allure. As he gets up to find out more about the bartender, he starts peppering Desirre with his own questions: "You single yet? What's your real name? You throw the cat around?"

Meanwhile, Gus, who works for a small broker-dealer, starts telling me how much he loves trading. "Yo, I had a buyer and a seller of Forest Labs today," he says. He keeps talking. He's coming dangerously close to being labeled Johnny Wall Street. Randy and I have names for guys like this—we just say "J Wall" for short. He's the guy who wears button-down shirts untucked over his khakis. In the office he tells you to protect him on the lunch print, his *cool* way of telling you to order him lunch. Johnny Wall says he's a size buyer when he sees a hot chick. He tells you at happy hour how he whacked a bid and sold another 250,000 shares behind it. At dinner he brings up commissions and research. He asks you what your favorite stock ideas are as you put a slice of buffalo mozzarella in your mouth. He doesn't own any stocks; he just wants to impress. Johnny is the last one to show up at your high school reunion, driving his new car and checking his Rolex. Johnny Wall is a douche.

"So you know what I did," Gus says. I wish Randy were here listening to Gus's trader talk. "I fucking plugged the buyer." I shake my head in acknowledgment. "The seller was my boy, so I took care of him," he says.

Then Randy comes back with his intel. The bartender's name is Lily, she's from Long Island, and she has a son, but she's single. He doesn't tell me if she's the freak of the week. Randy taps Gus on the shoulder, the signal for him to call the limo. "Should be here in twenty," Gus yells over the din of the bar. I have to work fast, but I'm fueled up and bulletproof. I'm on my third tequila on the rocks and my pocket is full of cocaine. I leave the other three guys at the booth.

Lily smiles and asks if I need another. I smile back and ask to borrow a pen. I grab a cocktail napkin. *You have a beautiful soul,* I write, *and a beautiful smile.* I then add my name, age, and telephone number. I'm just about to fold it and hand it to her when I realize that I couldn't be any less creative if I tried. I should put my journalism degree to work. I open the napkin up and add: *Best dance move: the Towel Dance.* There's no shot she knows what the towel dance is, and that's exactly my point. I neatly fold the napkin and hand it to her. Randy motions to me that the limo is waiting. It's 10:33 p.m.

The limo is white, with red leather interior. A shiny disco ball hangs from the center ceiling with purple neon undercarriage lighting. The carpet is leopard-print shag. "Rock the Boat" by the Hues Corporation blares from the oversize speakers. The car is so ridiculous, it's actually cool. The driver's name is Big Al; he looks like Ron Jeremy, the old porn star. Big Al has no rules. Randy and James sit on the upper-left side of the limo while Gus and I sit in the back. We pass a joint. "Did you guys see Intel's earnings after the bell?" Gus says.

I look over at Randy. "Strike two," I mouth as I hold up two fingers. As I look at Gus, I mull over my options of how to respond: a) politely ask him to not talk business; b) tell him to find the next PATH train back to Jersey; c) ignore him; or d) . . . "I took fourth place at the science fair in junior high," I say. I widen my eyes and nod a little to affirm it's really true.

Gus looks like he's just been voted off *American Idol.* He senses he said something wrong, but he can't figure out what it is. He seems like an okay guy, and so far I'm having a good night. But talking business when you're supposed to be out having fun is a pet peeve of mine. Gus doesn't realize it, but I know what he's up to. I knew it from the White House. He wants me to open an account with him. But he's going about it the wrong way. I respect people who play the game correctly: become my friend first, and then we'll talk business.

We pull curbside to the velvet rope at Suite Sixteen. Outside the club, a crowd waits for the bouncer's approval. Stoned, high, and drunk, we stumble out of the limo to the front of the line. Randy slips the bouncer a hundred-dollar bill and the gates open. Inside I see the general manager—his name is Jason, he's a friend of a friend of a friend, born and raised in New York, a blond-haired Jewish twenty-something. "Oh, man, we just slipped your boy some money—I didn't know you work during the week," I say.

"Always ask, Turney," he says. "Always ask. We're opening up a new club called Marquis next summer. You better come to the grand opening."

"Thanks, man, definitely," I say as he hands us over to the hostess. We tell her we need a table and she leads us to the curvy banquettes in the back lounge. The crowd that surrounds us seems to move to the beat of the music. As we pass through, I see a plethora of sexy women—it looks like a casting call for *The Bachelor*. The few men who are here have their downtown attire on: chain wallets, Puma sweat wristbands, and faded jeans. We're the only signs of Wall Street.

The waitress stuffs bottles of Veuve Clicquot into a bucket of ice. The bottles are only half liters, so we order multiple. Eminem blasts from the speakers as girls dance by our table. The bathroom here is worse than the one at the Wetbar. It has only one urinal and one stall without a door. I give it one Zip. Gus takes out his wallet and fumbles through some bills before he retrieves a hundred. He hands it to the bathroom attendant like he's paying a toll.

Back at the banquette, the thunderous beat makes it difficult to hold a conversation. But each bass note seems to pump the coke that courses through my body. The champagne makes it all fuzzy and warm. Everyone at the table must feel the same, because we just smile and nod at one another.

Two girls at the booth on my left lean over and tell me they're in college. Wide eyed, with smooth skin, and a bit gawky, they look the part. They also look uncomfortable. I pour them both a glass of champagne. They tell me they appreciate the free alcohol but don't usually drink champagne. Neither do I, I say. We toast to the universe for allowing our paths to cross. When they ask me what I do, I hesitate.

"I work on Wall Street," I say.

"And?" one of the girls says, expecting more. "Whaddya do?"

"I work at a hedge fund. I'm a trader," I explain.

"Cool, but whaddya do?" the other one asks.

I've had this conversation many times; normally, people have no idea what I'm talking about. They think I wear a blue jacket and make funny hand signals all day on the floor of the stock exchange. Even my family and close friends aren't sure what I do. Sometimes I'm even asked for stock tips, when they should be asking someone who researches stocks, like an analyst or portfolio manager. I pull a trigger. I'm told to buy 100,000 shares of JNJ. It's my job to know how, where, and when to do it. It's a high-wire act. The college girl persists.

It's one of the great mysteries of the universe. Everybody says they want to know how Wall Street works, but the truth is, all they really want to hear is how much money I make—or how much I can make for *them*. "Well," I say, struggling to be heard over the music, "basically, institutions and people give us money to invest because we're going to make more for them than they could make on their own. For that service, we charge a fee and take twenty percent of the profits." I have the girls' attention, and the coke is fueling my narrative. "It's like this," I continue. "Say you invest a hundred dollars, and for that investment you get a return of ten bucks. Not bad, right?" The girls nod. "But what if I was to tell you for the same hundred I could get you a return of fifty? Would you do it?" Now the girls nod enthusiastically. "All I ask for is ten dollars of the profits and a nominal fee."

"Wow," says the girl closest to me. "You can really do that?"

"Give me a hundred and I'll show you," I say, lifting my glass.

One of the girls spills her champagne. They both giggle as the one friend tries to wipe the other dry with a tissue. The scene is endearing. It reminds me of my college days, or the first years I was in New York, when I had only intimate friends. Everything changed when I went to the buy side. Now sometimes it's as if I can't trust anyone I do business with. *What do they really want?* I always have to ask myself. I'm envious of the innocent connection these college girls have.

Hours pass and the college girls have to go home—maybe they have a quiz in the morning. I'm sad to see them leave. If I liked them less, I would have tried to trick them into going home with me. I still live on Sixty-Seventh and Amsterdam. Sometimes I ask girls if they want to go to an underground club called Club 67. When the taxi pulls up to my building, they start to get suspicious. But my doorman is in on the ruse, and when I ask him if the club is open he'll say: "Yes, go on up." I've walked a number of girls into my apartment and only one has screamed and run back to the elevator. I exchange numbers with the college girls and watch as the crowd swallows them on their way out.

It's past two a.m. I can't speak. The drugs and alcohol have taken over. What initially allowed me to say and do whatever I want is gone, leaving only paranoia, guilt, and shame. When you're this fucked up, there's only one way to change the way you feel: do more coke. I motion to Gus, Randy, and James that I'm heading to the bathroom.

The door attendant snickers when he sees me. I've walked past him ten times already. I glance at the mirror. My hair is standing up and my face is red and sweaty. I duck into the stall and pull out my bag. It's almost empty. I shovel my apartment key into it and snuff the few remaining bumps into my nose and then peel open the bag and lick it. I pop the bag into my mouth and suck on it for a bit.

Back upstairs. Randy and James are gone—poof—vanished, and I'm stuck with Turbo. I turn to head out. From behind, Gus grabs my arm. "You want to make a move?" I'm torn: part of me wants to sneak off into the night and go home, but the other part of me knows the night isn't over. I shrug. Only for something good, I tell him. Gus tracks down our waitress and signs the check.

Gus has rented a room at the W Hotel for the night. We make our way back there to snort more cocaine. He has a lot left in his bag. I begin to regret shutting him down earlier in the limo. I decide to ask him about his business. At first he hesitates, but a fresh, fat line of cocaine gives him the shot of courage. He had Wall Street internships in college, he says. He knew from a very early age that he wanted to work on the Street. His father was in the business for many years and made a pile of cash. It's funny how small the Wall Street world is. Turns out, I met his dad once or twice, back when I was interviewing for jobs. My uncle is friendly with his dad. Gus is starting to grow on me.

"We can call some hooks if you want," he says. I assess the layout of the room, two double beds separated by a nightstand. Tempting offer, but I'm going to pass. The two of us take turns snorting lines, smoking cigarettes, and laughing. The next thirty minutes escape us.

"I'm gonna head home and try and get a couple of hours of sleep," I say. Gus picks up the remote and orders porn. I'm a huge fan of pornography, but watching it with another dude makes me uncomfortable. I thank him for the night and tell him we should hang out again real soon. I glance at his bag of cocaine. Before I even ask, he offers me half of it. I leave him with a nice little mound on the nightstand and stuff the rest in my pocket.

I'm just about at the door when he calls to me. *Shit,* I think, *here it comes.* He made a comeback—he was doing so well. He can't help himself. Right down the middle . . . Strike three.

"Do you think we could open up an account?" he asks.

I stop and turn around. I'm vibrating from cocaine. "Can I give you some advice?" I say with a rasp. For the first time all night I notice how coked-out he looks. His eyes bulge.

"Don't ever ask. And if you have to ask, wait a week, a month or two. Work it a little bit, ya know? Pretend we're friends, act like you don't care about the business, just play it cool, fake it." He sits on one of the beds, but hangs on my every word. "If you ask on the first night"—I put both my arms out and shrug my shoulders—"then I know, ya know?"

Yes, he helped pay for the cocaine in the White House, he paid the bill at the Wetbar and for the limo over to Suite Sixteen. Yes, he paid for the countless bottles of champagne. Yes, he even let me take half of the remaining coke, and, yes, he offered me a hooker. No! Don't ask. This is how the game is played, and it's still too early. If I wanted, I could take his room for the night, borrow his shoes, and make him dance barefoot.

"Thanks, man, I appreciate the advice," he says, looking down at the floor.

"Just let it happen naturally," I say. I'm practically in the hallway when I stop. *"Yes,"* I say.

"Yes, what?" he asks.

"Yes, I'll open an account with you tomorrow."

It's four a.m. I'm somewhere on Lexington Avenue and I'm looking for a cab. I remember I know someone who lives close. I scroll my phone for the number. When I call she picks up. Ten minutes later she unchains the lock and lets me in. Barbara is in her late forties and on the tail end of her escort career. Her apartment is lined with Christmas lights year-round, and there's a mattress with no box spring in the far corner just outside of her bathroom. The couch, television, and coffee table look like the ones I had in college that I shared with seven roommates. Like her, the apartment is well worn but not well loved. Barbara wears a black lace nightie.

"You still don't have a girlfriend?" she asks as she takes my hand and leads me to the couch. "I don't get it."

"I'm having too much fun," I say as I pat down my hair.

"Me too," she says. Barbara was listed under "mature" on the website where I found her six months ago. Her photo was sexy: blond hair, really large breasts. But in person, she wears the truth of her age in her eyes. A bird's nest of wrinkles sits on either side of them, and they have the tattered expression of a hard life filled with disappointment.

"I gave my number out tonight and took one," I say.

"There you go," she smiles. "Nice work." I like Barbara and I think she likes me. But like most everyone else in my life now she's a person whose sincerity I sometimes question. One of the first times we were together she told me I reminded her of Johnny Depp. I laughed because I look nothing like him. She told me she'd once spent several nights with the star, and he was very much the gentleman. I liked the story, and didn't care much if it was true or not. I dump the rest of the coke on the coffee table and she fixes me vodka on the rocks.

She asks if I want to take this party to bed, but I get the feeling she only says it because she feels obligated. She can tell that I've partied too much. No thanks, I say. Instead, we stay on her couch and chat. I ask her how her business is going and she shrugs as if to say that some nights are better than others. "If only I'd invested some of my money," she says, "then I'd be set." The statement makes me wonder. I want to tell her that it's a bear market and nobody's making money. "Then I wouldn't have to do this every night," she says. "I could pick my clients and only hang out with guys like you." Her comment makes me smile, but I now realize how similar we are.

I'm tired and feel dirty. Barbara asks if I'd like to take a shower with her. The hot water pelts my body. We take turns washing each other, and laugh as we do. It's the best twenty minutes I've had all day.

I'm dressed now, my hair still wet. I hug her at the doorway and try to hand her some money, but she refuses. "Please, just take it," I say. She begins to push me out into the hallway but not before I drop a couple of hundred-dollar bills on her table next to the door.

On the street, I look at my phone: it's 5:42 a.m. I need to go home and change my suit.

16

AN HOUR later, I'm at my desk next to Rich and Melinda. They both work on the trading desk with me. We hired Rich right after we launched. He was my Citigroup sales trader when I worked at Galleon. He executed my million-dollar Sepracor trade. When Gary called him up to tell him he couldn't cover Argus anymore, he must have chuckled. He was on his second interview with us. Rich is the skinniest ex–Division I hockey player ever, and has unruly black hair that sits on his head like abstract art. With his white pearly smile and his 'fro, all the girls love him. Melinda, who was Krishen's assistant at Galleon, is a dark-haired beauty who's part Hawaiian or Filipino or something. Melinda deserves her seat. She's the first in the office and the last to leave, and she's fully aware that she doesn't know everything yet, which makes her very wise. I enjoy coming to work: we laugh a lot and work hard, everyone is smart, and we function as a team.

Gus calls right after the opening bell. I knew he would. I give him an order: buy 15,000 shares of SPY. I don't have any interest in buying the stock, but it's so liquid that I can either sell it immediately or wait five minutes and see if I can make a little money. Both Melinda and Rich cast questioning glances my way. It's like they know I'm up to something. "He has great execution," I say, pinching my shoulders up. I want to take my words back. "Great execution" is code for "he has a big expense account." It's not like I can do *anything* I want, though. Krishen needs to approve any account I open, but when he asks me why I opened this one, I'll just make something up.

Gus calls back with the report. This time Rich intercepts the call. "Who the hell is this tool Gus?" he asks me. He sounds like he's joking. "I mean, seriously, man, who names their kid Gus?" Biting my lip, I'm thankful he didn't share his nickname: Turbo. It hurts to even think about last night. My guard goes up. Neither Rich nor Melinda knows about my drug use. I wouldn't know Gus's name if he hadn't supplied me with the pile of blow. On Wall Street, a bag of cocaine is like an after-hours name tag, but much more memorable.

"He's not a squirrel, I promise." A squirrel is someone to whom you give an order only to find that they keep coming back for more. Sometimes they're from a regional bank in the Midwest or some boutique outfit close by. Feed them once and they start calling you every day. And then it's a few times a day. Next thing you know the squirrel is driving you nuts. We now pay five cents a share on every trade, so the squirrel has two cheeks full of nickels and starts coming to your door looking for more. The problem is, I have a feeling that Gus is as squirrelly as a guy can get.

By the afternoon I need toothpicks to keep my eyes open. Fucking brutal. The only good news is, Gus hasn't called in a couple of hours. I'll never do what I did last night again, I tell myself. This is the time of day that sucks most. The two hours left until the closing bell are an eternity, and there's nothing to keep the feelings at bay. And now the worst of those feelings take control. I begin to hear a primal drumbeat inside my head. *You fraud,* it says. In the space of twelve hours, I go from king shit to just shithead. *I'm not making this firm money. They could train a chimpanzee to do what I do. Melinda and Rich will both find out I'm a coke fiend. Every time I sniffle they look my way. Krishen is about to fire me. I'm a buy side squirrel and I'm only thirty-two.* One ugly and negative thought after the other spills out of me like gray matter from a shotgun blast to the head. Then, right when I'm about to drown in my negative internal talk, right when I'm at my most vulnerable, the phone rings and I pick it up.

"Come on over to the White House after work," Randy says.

"No," I say. I quickly hang up the phone. I don't want to go back for at least a month.

I love Sunday nights. As a trader, there isn't much to do. Sure, I could be studying some charts or reading *Barron's,* but who wants to do that? I'd much rather be sitting on the couch with Jason and Ethan watching *Sex and the City.* My cell phone buzzes. I programmed Gus's number into my phone, but I did it under "Turbo." It makes me smirk every time I see it flashing. I click Ignore. Then my phone buzzes again. "Turbo can't take a hint," I say. But when I look at the caller ID, I see it's a number I don't know. I press the Talk button.

"Hellooooo," I say in my best Barry White.

"It's Lily," says the voice.

Lily? I repeat her name in my head a few times. But I have no idea who she is. It's not that unusual for an unknown female voice to be calling me—I'm social. I play it cool, ask her what's going on. When she says she's at a friend's house and just got done watching *Sex and the*

City, I grab the remote and mute the closing credits. Soon we both run out of things to say and an awkward silence ensues. "So, you're really good at the towel dance?" she asks. How does she know about that? "We should get together so I can show you in person," I say.

"Okay," she says sweetly. "I'm busy until Labor Day, but how about after that?"

I take Lily's number and agree to give her a call. After I hang up, I ask Jason and Ethan if either of them knows a Lily. They both shake their heads. It's not until later that night when it comes to me. *Lily!* The bartender at Wetbar with the Jennifer Aniston hair.

In September 2002, my roommates and I decide to move. Much of Manhattan—the Upper West Side high-rises in particular—is like an upscale Soviet Union. People live in apartments that all look alike, they awake at the same time, eat the same granola, dress in the same corporate uniforms, and line up for the crosstown bus or take the stairs down to the subway. The sameness can drive you crazy. We all agree: it's time for a change.

Right now there's only Ethan, Jason, and me living here. We knocked down a wall to open up the living room. Ethan is my cousin. He's an actor a couple years out of college. He'd be perfect for an afterschool special playing the morally responsible friend. I need to corrupt him a little bit. He *looks* like my cousin, Duff nose and all. Then there's Jason. He looks like a chubby Ben Affleck. The kid could make you laugh at a funeral. He's a media buyer; he purchases airtime on television for his clients. All my other roommates have moved out.

Now, it's not like I can't afford an apartment on my own. I can. My salary is up to two hundred grand a year at Argus. And that's not including my bonus. In 2001, I got six hundred grand. We didn't make any money, but Krishen rewarded me for taking the risk of leaving Galleon. *What would be the fun in living alone?* The thought of being unaccompanied, hungover, in a fancy one-bedroom apartment is depressing. I want to live with my friends until I fall in love, get married, and start a family. When I was a kid all I wanted to do was become an adult. Now as an adult, all I want to do is remain a kid. Anyway, I always told my friends that if I made it I was taking them along with me. It's time for me to back up my words.

Only one question remains: Where? Once, when I was headed to a restaurant downtown in Tribeca, I saw a converted factory building with a black wrought-iron staircase and porch across the front. At the time, I thought: I'd love to live in a place like that. But the idea of moving to Tribeca might have actually formed on a date that everyone remembers.

On September 11, 2001, Argus Partners had been up and running for only a couple of months and we were in our temporary space on Sixth Avenue in Midtown. Along with several other senior people, I was in a meeting that morning when an administrative assistant came into the room to tell us a prop plane had hit one of the twin towers. When the second jet hit, Krishen asked everyone to evacuate the office. We gathered on the sidewalk outside of our building. Looking down Sixth Avenue, I could see the smoke billowing from the upper floors of the north tower, which, by then, stood alone. I remember turning away to light a cigarette. When I turned back, the top of the tower was gone. In that moment, the building had begun to collapse into itself. I spent much of that day with Jason, Ethan, and some other friends in the Sheep's Meadow in Central Park. We smoked cigarettes and scanned a sky that was far too blue for more jets. Later that evening, we all went to a local bar. For once I didn't want to go. But I didn't want to be alone.

Three weeks later, I threw a party for the Twin Tower Fund, a charity that raised money for children who were left orphaned by the

September 11 attacks. I'd called every contact I had on Wall Street. The party was held at a club in Tribeca called Shine, and raised more than twenty-five grand for the charity. Wall Street still talks about that night. More than a thousand people danced until four in the morning just blocks from the still smoldering site of Ground Zero. Though I'd always thought of Tribeca, with its cobblestone streets and converted factories and warehouses, as a magical place, after 9/11 the idea of living there brought out in me an almost patriotic fervor.

It's Jason and I who go looking for apartments. One of the last we see is in the Sugar Warehouse building, a redbrick ten-story structure on a cobblestone block called Laight Street. When the structure was built, before the Civil War, it was one of the tallest buildings in Manhattan and part of the city's skyline. Now the building consists of duplex and triplex apartments. The doorman tells us that the apartment we're looking at is the only rental in the building—the rest are tenant-owned.

The door to 5A swings open to reveal huge floor-to-ceiling windows that look out onto the Hudson River. An orange sun sets over New Jersey and its rays form a shimmering path that cuts the river in two. A cruise ship slides by. The view is stunning. The living room is sunken and spacious; the shiny wood floors glisten at our feet. There's a full dining room and a kitchen filled with top-of-the-line stainless-steel appliances. A huge master bedroom is on the second floor. Here, with even bigger windows than in the living room, the view is even more amazing. The master bath has beautiful southwestern tiles and a monster steam shower. Across the hall is another bedroom with its own bathroom. The third floor is perfect for a pool table (if we stick Ethan's bed in the corner) and has a sliding glass door that opens up to a 1,500-square-foot roof deck. Jason and I stand on the deck. We can see up and down the Hudson River from the George Washington

Bridge to the Statue of Liberty. Like the iconic *New Yorker* cartoon, the rest of the country lies beyond the river. I light a cigarette and the white smoke curls and dances away with the breeze.

"I'll take it," I tell the broker.

"But I haven't told you what the rent is," he says.

I don't care. I have to live here. "How much?" I ask.

"Ninety-three hundred a month," he says, looking down at his sheet of paper.

"Okay, I'll take it."

We move in a week later. But it's not as if we carry box springs and mattresses up flights of stairs, especially after I break a cheap mirror trying to remove it from my wall. We hire professional movers. And from the Sixty-Seventh Street apartment they bring my almost new, custom-made, twenty-foot sectional velvet couch and my fifty-inch console television. I buy stuff in Super Bowl–party measurements. In the new apartment, my bedroom is enormous. I have a Charles P. Rogers iron sleigh bed that I position in the middle of my bedroom at an angle. Someone once told me that positioning your bed this way is rebellious, a fuck-you to interior decorators. That might be so, but I could have two beds at an angle and the room would still look empty. My new walk-in closet is bigger than the bedroom in my first apartment in New York. The third floor is empty too. And the roof deck also needs furniture. When I decided to take the apartment—I was willing to pay most of the rent—I hadn't actually thought much about furnishing it. Leaving aside the money it's going to cost, filling the apartment is going to take some energy.

But like a good team, the next day we come up with a plan. We'll begin by acquiring the essentials. Jason and Tridge, an old roommate who flew in from Ohio, take my cash and go to look for a pool table.

Ethan takes my credit card and leaves to go to J&R, a music and appliance store, to buy speakers, wires, and portable telephones. My old roommate Johnny Hong Kong, who'd moved back to Colorado, flies in to see the new apartment and lend a hand. He and I stay behind and wait for the cable guy to come. After the three boxes are installed and the cable guy leaves, I turn on the set in the living room to see if it's hooked up properly. The movie *Zoolander* with Ben Stiller and Owen Wilson is on. I love this movie. It's even better when I'm high. I tell Johnny where I've hidden my stash and we light up a bowl. Now, in the movie, Owen Wilson, who plays a rival to Ben Stiller's supermodel character, has an apartment with a "soil room." Essentially, it's a room filled with dirt. This is a terrific idea, I decide. I've come to this conclusion, of course, after several bowls of some very, very good pot.

"We need a soil room," I say to Johnny, whose face is plastered with a Mary Jane smile.

"Yes," he says, nodding. "We do." And so, red-eyed and giggly, we head out the door in search of one.

ABC Carpet, unfortunately, doesn't sell soil. But it has just about everything else. Walking into the store on Broadway is like walking into a Rockefeller garage sale or the plunder-filled hull of a pirate ship. It's not cheap. High or not, I would have never gone here before working on the buy side. But it is a trippy place nonetheless.

This day, the store is packed with customers. I bounce off of shoppers like a floating plastic carnival duck. Suddenly, the din that surrounds me seems to mute and I become laser focused. In front of me stands something called an Indian daybed. It has a beautifully hand-carved canopy with four wooden posts that stand seven feet tall. The sides are white Egyptian cotton see-through drapes. In the middle hangs an antique iron chandelier with tiny red cylinders and jewels hanging from it. I tug at Johnny's shirt without taking my eyes off the bed. I step closer.

"This is it," I say.

"What about the dirt?" Johnny asks.

"It's perfect for the living room," I say.

Johnny looks at the price tag and whistles. I flag down a sales-person on the floor. I'm wearing flip-flops and a T-shirt. My hair is unkempt and my eyes are red-rimmed. "I'd like to buy this," I say to the man. He looks back at me suspiciously.

"Are you aware of the price?" he asks. I'm not really paying attention to him. Instead, I'm looking over at the cashier's station, in front of which is an enormous line. It might be paranoia from the pot, but the line looks like a run on a bank—the faces are distorted in anger and frustration.

"Look," I say to the man as I hand him my American Express card. "I really want this bed thingie." The salesman glances down at the credit card and back up at me. His expression says he doesn't know what to expect next. "But I can't wait in that line." He completes the transaction in no time. Johnny and I practically run from the store. Twenty minutes later, we're home smoking the rest of the pot and clicking the channels to find *Zoolander* again.

"We never got the dirt," Johnny says.

"I know, man, I really wanted the dirt too," I say.

Over the next few weeks, I spend money like I'm getting divorced and my soon-to-be ex-wife's lawyer hasn't had my assets frozen yet. I purchase twenty thousand dollars' worth of artwork and photographs, including a few from Mixed Greens, a gallery specializing in mid-career artists. I buy a gigantic photo of a fish called *Bi-polar,* and a huge, out-of-focus photograph of James Dean; I buy floor lighting and tiny multicolored spotlights that shoot from the floor to the ceiling, a thousand-dollar shag carpet, and a three-thousand-dollar frosted glass bar with four stools. I buy a couple of TVs, assorted chairs and lamps, and a surround-sound system for the living room. I buy an original Ms. Pac Man video game. Each day, the triplex fills a little more until it looks like a cross between a lair and a nightclub. *The spoils of the buy side,* I say to myself one day as I lie on the couch. And, yes, it's only as substantive as a single thirty-two-year-old guy's fantasy could be. But it's a fantasy come true, and a long way from Kennebunk.

Once we're settled from the move, I decide to call Lily. For my date, I wear my favorite jeans that are perfectly frayed and faded, and a baby blue short-sleeved shirt with a name patch that says "Trenton" on one side and "Chrysler/Dodge/Plymouth" on the other. I look in the mirror for a quick assessment of the outfit. Not bad, I think. If the whole Wall Street thing falls through I see a future for myself in oil changes. I'm meeting Lily at Dos Caminos, a Mexican restaurant in Soho. It's just a short walk from the new apartment.

She sits at the bar wearing a cream-colored tunic that hangs from her shoulders by spaghetti straps. When she stands to hug me I realize how petite she is. Her golden-brown skin is soft. The hostess leads us to an outside table. I follow behind Lily and notice the way her tunic sways with her walk. We munch on chips and salsa while we wait for our margaritas. During our last phone conversation, she talked about her son and I immediately ask about him. He's seven, she says; he loves sports and really loves his dad. There's the slightest hesitation to her words, which leads me to believe that there's some bitterness between her and her ex. Lily lives on Long Island and commutes at night to the club. Geography and single motherhood aside, I find myself very attracted to her. Though unquestionably beautiful, she possesses something else that tugs at me. Over margaritas, she asks what I do for a living. The question catches me off-guard. I was sure she knew

I worked on Wall Street. When I tell her, she's surprised. "You don't come off that way," she says. I think she means it as a compliment. She has a bartender's-eye view of Wall Street. All she sees is guys in ties on the cocaine-fueled prowl. "I mean, you're not at all like your friend Randy."

Later, I ask for the check. The waitress tells me it's already been taken care of. I run through a mental checklist of people who might have picked it up. It certainly wasn't Melinda or Rich from the desk. Though they know about Lily, they didn't know I was taking her out tonight. Anyway, my relationship with them is much more of the locker room variety. Once, when Rich was out of the office for a couple of days, I told everyone who called for him that he was home with his sick cats, Mr. Buy and Mr. Sell. When Melinda picks up one of my calls and I'm off the desk, she often tells the caller, especially when it's a girl, that I'm having an episode of my chronic diarrhea. She learned that trick from me. It would be much more likely for either of them to send a clown with balloons than pick up the check. I don't think it's Randy—he's hosting at the White House and has just texted me, asking if Lily knows how to drive stick. There's only one other person who knows where I am and who I'm with. I'm really underestimating Turbo.

When we get to the sidewalk, I rush to establish position on the outside. I was told that when a man walks with a woman he should be closer to the cars in the street in case a vehicle loses control and takes out a few pedestrians—I *think* that's the reason. Lily allows me to claim my spot as we head down West Broadway. The shops and businesses are still open. It's a charming few blocks before you get to Canal Street. I reach down for her hand. It's small and soft. She looks up at me and smiles, and then quickly looks forward again. When we get to Canal Street, I ask if she wants to see my new apartment. In my head, I can hear Melinda calling it the "cockpit." With a tiny shake of her head, she declines. "I have a babysitter," she says with a small smile, behind which lies an inner meaning that I can't quite make out. I lean in and give her a gentle kiss on the cheek.

"Can I call you again?" I ask.

"I'd like that," she says.

BY OCTOBER 2002, the market is coming back from 9/11 and the summer lows that followed. Though we didn't expect to bust out of the gate, Argus has been struggling this last year just to stay even. Only in looking back can one see just how seminally dysfunctional 2002 was on Wall Street. It was the year that Tyco's Dennis Kozlowski, Enron's Andrew Fastow, and ImClone's Sam Waksal formed a Mount Rushmore of greed and underhanded dealing. It was also back then that a New York State attorney general had the temerity to believe that a stock analyst's rating should reflect what the analyst actually believed. Of course, that was before said attorney general became "Client 9" with midcalf socks. But as I'm living it, 2002 doesn't seem as much scandalous as challenging. The heady gyrations of the pre-9/11 market are a distant memory. Every day is a struggle, as if we're fighting an inexorable force.

By now, I've been a head trader at Argus Partners for almost a

year and a half. Though my off-the-cuff remark to the Goldman
MBAs at the Chelsea restaurant might have been decidedly un–Ivy
League, there was more truth in it than anything they received from
their famous-author faculty. In some ways, my tenure as trader has
let me understand Gary Rosenbach more. Maybe it's the pressure, or
the amounts of money we deal with, but traders do some crazy shit,
especially when it comes to people who want our business. I made a
promise to myself that I'd never use my position in the mean-spirited
way Gary did. And yet, for a laugh, I have no problem using my status
at Argus to make people dance a little.

Once, during my Argus days, Brad, my sales trader from Lehman,
calls. There are a dozen or more guys like Brad who'll do anything for
commissions. I've been out with Brad numerous times, for dinner and
at clubs. I like him. He's a couple of years younger than me and holds
a junior position on Lehman's trading desk. Actually, I see some of the
old me in him: he's a little overwhelmed and people like to pick on
him. Brad is a good sport about it. He went to Syracuse University and
comes from Jersey. Now he's on the phone, begging for orders. But
before he gets to business he rehashes a recent night out.

"You're like the Joan Rivers of Wall Street," he says. "You know
everyone."

I act like I'm offended, but I'm really not. I like that people know
me. I hang the phone up. *Click.* He calls right back. "I think we were
disconnected," he says. Nope. *Click.* This happens three times in a
row. Finally on the fourth, I let him speak. "You're really mad at me
for that?" he asks.

"Uh-huh," I say.

"Aw, Turney . . . please. Let me trade with you."

"Maybe," I say. "But first you have to get back in my good graces."

"Anything," he says.

"Okay, I want you to climb up on your desk and sing 'Milkshake.' "

"Come on," he pleads.

"You heard me: up on your desk and leave the phone open so I can hear." First comes the shuffling of paper and the squeak of his heels. And then I hear the rap hit coming out of his mouth, off-key and with something less than full gusto: "My milkshake brings all the boys to the yard . . ." In my mind's eye, I can see him on top of the desk as the crowded Lehman trading floor stops to watch and throw balls of paper at him. I call over to Melinda and tell her to pick up the Lehman line. We're both laughing. When Brad gets back on the phone, I tell him to buy me 69,000 shares of BBH.

It didn't happen overnight, my transformation into mischief-maker head trader. Like all my other jobs on Wall Street, this first year and a half has been a learning process. At first I thought becoming the head trader at Argus would be a smooth transition. I just wanted to continue to build on what I learned at Galleon, which was considerable. The shady stuff aside, Raj's ship was crewed by some of the best talent on the Street: Dave and Gary. I knew from them that a big part of being a successful trader was just showing up every day, being ready to work, limiting mistakes, and keeping the information—coming in and going out—flowing. But at Argus I learned there were new mistakes to make. I also learned that making mistakes is the best way to learn.

One day I overheard Krishen tell a potential investor in the conference room that I traded like a cat. I'd never heard him openly compliment my trading skills, nor had I ever considered those skills feline in nature. It fact, I'm not sure that what I have is even a skill. Much later in life, I was diagnosed with a low-grade depression called dysthymia, which I apparently had for a long time. But during my trading years I thought I just had an ability to stay even-keeled. The old adage on Wall

Street is "Don't get too emotional." "Don't get married to a stock" is how it's said. I never have that problem. I never get angry when a stock goes against me, and neither do I get too excited when one goes up. People around me see this as a kind of cool-headed detachment, but I really don't have control over it. And it gives me a clarity that many other traders lack.

Often, when the price of a stock is going against Angeli, our senior biotechnology analyst, she bolts out of her office, all anxious to sell. One day when I'm on the phone she asks: "What's going on with Biogen?" I hang up to see what she wants. The stock has been selling off for a couple of days on no news. Have the fundamental reasons we bought the stock changed? I ask. "No," she says nervously. "But we have to sell the position because it keeps going lower." As soon as she walks away, I buy more Biogen. Her threshold for pain is my buy signal. That's when stocks rally.

Maybe Krishen's right. I do like to sit and observe everything around me before I pounce. Some of my best trades are derived from watching others. Take Nate, for example. He's the most treasured guy in the office. The reason? He's just about always wrong. Whatever he gives me, I go the other way. And there's Vivek, a guy we hired from the sell side. Indian and super intelligent, Vivek, in my opinion, needs a bigger set of balls. He's a great analyst, but he doesn't know how to size his bets. When he says, "Buy twenty-five thousand shares of Medtronics," I buy fifty thousand. I know he's usually right, but he just doesn't appreciate how aggressive one needs to be if a stock is on the rise.

I read the body language of those around me and cast a wide net, sponging up information from our portfolio manager, our less senior analysts Karin and Zandy, my fellow traders, even the guy with the tiny 401(k) who brings me my bacon, egg, and cheese in the morning.

If he's got a bad feeling about his investment, I don't dismiss it. I'll usually take the other side of his trade. It's all information, and it all goes into how I work.

I guess that, partly, my unorthodox way of trading was born out of the lack of any other skill to rely on, at least any other skill in the traditional Wall Street sense. Reading research puts me to sleep, I don't get excited by market news, and I'm not into technical analysis. I trust my instincts. And, so far, it's working very well. *Meow.*

From Galleon, I also brought to Argus some experience in another facet of my job. In October, it's customary for hedge funds to develop a budget indicating the level of commission that will be paid to each broker in the coming year. Though the commissions are paid after each individual trade, the targets give me a guideline to follow. How much each brokerage gets is a decision that usually falls to the head traders and the research team—with the portfolio manager having the final say, of course. At Galleon, I wasn't making the decisions. But I did handle the spreadsheet that kept track of commissions. It was my job to alert Gary or David if we were ahead or behind in the commission budgets. It was during that time that I began to learn the science behind "bang for the buck," as they called it in the office. I saw that whether you pay the big houses, such as Goldman Sachs, a million or a half million, you get the same service and resources. If you pay them two million you reach another level, but we aren't going to do that. So the answer is to pay Goldman $500k. It's an art to pay as little as you can to get what you want.

Now it's my duty to evaluate our sales traders. This will be the second October I'll perform this task at Argus. Once I compose the list I hand it to Krishen and the entire research team. Overall, I try to be as honest and objective as I can, but I'd be lying if I told you I wasn't also protecting my friends and the guys who entertain me. I have to show that Randy and James are making money for us. Otherwise Krishen will question why we're paying their firms well above the going rate.

I tell Krishen that Randy gets me great info. Sometimes I use other people's moneymaking ideas and give Randy the credit for it. With James, I tell Krishen that his firm loses a lot of money when we ask for capital, but the truth is that his firm loses nothing. Sometimes when I'm trying to get a trade on the tape I'll just ask another broker to "put me up," meaning I want them to take the other side of my trade and take the risk. If the stock goes up like I think it will, he'll lose money until he covers his short. If the stock stays put or goes lower he can cover his short and get out flat or make some money. But the truth is, I'm usually on the winning side. The edge the house has in a casino pales by comparison. Honestly, the broker doesn't stand a chance. But the broker doesn't care because he knows it's part of the price he pays for a big slice of my commission budget. Even if he loses two hundred grand over the year in these types of trades, if I'm paying him a million in commissions during that time, he's still ahead $800,000. Gus's commissions are a lot less involved. His are on a level that Krishen doesn't even pay attention to. He's easy to hide.

The total we're paying the Street this year is somewhere between $30 and $35 million. Of that, I'm going to pay Randy's firm seven figures. That's a big milestone for his firm since it's all in one sector—healthcare. It puts him in a very favorable light with his bosses. James will get around $300,000. Gus is going to get $100,000. But his firm pays him 40 percent of the commissions he brings in. So $40,000 goes directly into Gus's pocket. Not bad for no research, no capital.

This time of the year is fun. I have a lot of mouths to feed, but a full pantry with which to do so. Maybe the best part of budgeting commissions is that the recipient won't know how much they're getting until we pay them—budget figures are never shared with the brokers. But I know, and that's what matters. I feel powerful and mag-nanimous all at once. Wall Street is nothing more than a bunch of boys and girls waiting for Christmas morning. And I'm the Secret Santa with all the gifts. Best of all, big commissions bring big expense accounts. And at Argus, there's no limit to the way the brokers treat me. Now I set my own limits on being entertained.

18

IN DECEMBER 2002, I'm invited to a big Wall Street charity event. Actually, I received the invite a month before, accepted, and then forgot about it. James calls and reminds me the party is tomorrow night. I'm about to blow it off when he begins to guilt me. "Come on, man, it's for a good cause," he says. I know he's more invested in the party than the cause, but his ploy works and I start thinking about what I should wear.

I haven't had my hair cut in six months, and I only shave twice a week. Not very Warren Buffett of me, I know. I'm also as skinny as I was when I was nineteen. I've hired a personal trainer and started going to the gym regularly. When I went to Equinox to arrange for the trainer, I told the salesperson I wanted a female, someone around my age and fun to be with. He asked me if I wanted a trainer or a date. Her name is Mavis, and she works me hard.

After my workout, I go down to Cheap Jack's, a vintage clothing store below Union Square. I like shopping in places like Jack's, thrift shops, and even the Salvation Army. Outside of my work clothing, I wear one-of-a-kind things, like my white and blue Indian-style sweater with huge buffaloes on the front and back (it's so ugly, it's beautiful), and my lace-up cowboy shirt. But today I'm on a mission.

The salesgirl at Jack's is about twenty-two, with multiple facial piercings and two full sleeves of tattoos. Her hair is dyed so black, it has a purple hue. "Can I help you?" she asks. Shopping for vintage clothing is like looking for love. You really don't know what you want until you find it. The process can't be rushed, and you can't be led.

"Nah, I'm all right," I say with a smile. I spend an hour on the first floor, rummaging through all of the circular racks. I find a few good shirts, including a powder blue ruffled tuxedo shirt, but I'm looking for something . . . daring. "We have more stuff downstairs," the sales-girl says, sensing my disappointment.

The basement is more like it: racks of clothing a block long, one after another. I stand on the bottom step and breathe in the pungent odor of camphor and dry-cleaning solvent. How many lives have been lived in these clothes? What kind of adventure have these threads seen? It's in this moment of contemplation that something clear across the room catches my eye. I walk directly toward it, pull it off of its hanger, and check the size. Like it was made for me. I have to have it.

The next night I make my way to Cipriani's on Forty-Second Street. The invitation said eight p.m., so I arrive around nine. At the very least, I expect there'll be forty or fifty people at the party I know, if not more. Argus is starting to exceed expectations. Although making money has been difficult, investors keep investing. We're inching closer to a billion dollars under management, which will put us in select company. A billion-dollar hedge fund is a big deal, but a billion-dollar hedge fund in only one sector (healthcare) is a bigger deal. I've started to develop a reputation on the Street, both during work and particularly after. Sales traders tell me they know they're in for a big night anytime they have a dinner planned with me. They're never sure what I'm going to say or do next. I know most of my sales coverage will be here, some ghosts from Galleon and maybe a few friends from my Morgan Stanley days. I get out of the cab and walk through the lobby. "Oh my god, look at him," I hear one doorman say to another.

The space used to be a savings and loan bank when they weren't afraid to show off. Glorious chandeliers hang from a soaring ceiling that is supported by towering marble columns. The floor is marble tile that shines with the reflection from the subdued lighting and squeaks under the soles of five-hundred-dollar shoes. The room is filled with Wall Street's elite.

I would imagine that wearing a bright orange prison jumpsuit to any event would garner some attention. But at this particular party, especially in this Eliot Spitzer, Enron, and Tyco era, my outfit is a bit more frightening than your average party costume. No doubt, it represents the worst nightmare of a few of the attendees. But I'm not trying to make some kind of political statement. If you asked me in this moment why I wore it, I'd tell you it was a business move, to get the room's attention. But maybe the reason is simply that I'm on the buy side and I can get away with it. It symbolizes freedom to me, not incarceration.

I make my way to the bar. The crowd parts to get a look at me. I stride through them. As I do, I get smiles, thumbs-ups, and high-fives. The bartender grins and asks me what I'd like. I'm sipping my beer when Gus almost tackles me. Randy and James follow close behind. "Outstanding," Randy says.

"Tendy," says James.

"Dude, you have to meet my bosses," Gus says breathlessly. "They're gonna love you." Gus and I walk across the dance floor. In the middle of the crowd he whispers that he has a present for me. I tell him I'm planning on meeting Lily later.

"Just take it, man," Gus insists. "I got three more in my pocket." I place my hand under his and open up my palm for the half-inch drop. Although it's done subtly, I feel like the entire event sees the pass. I quickly stuff the coke underneath my jumpsuit into my pants pocket.

When we get across the room, there are two men standing by themselves next to a high round table on which lie two cocktail napkins with watery rings. The men now clutch their drinks. Vinnie and Robert are Gus's bosses. Vinnie's bald and wears a double-breasted suit that looks like a remnant from his eighties clubbing days. But he has a charming smile. He probably got a raft-load of chicks back in the day. Robert is obviously Vinnie's lesser half. He smiles and nods a lot. He has a thick brown mustache and eyes to match. I doubt he got many chicks at all. "I hear orange is the new black," Vinnie says, pumping my hand. "Great to finally meet you."

Over the next few hours I talk with people from all over the Street: Goldman, Morgan, Citi, Credit Suisse, Bear Stearns, Lehman, and on and on. And every conversation goes just about the same as the sales pitch I'm getting from Vinnie: "We have the best execution . . . We're on the floor next to the Big Pharma specialists . . . We can do this . . . We can do that . . ." After a while, it all folds into one squawking disharmony. Not even my outfit can throw anyone off their sales pitch. Big Banking couldn't care less what you look like as long as you are putting money in their pockets. I'm not sure exactly when it happens, whether it's while I'm talking with Vinnie or Lehman or Credit Suisse, but the scene cuts to a bird's-eye-view camera angle. There I am, an orange robin surrounded by flock of black crows. Suddenly I have an urge to do the entire bag of cocaine, anything to escape. "I have to use the bathroom," I say. I look around the room and see that all the wings have been clipped. Everything is so corporate and homogenized. If everyone grew their hair, dressed with flair, and spoke their mind, I'd be the first one in line at the barber shop, shopping at Brooks Brothers, and picking up a copy of *Barron's* to have stuff to talk about on Monday.

As I walk out of the bathroom, I can feel my heart beat from the hit of coke. The huge room seems to have shrunk, and everyone is looking at me. I start desperately searching for Randy and James. When I finally find them, I beg them to leave with me. When we get out to the street, I feel exactly the way I look: like an escaped con. We leave Gus behind. The last I see of him, he's pitching some hedge fund guys from Connecticut. We head over to the Wetbar.

Inside, the place is packed. Lily sees me and breaks into a beautiful smile and then blows me a kiss. After she takes care of her customers, she makes her way down to me. "Hey," she says, her eyes gleaming. "What's with the orange jumpsuit?"

"It felt right," I say.

"You look cute," she says.

For the rest of the night, I have most of Lily's attention. I think about the coke in my pocket a couple of times, but I don't want her to see me higher than I already am. I stay only for a couple of drinks, then I grab her hand and let her know I'm going to leave; I need to get some sleep, I say. She smiles sadly but says okay. She asks me to wait one second. She runs to the other end of the bar and grabs something behind the cash register. She hurries back and hands me a crumpled-up napkin and makes me promise not to open it until I get home. "Of course," I say as I stuff it into my pants pocket.

When I get home, I reach into my pocket and feel the present from Gus. It's still practically full. Then I open up the napkin from Lily. It's a Hershey's Kiss. I strip down to my boxer briefs and place the bag of cocaine and the chocolate kiss from Lily in my sock drawer. I ball the jumpsuit up and toss it into the hamper and crawl into bed.

19

BEFORE I fall asleep I realize I need to tell Lily something. I go see her the next night. The doorman at Wetbar recognizes me immediately. I've been coming here at least once a week with various sales traders who want to meet for a drink. Usually I don't say a word about Lily to them and just wait to see their reaction when she comes up and plants a big kiss on me. But this night I'm here by myself.

When I see her from a distance, my breath catches in my throat. I'm standing in the middle of a crowded bar, but the only thing I can see is her. She doesn't see me. She's working hard pouring drinks, taking orders, and hitting the cash register. I turn around and head for the exit. I came to break up with her. My relationship with Lily never broke the surface; it was cocktails, laughs, and some sex. I just don't see how it'll work. I can't see myself slowing down or her moving faster. She's got a son. Actually, all of these excuses are garbage. I'm not in love. I don't know what love is, but I assume I will when it happens. This is not it. Maybe it's the trader in me that knows to pull the trigger. I hear it all the time: Don't get married to a stock. Don't be emotional. If I'm in a bad trade, I bail. But I realize breaking up with someone while they're at work is not the right thing to do. I'll call her tomorrow or maybe the day after.

20

IN LATE February 2003, I have flu-like symptoms: a fever, lethargy, gastrointestinal issues, a cough, and a sore throat. It can mean one of two things. Either I have SARS or I'm hungover. The fact that I went to Café Noir and drank a lot of tequila and then stopped by the White House makes me think it's the latter. But who knows, because everyone is afraid of the SARS virus. People are talking about a pandemic, and the Asian markets have been in a free fall. Just last week, an American businessman traveling from China developed the symptoms. The plane was diverted and he was taken to a hospital. He died there along with the doctor who treated him. Now the World Health Organization has issued a global alert. This is serious. There are traders on the floor of the Hong Kong exchange wearing surgical masks.

They say for every action there is a reaction, but on Wall Street it might be more fitting to say for every tragedy there's a trade. And right now the SARS virus has the attention of the healthcare investment universe. Just about every day, research tells us of a new, tiny biotech company that either is working on a vaccine for the flu or has uncovered a new strain, which could be good for healthcare stocks, though very bad for the human race. These days, our morning meetings are almost entirely focused on the topic of SARS and the moneymaking opportunities it provides. And these opportunities are not just confined to drug makers and medical supply companies. The virus has the potential to seriously affect the airlines, tourism, restaurants, air filter companies, quarantine centers. You can cast the net as wide as you want.

At the morning meeting I'm sitting at the conference table pinching my nose with a tissue. I've already made three trips to the wastepaper basket with balled-up snotty ones. As I grab a fresh Kleenex, a curious thought comes to me. Maybe I'm not a capitalist. I have to look around to see if the trading gods are about to strike me down with a bolt of lightning. No? Okay, I'm good. But what am I doing with my life? Our country is about to go to war in Iraq and you can still smell the fumes from the pit at Ground Zero, and I'm sitting here trying to figure ways to make money off of SARS.

It's not the first time I've questioned my career. Back when I was trading for Galleon, we were short a ton of stock in a company that had a phase-three cancer drug we thought wouldn't get approval from the FDA. I remember feeling sick to my stomach at the idea of rooting against a drug that could possibly let cancer patients live longer. I drank myself into a stupor that night. At some point, maybe halfway through the bottle of Patrón, it came to me. This had nothing to do with the cancer patients. It was purely an investment decision. Like Hyman Roth once said on the roof of a Cuban hotel: "This is the business we've chosen." We weren't rooting against the drug. We just didn't think it would get approved. It's business, that's all.

The thought of Hyman Roth snaps me back to my senses just before I suggest a group hug or a candle-lighting ceremony to the analysts and traders. I remind myself of my plan for 2003. I want to make a bonus of a million dollars. That's my goal. And it looks like the market is about to cooperate.

After an end-of-the-year rally in 2002, stocks dipped in January and February. But despite SARS, there are signs of a bull market on the horizon. Over the past two months, the market held the lows of 2002, which is a bullish indication. And then there's what's happening in Iraq. The old adage goes "Buy on the cannons, sell on the trumpets." Going to war is good for the stock market. But to take advantage of the brightening financial situation, I need to make some adjustments. I need to change the way I trade.

For the most part, traders at hedge funds can be divided into two categories. Either you're an execution trader or a proprietary trader. Though I've prop traded a bit before, first at Galleon, then at Argus, the majority of these trades were small: fives and tens. For most of this time I've been an execution trader. An execution guy's primary job is to not fuck anything up. You follow instructions from analysts and portfolio managers as literally as you can. I remember one of Melinda's first trades on the desk. Krishen walked by and told her to buy ten Amgen. So she called up Morgan Stanley and bought ten AMGN, just like she was told. It wasn't until the next day, when Krishen asked where the ten thousand shares of AMGN were, that she realized "ten" was shorthand. A billion-dollar fund would never buy only ten little shares of anything.

There's nothing wrong with being an execution trader. It's safe. But by this time in my trading life I'm like an eighteen-year-old with his Camaro. I want to start taking bigger bets on my own and making more money for Argus. Because, at the end of every day, or year, as a prop trader I can go to Krishen and say, "This is what I made." Being a prop trader is the best way to quantify your worth. It's the best way to make a million-dollar bonus.

Of course, this doesn't come without risk, and each day your worth is documented on paper in red or black ink. But the freedom of it is exhilarating. As a prop trader, I'm given capital by Argus to initiate my own trades; there are no analysts or portfolio managers telling me what to do. I buy, sell, short, and cover. It's all up to me.

I start modestly by buying 25,000, then 50,000 shares at a time. Then one day I get an idea. Every trade has to be printed so it can scroll across the ticker, or "hit the tape," as we say. We get the same information as the ticker on our "times and sales" quote screen, but faster. Whether it's on the ticker or on our computer, though, when a trade hits the tape, everybody on Wall Street can see it.

So I punch the UBS light and tell my sales trader to buy 69,000 shares of BBH, the same buy I gave to Brad. The BBH is an exchange-traded fund made up of eighteen different biotechnology companies. It's a basket of stocks. For me it's a bet. I think the whole group is going up. And I come up with the number 69 as a way of embedding the trade in the juvenile minds of my fellow traders. Later I sell the 69,000 shares with Goldman. The next time I do it I use two different brokers, but always in blocks of 69,000 shares. In less than a week, I've used every broker I deal with several times, so they all know that when they see the 69,000 shares of BBH hit the tape, it's me.

Now, except for a couple of immature giggles (mine included), my mark wouldn't mean much if I didn't work for one of the largest healthcare funds on the Street, which I do, and for a portfolio manager whose performance at Galleon is legendary, which Krishen's is. We're considered smart money. So when my 69,000 shares are printed in the BBH market, it not only draws attention, but makes the sell side begin to wonder if Argus knows something. And the last thing anybody on the sell side wants is to be in the dark. My phone starts ringing with sell siders telling me they could have done better on my last print, saying they can be more competitive. With each order I give out, my pricing gets tighter. Give me a chance, they plead. The dogs begin to howl for my business.

Though using 69 is an original idea and as far as I know unique, smart traders have been finding ways to separate themselves from the crowd for years. Wall Street isn't like slots in Vegas, where you are playing against the house. This is poker, with winners and losers sitting at the same table. Picture two hedge fund traders, one from Hedge Fund A and the other from Hedge Fund B. Both have identical educational backgrounds, identical resources, and identical ability to process the same information. But that doesn't mean they'll make the same amount on the same idea. It's the art of making money. It's a skill.

I don't have the same educational background as many of the people I trade with and against. I don't have the advantages other traders have or have been given. So I have to find my own edge. I take what I've learned in my first eighteen months at Argus, the ability to read people and nuances, add my alliances with the other members of the Healthcare Mafia and the courage of a teenage Camaro driver, and then stamp all of it with the number 69. And guess what? I start to get really good at what I do. Soon I'll be sitting at the poker table with everyone's money.

Sometime later, I'm at another morning meeting. Though I'm physically feeling much better, I'm about to fade out from all the biotech research babble when I hear Vivek say something about hospitals using temporary staffing companies instead of hiring nurses full-time. He says he's noticing a new trend. I sit up in my seat. This is a shift. A change. This could be a big deal.

Krishen, Vivek, and I work together to quickly identify which companies stand to benefit most from this new trend. We find three major players and a couple of secondary players, all big healthcare staffing firms. But none of these stocks are liquid. There's a saying on the Street that some stocks "trade by appointment," which means that the stock is difficult to buy or sell because the average daily volume is tiny, usually less than 100,000 shares. A large buy order would drive the stock up dramatically and send up rockets and flares to all our competitors. Establishing a position in companies like these, at least in the size of the portfolio we envision, has to be done gently and over time, of which we don't have all that much. In three weeks these companies are due to report earnings. Undoubtedly the report, held on a conference call with potential investors, will include a discussion of this new trend. Once it happens, the proverbial cat will be out of the bag.

Each day I buy as much as I can. I don't want to show the pair of aces I have in the hole, so I call a few of the bigger bulge bracket firms to see what's going on with the stock. I don't tell them if I'm a buyer or seller. I just want to get a feel for the market. I buy in small increments on the machine, Instinet, so as not to move the stock too much. I also try to find a natural seller, so we can just cross stock without drawing attention. But I don't have any luck.

It takes me close to two weeks to secure our full position, about three or four hundred thousand shares for each stock. Then I call two of my fellow Healthcare Mafia members and tell them to meet me at a place called Mexican Radio after work. They know what this means:

I have information they'll want to hear. I'm not just being a nice guy. I know if I help them, and make them look good in front of their bosses, they'll owe me. I also want them to create buy interest in the stocks when the time is right.

When I walk into Mexican Radio, they're sitting at the bar. Roger works at a billion-dollar macro fund that trades a lot of healthcare, and Trevor is at a multibillion-dollar healthcare fund. The protocol for our Mafia meetings is to never start with business. We spend the first half hour drinking margaritas and discussing the usual bullshit: What's new? How's work? Any new chicks? That kind of stuff. Once the warm-up is out of the way, I tell them about the staffing call we have, which companies are involved, and how much we think the stocks will rise. We suck down a few more Shortwaves, the signature margarita at the Radio, smoke a few cigarettes, and then head home for the night.

Over the next two days, the stocks continue to rise; my allies have clearly convinced their portfolio managers to buy. I then let the story out to a few more hedge fund traders I know. Now the stocks are really starting to move. By then, we've already made a significant amount of money. So much so, the prudent move might be to get out. But Vivek tells us the stocks still look cheap and should go higher. We wait.

By the time the staffing companies release the news about the new trend, the stocks are up over 10 percent on the day, a huge move in the premarket. The short interest (the outstanding shares that are shorted) is high, as a lot of hedge funds had a negative view on the sector before this morning's news. I wait for the opening bell as the stocks continue to climb, now up nearly 15 percent. It's time for me to go to work.

I call five brokers on the Street: Goldman, Morgan, Merrill, Citi, and Credit Suisse–First Boston. Though I want to sell, I don't want the Street to know that yet. So I tell the big five that I have a large buy I need to make in the staffing sector. I act like I'm losing money, tripping over my words. It's a hand I can't overplay. I'm not dealing with idiots (well, maybe one or two of them are). But I've seen plenty of traders in this situation for real—I've been there myself. I know how to make it sound believable. They tell me they have to call me back. I know as soon as they hang up the phone they'll be screaming that they have a large buyer for all staffing company stocks across their trading floor. Then all of their coworkers will start to make outgoing calls with the same information. Meanwhile, I'm at my desk getting my sell tickets ready. Each return call I get is about the same: "Sorry, nothing for sale." And by now, the sell side firms have told most of their accounts that they have a large buyer of my stocks. The entire mood has changed. The smart money is buying, and everybody wants in. Perception becomes reality. I do run the risk that someone might find a seller and I'll get a call offering me a shitload of stock, but I'll deal with that if it happens. It doesn't.

By the end of the day the stocks are up nearly 30 percent. I give Gus a call to sell some of our positions, not only to throw Turbo a few poker chips, but because I want to use someone who wasn't involved at all. The longer I keep my identity as a seller from the Street the better the stocks will continue to perform. But I can only keep it secret for so long, and over the next two days I sell off the remainder of the stocks until we're flat. In the end, Argus is nearly seven million dollars richer. Not bad for three weeks' work.

In the office, most of the credit goes to Vivek, for coming up with the idea in the first place. That's fine with me. I'm not looking for applause. I'm looking toward bonus time, and my million-dollar goal. That night I'm at the Radio again with Roger and Trevor. "Nice trade, my man," says Trevor. I nod and order a Patrón Silver on the rocks with three limes. "Any new chicks?" I ask. There's nothing more about the staffing deal to say. We all know what we made, and what is owed. After a few laughs and another round, Roger asks for the check. I watch them walk out the door and then I order another Patrón. On the bar, my cell buzzes. I look at the text. It's from Randy. "Come over," it says.

21

BY THE spring of 2003, Argus Partners assets under management exceed the one-billion-dollar mark and we continue to grow. It's as if we're printing money. We're up, so we press. As we make more money, our bets get bigger. Galleon healthcare is a distant memory. When the Street thinks about healthcare, they think about Argus. When the Street thinks about trading healthcare, they think of me.

You really don't see it coming, the change. It's not like you get a memo or a tap on the shoulder from your boss telling you you're relevant now. No, you just wake up and your entire world is different. You're on every guest list, the tab is always picked up, and you're invited everywhere by your new "best" friends. I'm not saying it isn't exciting—it is. I sat on the fifty-yard line at last year's Super Bowl, one of the greatest ever played. The Patriots, a two-touchdown underdog, beat the Rams in overtime on Adam Vinatieri's field goal; I had even better seats at the double-overtime championship game the Miami Hurricanes and

Ohio State Buckeyes played in Tempe; I went to the Sundance Film Festival. There, I stayed in a seven-bedroom chalet on the ski mountain. I've taken helicopters to the Hamptons, and private jets to Vegas.

Although things are great, I feel like something is missing. I wonder what Lily is doing. The main reason I don't ever get serious with women is because I hate the breakup. Anything after a few dates requires "the talk," and I hate the talk. When I called her, we didn't make plans to meet again. We just said good night. The phone calls back and forth started to become further and further apart, with no plans being made. One day the calls just stopped coming and she faded to the background. I'm not sure if I left her in my wake or she left me in hers. I guess it doesn't really matter. I think I miss my old life. Because of business dinners and spending too much time with Randy and James at the White House, I rarely spend time with my roommates anymore. Before I started working on the buy side, Jason and I were always out together. We had a schedule: on Wednesdays it was Gentleman Jacks on the Upper West Side, Thursdays we went to Dakota on the Upper East Side, and Friday and Saturday we'd bar hop and always end up at Red Rock West. We also had our own bar routines. Sometimes we'd start with the invisible double Dutch move. We'd clear a circle and get two guys to pretend to be turning the ropes as we jumped. Or we'd do our Annie bit. We'd get on our hands and knees, pretend to scrub the floors, and sing "It's a Hard Knock Life." We were a team, like Bert and Ernie, Butch and Sundance, or Laverne and Shirley. We'd been performing together for so long, we no longer had to rehearse our lines. It all came naturally. I might be talking with a girl and Jason would interrupt and say, "Oh, Turney, I forgot to tell you, your agent called this afternoon." Then he'd just walk away. From there, I could tell any lie I wanted. I could be an actor, an artist, or a writer. But rarely a Wall Street trader.

But one day I get a phone call from a guy named Drew and I see an opportunity to bring Jason back into my social life. Drew acts like he knows me, but I've never met him. He explains he's the head of trading at Susquehanna, a Philadelphia-based firm that recently made a push into sales and trading, the customer facilitation business. Drew invites me to South Beach for the weekend with a bunch of their guys from Philly and some of their clients from New York. He tells me they're renting a jet, a BBJ 737. The BBJ doesn't really mean anything to me—it sounds like part of a personal ad on Craigslist—but the 737 tells me it's big, real big. I say I'll go, and I'm just about to hang up when a thought comes to me. Would it be okay to bring a new hire on the trip? I ask. When I tell my roommate Jason we're going to South Beach on a private jet, we're staying in a sweet hotel, and everything's paid for, he screams like a schoolgirl. There's just one catch, I say. "You gotta pretend you're my trading assistant."

That Friday, Jason walks into the apartment with an exaggerated shoulder swing. With each step he takes, he thrusts forward his hips and pouts his lips. "Dude!" I say.

"This is my trader walk," he explains. When he asks what he should wear, I tell him a button-down shirt and khaki pants. Fifteen minutes later he comes down doing the same exaggerated walk but now pulling his Tumi bag on wheels behind him. He looks like a flight attendant on the catwalk. He's wearing a blue button-down and khakis, though. He looks at me and notices I have on tattered shorts, flip-flops, and a white T-shirt. "Why are you wearin' that and I'm wearin this?" he asks. "Because you're dressed like someone who works on Wall Street," I say, "and, well, I'm not."

On the ride to the Westchester airport I try to brief him on the ins and outs of what to say and, more important, what not to say. "What's the name of the firm again? Sushsquash?" he asks. I hold my head in my hands.

"Susquehanna," I say. "Write it on your hand if you have to."

The car service drives us right out onto the tarmac. The only thing missing is a red carpet. A Boeing jet this size, at least one outfitted for commercial use, seats at least a hundred and fifty. But inside the plane, there are only twenty or so guys—each dressed exactly like Jason with their blue button-downs and tan pants. I hear the pop from a bottle of champagne being opened. Then another. The comfortably spaced seats in the back of the plane are full, so we find a spot up front. The leather chairs recline. There's a couch and a coffee table. An oriental rug covers the floor, and recessed lighting gives the space a muted glow. The kitchen galley looks bigger than most apartments in New York City. A flat-screen TV is lowered from the ceiling. Before we even sit we're offered a cocktail. I almost forget we're on a plane. It's like a gentlemen's club with wings. Jason and I settle in and sip our beers. The pretty blond flight attendant smiles at us and then begins the instructions for takeoff.

"I love stock trading!" Jason shouts.

After we reach our cruising altitude, I meet Drew. He looks exactly how I thought he might, like any number of Wall Street brokers: brown hair, forty-something, ex-athlete. Probably has a seven handicap on his home course but plays to a fourteen anywhere else. His smile is part salesman and part aging frat boy. He's a little buzzed. But he still has the amped-up demeanor of every sales manager I've known since the days I was interviewing for my first job on Wall Street. "How are you?" he says as he glad-hands me. "Excited for the weekend?" He spends the next few minutes telling me how great I am. "You have a terrific feel for the market," he says at one point.

"Terrific feel," Jason agrees.

In Miami, we're booked in the Delano, one of the first art deco landmarks in South Beach to be restored to its original glory. Staying there makes you feel like a 1940s movie star. Perfect. We have reservations at a hot new restaurant for tonight.

When we arrive for dinner, I steer Jason to the end of the table. This way, I figure, we can avoid as much business talk as possible. But there's no keeping Jason quiet, and after a few cocktails he begins telling stories, and all of them are about me. Jason is funny, a good storyteller, and his audience of brokers are enjoying themselves. He's starting to sound more like a friend than an assistant. I'm getting nervous. Then he tells his favorite story, about how after a big night I woke up in my bed and found it filled with hay. "I think he got down with one of the horses in Central Park!" Jason exclaims to peals of laughter. I laugh and then excuse myself, and head outside to smoke. It's time to stop the Turney stories before Jason blows his cover.

In front of the restaurant, I see Sam, one of the Susquehanna clients, talking on his cell phone. He smiles at me, then turns his back and continues talking in a hushed tone. I'd noticed him texting throughout dinner. I light a cigarette. Sam now is off his phone. There's something about his body language, his expression, that sends me a signal. "Nice night," he says. I nod. We stand there for a moment in silence, looking out at the decorative palms and expensive cars that pass on Pennsylvania Avenue and sharing the uneasy bond of strangers who have something unsaid in common. I flick my cigarette out into the drive in front of the restaurant. "Anybody party on this trip?" I ask. He looks at me with the smile of an old friend.

"On its way," he says.

When I get back into the restaurant, our end of the table has moved to the bar. Jason sits on a barstool, talking animatedly. Four

Susquehanna traders circle him and seem to be hanging on his every word. Uh oh, I think. This could be trouble. "I trade the Qs," he's saying. "The QQQ." All four guys around him nod like he's the Delphic oracle. This is hilarious. Traders know what the Qs are their first day of work. It's an ETF just like the BBH, but it represents the Nasdaq 100 and is primarily made up of technology stocks. Saying you trade the QQQs is like announcing you breathe air.

Jason then notices that a Susquehanna guy's concentration has begun to wander. He's looking down the bar at a girl. Jason gently lays his hand on the guy's shoulder, as if to say: "Pay attention." The guy gives him an apologetic smile, and Jason continues. "I trade 'em tight," he tells them. Now even the bartender seems to be listening to Jason. "I like to cross shit," my roommate says. "Mix it up, keep 'em guessing. That's my style." The Susquehanna guys' heads are now bobbing up and down. Jason chooses his words like an exchange student from Bolivia who learned English from watching MTV—but like a puffed-up actor, he teases his audience with dramatic pauses. "I even trade teenies," he adds, folding his arms to allow his words to marinate. Though "a teenie" is a price—one-sixteenth of a point—and not something that can actually be traded, the Susquehanna guys say nothing to Jason. Instead, they smile and look at one another with blank stares.

"That's great," one finally says. "You know," another says to Jason in a voice just above a whisper, "I want to get to the buy side someday." Jason takes a moment to ponder this, and then he forms a phone with his pinky and thumb, lifts it to his ear, and gives it a little shake.

"Call me," he mouths.

I pull Jason away from the group. I tell them we're going outside for a cigarette. We barely make it out of the restaurant before we burst into laughter. I trade the Qs? I trade 'em tight? Teenies? Just as I'm thinking about how funny my roommate is and how great this weekend with him is going to be, a white Lexus pulls up. Sam emerges from the car with a glorious smile, like he just hit the lottery numbers. As he approaches, I see him reaching for his pocket. I don't want Jason to see me get the handoff. He doesn't know half of my Wall Street dealings. Sam and I lock eyes for a moment. I send him the "Be cool" signal with my eyes. He picks up on it immediately and moves in to shake my hand. He slaps my palm with a medium-size ziplock bag and what feels like a lot of pills. I close my fist and slide it into my pants pocket. When nobody's looking I pop two of the pills in my mouth. The courage of my tequila buzz squashes any fear of ingesting a stranger's drug. Let's hope for the best.

Jason and I make our way back to the bar, and right next to three girls with tans, short skirts, and big earrings. They look like they're from Miami. They're hot. They barely notice us, so Jason takes it upon himself to introduce us as Trevor Licious and Turney Me-On. The girls laugh. It's right about then that it starts to happen. First I feel a tingle coming from deep inside, which begins to move outward, like an ocean's current. Now I'm smiling. Everything s-l-o-w-s down and all is okay. It's better than okay: it's perfect. This f-e-e-l-s nice. Look at the pretty lights shining on the bottles behind the bar. That's c-o-o-o-l. The tingle is now vibrant and engulfs me. There isn't a problem in the whole world, but if there were I could solve it. My words slice the room like Hemingway's; I have the edge of James Dean and the rhythm of Michael Jackson.

My body acts in concert with the beat of the music. Inhaling the scent of the girl's perfume is like being wrapped in fragrant silk. Everything I touch emits the energy of love. I hit every beat; my timing is perfect. The girls laugh. Our group is getting up from the table. The girls start to gather their things. They head for the exit. I need a cigarette. Back outside, I light up. The valet has pulled the girls' convertible Bronco around front. I turn around. Jason is inside talking to some guys. I look back at the girls. They wave me over. I look back. Jason, Sam, and a few of the other guys make their way toward me. The girls, now in the Bronco, are waiting for me to make my move. I run to the truck. I jump into the backseat. We take off. The way we head is a dead end, so the girl driving the Bronco makes a tire-squealing U-turn and we fly back past the restaurant. Jason, Sam, and a herd of Susquehanna guys are screaming at us. They chase us for half a block. I reach into my pocket for the bag of ecstasy pills. I count them with a glance. There are seventeen left. I take two more and give one to each of the girls. The night has started.

Now I'm in a hotel room. I guess the girls aren't from Miami. I start to kiss one while the other two begin to make out. We're all naked on the bed. More ecstasy. Now we're in a club. The music is loud. More alcohol. I'm making out with one of the girls again. I think it's the same one. Back in the jeep, the cool Miami night air blows through my hair as we speed along Collins Avenue. More ecstasy and more alcohol and back in another club.

It's six a.m. and I realize I'm alone. I'm standing in the middle of a club called Space. The music is obnoxiously loud and the same beat over and over again. I think there are smoke machines on the dance floor. Everyone is walking around like zombies. And then it's as if someone abruptly flips a switch. My brain zaps. The noise in my head is unbearable. I need to go home. I bump into a couple of guys from the trip. They want to know where the ecstasy is and how I got here. But then they ask the most bizarre question. "Dude, what are you wearing?" I look down and see that I have a woman's pink Izod shirt on. It hangs right above my belly button like a girl's half shirt.

I know I'm not the most honorable person in the world, but I try to make good decisions. It was wrong to leave Jason and all the

Susquehanna guys. It was wrong to keep all the drugs to myself. I don't want to be that guy. It's not the first time I've made poor choices that contradict the person I want to be. Maybe that's the problem. I want to be someone.

Early the next afternoon, I'm by the pool, stretched out on a chaise lounge. Even with my sunglasses, the bright glare bores right through my eyes into my head. My mouth feels like it's filled with beach sand. In ones and twos, the Susquehanna guys come over and tell me how much fun they had with me last night. They say nothing about the ecstasy I took from them, of course. Nor do they mention anything about my going MIA. They're the same as they were on the plane down, or at dinner last night. I'm the client, no matter how bad I behave. Jason lies on the chair next to me, uncharacteristically quiet. Finally, it's just us two. "What happened to you last night?" he asks. I close my eyes to block out the sun and shake my head.

22

IT'S THE early summer of 2003, and my parents are coming to New York and are going to stop by my Tribeca apartment for the first time. When I get home from work on a Friday, I begin to tidy up. For the most part, my roommates and I keep the apartment clean, but there's always the odd empty beer can or pack of rolling papers lying around. I notice Jason has strategically placed a couple of porn DVDs on the coffee table along with a bong and my bag of weed. That's funny. He's getting back at me. One night, when we lived on the Upper West Side, we threw a party. When he was in the shower beforehand, I stuffed a bunch of porn magazines underneath the couch cushion in his bedroom. Once the party got rocking around midnight, I lured Jason and a few girls into his room. When I sat on the couch I acted like something was wrong with the cushion. I pulled it off and six or seven triple-X porn mags came tumbling to the ground at the girls' feet.

My parents are in town because they're on a flight out of Kennedy to Paris tomorrow. My sister Kristin lives there now with her husband and three children, and this past Christmas I bought my mom and dad round-trip tickets on the Concorde so they could visit her. When I handed my mom the envelope with the plane tickets, on Christmas morning in the kitchen of our house in Maine, she gasped with joy. Dad said something like: "What'd you go and do that for?"

I put the pot and DVDs behind the bar and look around one final time to make sure I haven't missed any more of Jason's booby traps. Everything in the living room is either new or expensive. With all the artwork on the wall, the Indian daybed, and the modern furniture, it's like I live in some sort of Spoils of the Buy Side exhibit. I decide to turn on CNBC but mute the television to complete the set.

Just then the buzzer rings. Over the intercom, the doorman tells me my parents are at the front desk. I take the elevator down to meet them. In the lobby, Dad is making small talk with the doorman. Mom is talking to Uncle Tucker, who'll be joining us for dinner. Tucker is back in New York from San Francisco, working for a new firm and on his third wife. It was nine years ago that I moved into the tiny room in the Upper West Side apartment and called him for a job in anything related to my writing degree. It's weird how things work out. I walk down the long hallway to the front desk. My mom hugs me, and Dad and Uncle Tucker shake my hand. I lead them back to the elevator. Once we're all in, I tell my dad to hit number five. I turn to start talking to my mother, but I realize the elevator hasn't started moving. "Dad, hit five, please," I say.

"I did," he says.

I watch as he tries again. He presses his thumb as hard as he can on the number five, but he's hitting the actual number, not the button to the right of it. I reach over and push the button for him. I wonder in this moment what would've happened to me if I never left Kennebunk. Would I know how to operate an elevator?

My father grew up in Pittsburgh. I know very little about his youth—only what I heard over happy hour at Duff family get-togethers. The stories I do remember involved the usual teenage high jinks—firecrackers in mailboxes and midnight cemetery raids. I know even less about his relationship with his father, although I guess it couldn't have been great. The whispers I've heard about Grandpa's drinking and his ultimate demise in business lead me to this conclusion. It's strange. Looking back, the extended Duff family, as many as twenty-five members, spent every summer vacation in a house in Land O'Lakes, Wisconsin. We gathered at least once, sometimes twice, a year on Thanksgiving or Easter, at my grandmother's house in Upper St. Clair, just outside of Pittsburgh. And yet these memories are nearly empty of family stories. Maybe it's just that I was too young then to be interested in them. More likely, though, it has to do with the way my family keeps secrets, many of which are to this day locked in the Duff family's attics.

There are secrets on my mother's side, too. I know my mom's mother drank martinis out of milkshake glasses and smoked cigarettes in bed, where she stayed most of the time. But I found this out from Uncle Tucker only recently. I wonder if my parents' reluctance to talk about their childhoods was something they each brought to their relationship or was something that was formed because of it.

They met in high school, and then reunited when they both showed up on the campus of Bucknell University. There were pins, proposals, and a pregnancy before college was over. My father took an extra year to finish up his chemical engineering degree. My mother, then pregnant with my oldest sister, Debbie, lived on campus with him. The births of my sisters Kristin and Kelly came after graduation. And then, at my grandfather's urging, I came along—the youngest, and the only boy.

I don't have any of those clichéd memories of playing catch or going fishing with my father.

Instead, we did yard work together, or at least we did it together for a while. It was not unusual for my father to spend every daylight hour of a weekend working around the house. It was impossible to keep up with him, or to live up to his standards. If I couldn't stack the firewood in a perfect pile, if I couldn't paint the garage without streaks, he didn't want me to stack or paint. I remember I once mowed the lawn without him asking me to. When he saw that my mow lines weren't perfectly perpendicular, he told me never to mow the lawn again. It didn't take me long to figure out that if I wanted to get out of doing chores, all I had to do was do them imperfectly. That was fine with me. I wanted to be running around with my friends, playing games or just goofing off.

Dad tolerated my mediocre grades, but he was proud of my athletic achievements. He and my mom showed up for every one of my games or meets. There they never embarrassed me; they stayed on the sidelines with their mouths closed.

But even though we shared a love of sports, we had far more differences, such as our attitudes toward wrestling. In my senior year in high school I was voted an all-star in our conference football league. My parents wanted to come to the awards ceremony, but I told them it was only for the players and coaches. It was a lie. And if you ask me now why I didn't want them there, the only excuse I can come up with is that I was eighteen and being out with my parents, I guess, still embarrassed me. But at family dinner on the night of the event, I was overcome with guilt, told them the truth, and asked if they'd attend. My father refused to go. I'm not sure whether it was his way of punishing me for lying to him or his way of saying the heck with me. My mom was upset with him, though, and later came to the ceremony by herself.

Nowhere was the discord between my father and me greater than at the dinner table, where we sat as a family every night. We had our assigned seats and our unconsciously assigned roles. My father sat at the head of the table, my mother to his left and me to her left, and my three sisters sat across from us on the bench. We used to joke, but there was truth to it, that you didn't want to sit within an arm's length of my father at dinner. If your elbows were on the table or you were engaging in some other unforgivable act such as chewing with your mouth open, wearing a hat, or not wearing shoes, you paid the price with a swift backhand smack. Usually it was just to knock your elbow off the table, but as a child the shock of it was what hurt. To this day, I'm uncomfortable at a dinner table, though I can't lay all of the blame on my dad.

As the youngest and the only boy, I would constantly field questions from my sisters about my social life. When they heard through the Kennebunk rumor mill about a girl I was dating or something I was doing in school, they'd try to tease the information out of me. It felt like an attack. And I gave nothing up. In fact, I rarely talked at all at the table. In my senior year of high school, I was voted class flirt and most talkative. When my sisters found out from a friend of mine, they were shocked. They thought it was a joke—they didn't know I talked. But I knew that the less information I gave them, the less ammunition they had. I'd quietly finish all of the food on my plate, then ask to be excused. I just wanted to get out of the kitchen and go to the living room by myself. Even now, when I finish a meal I'm filled with anxiety. I have to get up and smoke a cigarette and then hang out at the bar. But since I'm the client, it doesn't matter.

On the outside, the Kennebunk Duffs were the picture of the perfect family—literally. We once posed for an advertising photo shoot for
Yankeeland Campground. My mom still has the brochure with the six
of us on the cover: my handsome parents and us four towheaded children, all with perfect noses. I don't, however, ever remember hearing
the words "I love you" growing up. They were never said to my sisters,
they were never said between siblings, and I never heard them between
my parents. And they were never said to me. But outside of an occa-
sional swat from my father at the dinner table, there were no arguments
and no malicious behavior. How could anything be wrong when you
have three daughters all at the top of their class, who are polite, respectable, and athletic, and a son who is creative, athletic, and—outside of
a few childish antics—respectful? What could be wrong when your
marriage has lasted forty-plus years? What could be wrong when you
live in a nice tidy house with a well-kept lawn? What could be wrong?

At some point, I guess when I entered my teens, the relationship between my father and me became the kind of war that nobody
wins—ever. It was just lots of firing missiles back and forth into enemy
territory, trying to make a direct hit. If he wanted to punish me, I'd
hide behind my mother and flash a smug smile his way. He'd flash one
back. He had all the time in the world, his grin said, and there'd be a
day when Mom wouldn't be standing between us. As I got older our
relationship matured into a respectable struggle, a gentlemen's duel
with lots of underlying causes and triggers. There's no anger in it, at
least on the surface. And that's where both of us stay.

When I look at him in the elevator I see everything that I couldn't
wait to leave behind: his small-town attitudes and values . . . his lackluster, simple life . . . his perfect stack of firewood. I don't see the man
who has the strongest work ethic I've ever known. I don't see the guy
who took a second mortgage out on our home so I could go to prep

school and then college; I don't see the breadwinner who paid for my three older sisters' education. I don't see any of that. My father once built an extension on our house—executing every step from laying the foundation to hanging the last door, all by himself. He tried to teach me how to use tools, but I didn't want any part of them. I saw no future in knowing how to use a level. If only by osmosis, some of what he tried to teach me was absorbed. I remember being on a road trip with Chris Arena, Jayme, and Jason when we blew out a tire. I was the only one who knew how to change it. My dad made me learn how to do that before he allowed me to drive a car. He wanted me to be prepared for life. He taught me how to be respectful to people, to be loyal, and to do the right thing. But on this night I can't see any of that. All I see is a man who doesn't know how to operate the elevator to my $9,300-a-month rental in Tribeca.

23

OCTOBER 2003

I'M ALONE on my roof deck the morning after my thirty-fourth birthday party. I'm not sure what time it is, but if I had to guess I'd say it's around five. The sun is just starting to rise and the clouds are edged in purple. I'm still wearing my sleeveless flannel, but I've lost my sunglasses. I have khaki shorts on and a red bar stamp from the Canal Room on my trembling hand. Sleep isn't an option at this point, not with the amount of cocaine running through my system. Fifty or so people came back to my apartment for the after-party. I grab an industrial-size garbage bag and begin throwing into it cups, bottles, cigarettes, and god knows what else.

After just a few minutes, I set the garbage bag down. I need to take the edge off. I pack a one-hitter and sit on one of the deck chairs. I look around at the carnage. The place looks like Mötley Crüe's hotel room. I guess there's really no worry that I'll become like my father. When my father turned thirty-four, he was working as a chemical engineer at American Cyanamid. He already had four kids and was struggling to pay the mortgage on a small house in Painesville, Ohio. I push the image of him, the hardworking young dad, from my mind and in its place come flashes of my birthday party, an out-of-order slide show: Treach singing "OPP," shots of tequila, ecstasy handed out like breath mints, and countless trips to the bathroom to snort cocaine. The marijuana slowly takes charge, soothing my cocaine jitters. Somewhere, deep in my ear canal, a Pink Floyd song plays. With my fingers, I comb back my almost shoulder-length hair and hold it at the base of my neck. I close my eyes and lean back. The early sun warms my face. I want to stay in this position forever. *I have become comfortably numb* . . . Then, slithering into my thoughts comes a question I keep asking myself: *Why do I feel so empty?* There's no reason I should be sad right now. I just threw a great party. Everyone had fun. I should be happy. And yet, I feel detached, like I'm watching myself in a movie. The character I play is happy. But I wonder if I am.

24

THE MARKET is going straight up and has been for months. It's like the heydays at Galleon all over again. And I'm sprinting toward bonus time and my million-dollar goal because I need the money. My salary, two hundred thousand, barely covers the bills. Along with the rent on the triplex, I still have my personal shoppers at Barneys, go on a couple of vacations a year—the last one was a trip to Cancun with Randy and a few other White House guys—and, over the summer, I shelled out fifteen grand for my share of a rental out in the Hamptons.

It's not like I'm worried I'll run out of money. If I don't make a million—a "stick," as it's called on the Street—I know my bonus is going to be at least seven or eight hundred thousand. And I think I'll make that much and more for the next twenty years. I took Looks-Like-a-Larry's advice and attached myself to revenue. And the best part of making this kind of money is the freedom it brings. I never look at a price tag anymore. If I want something, I buy it. If I want to go somewhere, I go. I don't owe a cent to anyone.

And in large measure, I've acquired this freedom by doing the opposite of what most successful Wall Street traders do. There is an axiom on the Street that goes something like this: If you want to make real money, you have to be willing to make real enemies. If Gary Rosenbach had a family crest, those words would be on it. And he certainly has real money. In 2003, the top one hundred financial traders in the world will earn a total of nearly six billion dollars with an average income of twenty-five million. And Gary's one of them. But you could fill a Gulfstream G6 with Wall Street people who despise him. I don't understand how he can live that way. I don't know what I'd do if I knew people hated me. Being liked is more than my business model. It's the most important thing in my life.

In most Wall Street careers there are lines drawn and then erased. Greed and power are maybe the biggest erasers. But there are also subtler reasons for lowering standards: the wife wants to move to a bigger house, the kids are about to go to college, you're having an affair with a girl in the intern program, all of which means you need more money and the line you thought you'd never cross doesn't seem so uncrossable anymore. I understand that. But I also know that no matter where my career goes, I'll never put myself in a position where people hate me. I'll quit before that happens.

Then one morning, the J. P. Morgan light on my turret rings. My sales trader tells me a tech company that deals in healthcare information services is having a spot secondary, which is like an IPO for stocks that are already publicly traded. The company's called Allscripts Healthcare Solutions, symbol MDRX. At Argus we have a focus list of stocks we want to own, and we've been waiting for the right price on this one for a while. My J. P. Morgan guy tells me they're offering two million shares at a discount from last night's closing price. Perfect. I tell Krishen. "Buy the whole thing," he says.

There's no chance we'll get the two million shares. J. P. Morgan has to keep many clients happy. But by asking for the full allocation, they now know how badly we want the stock. And since we do a huge amount of business with them, I have every reason to believe we'll get a healthy piece. I call the J. P. Morgan sales trader back.

Now, it usually takes some time to get your allocation, but it always comes before the stock starts trading. I have a pretty good idea of what we'll get. It has to be at least 100,000 shares. The deal is priced at seventeen dollars, and when MDRX's shares open it immediately starts trading at nineteen—I'm starting to count my money. But as the minutes tick by, my coverage hasn't called. So I call him, but he doesn't pick up. I call again. Some guy I don't know gets on the phone and then puts me on hold. I slam down the phone. Krishen walks over to my desk and asks what's wrong. I tell him we don't have our allocation yet.

I don't get angry easily, and I hardly ever raise my voice. A few months after I first started at Morgan Stanley, Uncle Tucker took me out to dinner. When he asked how it was going, I told him about two brokers who scream all day. "There are a lot of screamers in this business, Turney," he said. "They scream so much, no one listens to a word they say." But, he said, "If you're not a screamer, when you do scream people tend to listen." When the J. P. Morgan guy comes back on the phone, I tell him I want my allocation. I'm not yelling, but my words are forceful.

"Now," I say. He gives me some bullshit response about the deal being oversubscribed. It's like he's reading out of the *How to Talk to an Angry Client* manual. And that's when I lose it. "Get me my fucking allocation!" I yell. I slam down the phone. Ten minutes later, my coverage calls and tells me what he really knows.

"Sorry, Turney," he says. "You guys were shut out."

At first, I'm not sure how to react. I've never been shut out of a deal, not at Galleon or at Argus—not even a non-healthcare deal. And MDRX is a healthcare stock. This doesn't make any sense. But bewilderment quickly gives way to suspicion. "Who made this decision?" I ask the J. P. Morgan guy. He swears he doesn't know.

"I'll try to find out," he says, his voice a high-pitched squeak.

"Do that," I say, as I hang up the phone.

I'm fired up. One by one, I call people who might know what's going on, and one by one, I get the same runaround. I call other Healthcare Mafia traders. All of them received an allocation. They don't tell me how many shares, and I don't ask. If I pressed them, I could find out. But it's an unwritten rule to not share this information. The sell side would get really pissed if we ran around telling one another how many shares we received on a deal. At this point, I don't really care if the sell side is pissed. But all of the healthcare hedge funds I talk to are smaller than Argus. Typically, their allocations would reflect that—we should always get more shares than they do. I call my coverage at J. P. Morgan back. This time he has more information.

For some reason, he says, this deal was orchestrated directly from his bank's trading desk, a transaction that hardly ever takes place. I ask who was on the desk. When he tells me, I can feel the veins popping out of my neck. I know the trader. He'd interviewed at Galleon when I was there. He wanted the job badly but didn't get it. But I know he hasn't given up on the idea. I also know he's been kissing my old nemesis's ass.

I haven't had any real interaction with Gary Rosenbach since he tried to sabotage my start with Argus. But it isn't like he's completely disappeared from my mind. He hovers in the background like a vulture on a distant telephone line. I know I'm still in his thoughts, too. Through scuttlebutt, I've heard he was saying disparaging things about me, calling me America's Guest and a Wall Street diva. I also believe, with absolute certainty, that if ever he has the chance to fuck me over, he will.

I get Rosenbach's friend on the J. P. Morgan trading desk on the phone. He acts as if he has no idea why I'm angry. He tells me it was his firm's decision. They placed the stock where they saw fit. "Relax, Turney," he says. "Take a deep breath."

I repeat his words back to him: "Relax?" I say. "Take a deep breath?" It feels like my face is on fire. I'm holding the phone so tight, my knuckles are white. Put your boss on the phone, I say, using every ounce of my energy to keep my voice level. The thought that he's deriving pleasure from my discomfort makes the task almost impossible. "Nobody's around," he says.

"We'll see about that," I say.

I call our research salesman and get the number of J. P. Morgan's head of equities. His last name is vaguely familiar. He used to be a top producer, but now he sits in his office every day being a manager, one of Wall Street's many inexplicable misuses of talent. They like to take top producers and make them managers. When I learned about the transitive property in eighth grade, I don't think this is what they were talking about. One doesn't equal the other. He says he has no idea what I'm talking about. I explain the whole story without raising my voice. When I finish, in a calm and collected way, I tell him if he doesn't correct the situation I'm pulling the wire.

Now, when you tell your coverage you're pulling their wire, it's a big deal. The "wire" is the phone connection over which all their business takes place. It's a threat taken seriously. You pull someone's wire and you're killing them off. The manager at J. P. Morgan apologizes profusely but says there's nothing he can do about the MDRX deal. The two million shares of stock they had for sale are already in the hands of other clients. The stock is now up three dollars from where they priced it this morning. "I'll make it up to you, Turney," he says. "I promise."

"That's not good enough," I say. And before I hang up the phone, I add: "This is unacceptable. And just so you know, other hedge funds told me their allocations."

There are few reasons why you don't share information about your allocations. First, like bonuses, you run the risk of pissing off other traders. If I got, say, 100,000 shares and you were given only 25,000, you might be offended or resentful. You might even go to the seller and ask what the hell is going on, which could affect my future deals. But it's also a code by which we traders live. It seems almost ludicrous that in the cold-blooded, cutthroat world of Wall Street such gentle-manly agreements exist, but they do. They have to exist to keep the business from descending into total anarchy. People who break these codes are labeled "bad guys." And for someone like me, having so much invested in people liking me, nothing could be worse than being ranked among them.

Whenever you lower your standards, however, justification follows. I crossed this line for a business reason, I tell myself. The manager at J. P. Morgan now has little choice but to investigate the deal. And when he sees the list of allocations, it'll become obvious to him that Argus got screwed, and he'll want to know why. This is no longer about business for me. This is about my getting even with the people who I believe have conspired against me: Rosenbach and his friend on the trading desk.

The next day I'm back at my desk when I get hit on my instant messenger. It's a friend of mine who's still at Galleon. He asks if I can call his cell phone. "Dude, what the fuck are you doing to us?" he says. He then tells me Gary called every single Galleon trader into the conference room and accused each of disclosing their allocation on MDRX to Turney Duff. "Everybody here is pissed at you," my friend says. "They think you said something." I'd given little thought to any collateral damage my actions might have. I don't know what to say. "Did you?" my friend asks.

That night I go to bed and the only thing can I think about is what my old coworkers must think about me. I can't sleep. I get up to smoke a cigarette on my roof deck. It's past midnight. I sit down on one of my deck chairs and light up. I understand why the guys at Galleon are angry. They're worried about their reputations on the Street. But mostly they're pissed because Gary is making their lives miserable. Maybe I shouldn't have tried bluffing J. P. Morgan. It was a knee-jerk decision; I did it out of anger. The only thing it accomplished was to get people upset with me. I know exactly how those guys at Galleon feel. I watch the smoke from my cigarette dance and disappear in the black night air. All of the gratitude I have for everything Galleon taught me and the opportunity it gave me disappears. I'm thankful I don't work there anymore. Gary continues to believe he can have his way with me. But when I think about it, there's no reason he should believe any differently. It's the culture he swims in and has swum in since I've known him.

At some point at Galleon, I just became numb. They could yell at me as loud as they wanted and it wouldn't affect me. But when I seemed unfazed by the volume, it only made them turn up the rhetoric. And it wasn't only me. Belittling was a way of life there. Always politically incorrect, Raj and Gary one day walked into the office with a dwarf, whom they introduced as an analyst hired to cover "small-cap" stocks.

Other stunts weren't nearly as innocuous. Once, after I'd left Galleon, Taser International came up to the offices for an investor's road show. Raj offered five thousand dollars to the most attractive woman in the office if she agreed to get zapped. A fellow employee pointed the Taser as the woman braced herself. Her legs buckled and she collapsed to the floor when she was hit by the darts. The story goes that she may have had an accident in her pants. The odor of burnt flesh and defecation lasted longer than the laughter. Fuck those guys.

I'm not sure how much Argus lost out on the MDRX deal, or how much Gary Rosenbach and Galleon made. Maybe the amount was a few hundred thousand dollars. Yes, it's a lot of money, but for a billion-dollar fund it really doesn't move the needle. But that's not the point. The point is, I have to change. Here I am, hitting full stride in my career, and I'm caught up in this bullshit. I don't even care about the money. Yes, I'm still upset that my friends at Galleon think I used them, that I put their jobs in jeopardy. But I'm not going to let people like Gary push me around, and I'm not going to feel guilty about pushing back. And if someone else gets hurt in the process, well, that's the cost of war. You do more damage being tentative than making a wrong choice. From now on, I'm all in. If I'm going to be a successful trader, I can't do it by just trading stocks. I have to be willing to club baby seals, park in handicap spaces, and demolish an orphanage to build a strip club. On Wall Street, the timid get trampled. I'm tired of the hoof marks.

25

A BLACK Cadillac Escalade is waiting as I walk out of my building on a Saturday afternoon in late October. Carlos, the driver, has a cooler full of Corona in the back. We drive up past Canal Street and head over to the East Side. Randy, casually dressed, is standing on the corner of Fortieth and Third Avenue. He jumps in and I trade him a chilled beer for a bag of cocaine. I peel open the bag, wet my pinky, and stuff it right into the heart of the coke. My finger comes out looking like a sugarcoated biscotti. I jam it up my nose and snuff it. The Escalade turns onto the East River Drive. Traffic is thick, but moving. I continue shoving coke up my nose, but I count the ride in beers. Two Coronas later, we can see Yankee Stadium.

The usher takes us to the first row above the dugout. The stadium is full, but our row is empty. We make it just in time for David Wells's first pitch. We get two draft beers and two hotdogs, but the dogs are out of some sense of tradition. As coked-up as we are, there's no chance of us actually eating them. I stick mine under the seat and look up at the crowd. Hundreds of rows of smiling faces climb to the sky; World Series bunting hangs from the upper decks.

We're so close to the field that we can hear the pop of the catcher's mitt, see the glistening sweat on Wells's forehead. The score is 1–0 and the Yankee fans are a little restless. They always expect to win the World Series. I grew up a Cleveland Indians fan but also rooted for the Red Sox when we moved to Maine. I remember going to a game in July with my mom and dad when I was about seven or eight. Boston was a two-hour drive and we took the family station wagon, the Green Machine. It was a big deal. I remember being startled by all the cars and people but amazed at Fenway. The green field looked almost neon. I think Luis Tiant was pitching. We sat on the field level, behind third base, but way back. My father paid something like six bucks each for the tickets, whereas Randy, no doubt, paid a couple grand or more for our seats—and he bought eight tickets for just the two of us.

"You gonna get paid this year, right?" Randy asks as he wipes away his beer foam mustache. I give him a *What do you think?* look, a coked-up version of Tony Soprano. "If I don't make at least seven hundred and fifty k, I'm leaving," he says. Along with the market, the trading volume is way up. If people are trading, then the sell side is making money. "I should know by December," he says. Randy flags down the beer guy and orders two more. "Once the check clears I'll decide." No need to let anyone know you're looking for a new job until that check clears. In January everybody's a free agent.

Wells is struggling. There are runners on base. The pitcher looks like someone you'd meet at Red Rock West. Maybe I did.

"Dude . . . so funny," Randy says. "Last week we had a sales meeting." He grabs the two beers. "They used your account as an example on the slide presentation," he says, laughing.

"Come on," I say, wondering if he's putting me on.

"Yup. They said this is the correct way to grow an account and they showed your commission growth for 2001, 2002, and the first three quarters of this year," he says.

"Did they show slides of eight balls and bottle service?" The Marlins hit into a double play. Inning over.

"Let's use two of the tickets," Randy says. We get up and make our way to the bathroom, find two stalls in the back. I jam my apartment key into the bag and rip three quick bumps. Yankee Stadium is one Zip. I hate doing blow here. So many people in and out, no privacy. When we're done in the stalls, we head for the exit. The ticket taker warns us that there is no reentry.

"We know, we know," I say. Six extra tickets for three smoking-breaks. Once outside, we fire up two cigarettes. We finish them and light another. After we smoke our second we hand the same ticket taker two new fresh tickets. He should be an undertaker. His smile indicates nothing.

By the time we're back to the seats, I already want another bump and cigarette. I look up at the scoreboard. It's the top of the second—no, it's the third. The game is still 1–0, and Florida has a couple of guys on. "So, you think you can get me a new job?" Randy asks.

"Dude, in fifteen minutes," I say. I pull out my phone like I'm going to make a call. He asks me where I think he should go and I tell him Lehman or Merrill. "They do big business and there's not a lot of office drama," I say.

"You sure you can get me in there?" he asks.

"Yes," I say. "If I hooked Pete up, you should be a layup."

It was this summer that I met Pete. I awoke with a hangover in the beach house I shared with a few other Wall Street guys. In the pocket of the shorts I wore the night before was a bar napkin on which was written a phone number under the name "Pete—White Squall."

Over bagels and Gatorade on the porch, my housemates tell me that Pete is the bartender at John Scott's, a local beach bar. Slowly, the previous evening's festivities came into focus. I was calling Pete "Bailey" after the character from the TV show *Party of Five*. Pete was insane. At one point he put twenty cigarettes in his mouth and lit them. He didn't charge us for a thing. I loved him.

"But why do I have his number?" I asked.

"You promised you'd help him get a job," came the reply.

Pete told me he works in the back office of a firm called Knight Securities. That Monday morning I called Knight's trading desk. "This is Turney Duff from Argus Partners," I said. "We have a couple billion in assets and we want to open an account." There was the appropriate moment of silence on the phone. Imagine a lotto agent calling your house and telling you that he wants to sell you the winning ticket. What I'd just dangled meant hundreds of thousands of dollars in commissions for them.

"Just one request," I said to the stunned trader. "I need Pete in the back office to be my sales trader. No Pete, no deal." And that's how Pete went from the relative obscurity of the back office to the trading desk and the beginning of a very profitable Wall Street career.

"Listen," I say to Randy, "I don't want to sound like a dick, but you should know this: I can get you in anywhere." The coke is beginning to tweak me out. I start thinking about Randy and his questions. I don't even know who he is, really. I've never seen him outside of a party setting. What does he do besides party and trade stocks? Randy catches me looking strangely at him.

"What?" he says.

"What's your favorite color?" I ask.

"Blue," he says.

"When did you lose your virginity?"

"Thirteen," he says.

Gross. "Who'd you take to your senior prom?"

"Tina Trombone of the Trombone sisters," he says.

"If you could watch only one movie for the rest of your life, what would it be?"

"Boogie Nights," he goes. I talk to Randy every day and I don't really know anything about him. We've shared hundreds of war stories about drinking, drugs, and women. But I don't know him. And he doesn't know anything of substance about me. The crowd roars as Jeter drives someone in.

"I wanted to be a journalist," I tell him. Randy looks at me like I'm bleeding from my ears.

"Really?" he says.

"Yeah," I say, "and when I was at Morgan Stanley I took a course in screenwriting at the Gotham Writers' Workshop."

"The place with the yellow stands?" he asks. "I always wondered what that was about."

"I have a friend from college who works in television commercial production out in L.A. We wrote a horror screenplay together and called it *Horrorscope.* We emailed the script back and forth. It even was read by someone at Miramax but didn't go any further than that."

"That's cool," Randy says.

I tell him that when I was at Galleon I produced a small film. I titled it *I Killed Eminem* and my friend Jesse Itzler wrote and performed a track for the movie. "No shit?" he goes. The film ended up being shown at an independent film festival in California and a hip-hop festival in the Bronx. Not Sundance, but pretty cool nonetheless. "I didn't know. That's really something," he says, but his eyes now are flat and have a cocaine sheen. Now I'm sorry I said anything to him about my writing, my producing. I decide not to tell him about my dream. I don't tell *anybody* about my dream: I see myself on the cover of *GQ* or *Vanity Fair*. I'm holding the strings to two puppets: one represents Wall Street, the other Hollywood. When I look up at the scoreboard it's now 3–1, Florida Marlins. How'd that happen?

"Whaddya think about the execution model? I know it's hard without any research, but Gus is getting a forty percent commission payout," he asks, as if we haven't been talking about anything other than business.

"Everyone says it's going away, people have to justify their commission dollars with a research product," I say. "They've been saying it for years and it hasn't happened yet. If you have me and a few other guys and put up about three million dollars in commissions, you can make over a stick." Wall Street loves to play with the language. For example, if a stock is trading up a dollar you might say it's "up a taco," thanks to Taco Bell's ninety-nine-cent menu. Or if you trade your own money and you lose $125,000, you might say, "Fuck, I rolled a Ferrari today."

"Let's hit the stalls," Randy says. We head up the aisle and back to the bathroom. When we exit the stadium again, the same ticket taker eyes us. This time he says nothing about needing tickets to get back in. Instead he just gives us that funeral parlor smile.

The score is 3–2 by the time we get back to our seats. Someone hit a homer when we were outside. Bernie Williams, I think. We heard the roar. We begin to talk about my bonus. I tell Randy I've figured out Krishen's philosophy of paying his employees. On down years he pays up. And in up years he pays people exactly what they deserve, relatively speaking, of course. This way he ensures loyalty from everyone

192 ■ TURNEY DUFF

who works for him. If someone takes care of you in a down year, you really remember it and it's hard to complain on the up years because you are making good money. The Marlins bring Dontrelle Willis into the game to pitch. I like him. He's got swagger.

"Whaddya think you'll get?" he asks. "If you don't mind me asking."

I hold up seven fingers.

It's the bottom of the eighth. The Yankees are losing 3–2, but have a rally going: back-to-back singles by Williams and Matsui. The crowd is on its feet. Randy still has two unused tickets in his pocket. It's dark now and cold, but no one else seems to care.

"I have a surprise for you back at the White House," Randy says. Posada digs in at the plate.

"Let's go," I say.

26

IT'S THE next Thursday, or the Thursday after that, or maybe some other Thursday—I'm not sure. Thursday is Wall Street's Friday. I'm getting ready to go out. I have a business dinner with some guys from Bank of America. I put on my cowboy shirt with a lace-up tie in front. It's navy blue with white shoulders that meet down into a V right where the lace-up part of the shirt starts.

When I get to Pastis there's a crowd standing on the corner of Ninth Avenue, smoking cigarettes and talking. Some people think the Meatpacking District is becoming a little "bridge and tunnel," but new clubs and restaurants are opening up every week. There's electricity in this neighborhood that charges you. The gravity feels stronger, like you go out for two drinks and get sucked into a good-time version of a black hole and come home two days later.

Inside, the bar is two or three deep. I wedge my way to the service end. Waitstaff cruise in and out in their white aprons, white shirts, and black pants. A few minutes later I see Rob, the pharmaceutical trader for Bank of America. He walks in with a big smile and opens his arms to give me the Wall Street hug: one shoulder leaned in to make body contact and the other arm reaching around to fist bump my back. I reciprocate. "Dig the shirt," he says. He tells me we're waiting for two other guys but asks me if I want to sit. The hostess is beautiful. She has short blond hair with one streak of jet black that hangs to the side. Her skin is flawless, like Egyptian cotton. Rob tells her we have a reservation and we'd like to be seated. She asks if we're just two. No, he tells her. We're waiting on two other guys. She can't seat us until our whole party has arrived, she says with a polite smile. Rob thanks her and turns for the bar. But I don't move.

"I don't think you understand," I say as I gently touch her elbow. "I'm on the buy side." She looks at me, expecting an explanation. I just stand there looking at her.

"I'm sorry, sir," she says. "I can't seat any party until they've all arrived."

"But I'm on the buy side," I say, with deadpanned precision.

"I'm sorry, sir," she says, trying to stay polite. She thinks I'm rude, but I'm trying to be funny.

Once the other two guys show up, we get seated immediately. At dinner, they know the deal. They don't bring up business unless I give them a window. I try not to, but sometimes it just comes up. We order our meals and another round of cocktails. Once the food comes we order another round of drinks and my whole body chemistry begins to shift. I'd love to do a bump of cocaine in the bathroom right now, but I don't have any. When the waitress removes our plates, I get up and excuse myself to smoke a cigarette.

Then I'm in a cab. I just leave. I don't say goodbye or thank you. The Bank of America guys are sitting at the table, waiting for me to come back. I hate this feeling. I'm going to have to trade at least a million shares with them tomorrow.

The doorman nods in recognition when I enter the lobby of the White House. I blaze past him to hit the elevator button. Inside the apartment, I notice Randy's door is ajar and there's porn playing on the television, but nobody's in the room. I turn right and try to get into the bathroom, but the door's locked. While I'm still holding the handle, the door flies open. It's Victor, another buy side guy. His eyes are stretched wide and his lips look like rubber, but his jaw is cemented in place. He attempts to say hi, but his teeth are grinding so badly that it comes out more like a groan. There's cocaine caked all around his nostrils. He darts past me into Randy's room, where the porn is playing, and shuts the door. Thank god I don't live here. I hear Victor lock the door before I even get into the bathroom. I feel bad for his wife and kid.

I make my way into the living room, where I see a few guys I know. Dr. Fish and two of his coworkers are off to one side, bitching about drug dealers. They barely acknowledge my presence. Then I see another guy by himself in the corner, rocking back and forth just talking to himself. It looks like *Night of the Living Dead* in here. I move to the kitchen. Gus is there. But he's so wired from coke, he scares me. He starts telling me about some hooker he had sex with about three hours ago and how great it was. It's hard to follow him because he's speaking in fragments and he keeps launching tiny beads of spit from his mouth. I do whatever I can to avoid being hit by his saliva. Randy and James are in the kitchen too. Randy gives me a smile and nod, but James just glares at me. Randy pours some cocaine onto a plate and slides it over to me.

Then I'm back in a cab, heading to Brother Jimmy's on the Upper East Side. The cocaine in the White House has evened out my tequila drunk. I have a folded-up twenty-dollar bill in my pocket filled with the hefty amount Randy gave me.

Pete is at the corner of the bar doing flaming Dr Pepper shots with a few of his high school friends from Garden City, New York. I know them from out at the beach. This is a going-away party for him; he moves to Chicago on Monday. White Squall, as I prefer to call him, has done quite well for himself since I got him promoted at Knight Securities. He chuckles when he sees me. He orders me a flaming shot. I excuse myself and hit the bathroom for a quick bump. Two Zips. When I return to the bar, I fire back the shot and then tell Pete I have to make a phone call. On the street I light a cigarette and scroll through my contacts. I click Call and wait for Barbara to pick up. Finally, in a raspy voice, she says hello.

"Hey, it's Turney," I say.

"Who?"

"Turney," I say louder.

"Ernie?"

"No, Turney," I repeat. "Can I come over?"

"Umm, sure," she says. "Do you have my address, Ernie?"

"Yes."

When she opens the door she's pleasantly surprised—as if I'm the last person she expected to see. She has dark circles under her eyes. Her hair is now fifty percent blond and fifty percent black. She looks like she's aged ten years. Her apartment is even lonelier than I remembered. The mattress is still on the floor and the Christmas lights still line her apartment walls. The television has a crack in the screen and there's tons of empty Cheez Doodles bags and beer cans on the coffee table. She pulls out a heap of magazines and newspapers embedded into the couch and invites me to sit down. I notice the bruises on her arms and the burn marks and spiderweb veins up and down her legs.

She sits on the couch next to me and puts her hand on my knee. She leans over and kisses me on the cheek. "Soooo," she says. "You wanna do me?"

It's hard for me even to look at her. Her eyes are empty. I offer her some of my cocaine because I don't know what else to do. She's very thankful and offers me a beer, but then tells me she's out. "I'll go to the deli," she says. "No, I'll go," I tell her. "I'll be right back," I say as I close her door behind me.

I run to the deli as fast as I can. I buy a six-pack of Bud Light, the same as the empty cans I saw on her coffee table. When I return I set the six-pack down outside her door and stuff a couple of hundred-dollar bills in between two of the cans so the cash is sticking up and noticeable. I knock on the door and run back to the elevator.

It's past midnight. On the street, I get a text from a guy named John at Credit Suisse. He's with a group at Lotus back in the Meatpacking District. I jump in a cab. There's a line of about twenty people waiting to get in when I arrive. I walk directly to the door, but the tree-trunk arm of the three-hundred-pound African American bouncer stops me. "I don't wait in lines," I tell him. "I snort them." He looks at me curiously for a moment and then he opens the velvet rope. I see John and the guys hanging out at the middle of the bar, so I head their way. John turns to the bartender and orders me a Patrón Silver on the rocks with three limes. I notice a girl standing off to the side, talking with a couple of her friends. She looks really cute. She's got a silky black sleeveless shirt and white pants on. After Labor Day—I love it. I catch her eye as John hands me a drink. She's petite and her hair is all done up except for one loose strand that hangs to the side of her head. I like the way she smiles. I walk directly up to her.

"Do you think I'm cute?" I ask.

"I—I guess," she says with a giggle.

"I'm thirty-four, single, live in a triplex in Tribeca, and make seven figures," I say, and then wait a beat. "How cute am I now?"

"You're funny," she says. I don't even say goodbye to the guys from Credit Suisse. I grab my new friend's hand and leave.

By four fifteen a.m. I'm standing naked in my bathroom. I drop the used condom in the toilet and look in the mirror. My hair stands straight up and my face is bright red. I have two thoughts. How am I going to get this girl out of my bed and how am I going to get out of work today?

In the bedroom, she's awake, sitting naked on the edge of the bed, smoking a cigarette. She looks like she's striking a pose. Her silky sleeveless black shirt and white pants are nicely folded on the red velvet chaise lounge next to my bed. I force a smile, grab my pants off the floor, and quickly turn back into the bathroom. She doesn't say a word.

I tap out a hefty rope on the countertop next to my toothbrush and toothpaste. I pull out a crumpled-up dollar bill from my jeans, roll it up, and inhale the line. I see myself in the mirror again but look away immediately. I pour a tiny bit of cocaine onto my toothbrush and give my gums a quick scrub. I force myself to look in the mirror again and take a few deep breaths.

When I return to the bed I climb under the covers. What time is it? I ask. We're both looking at the same alarm clock. "Almost four thirty," she says. I jump up out of bed in a panic. "Oh, shit—I have to trade Europe today," I say. It's something I have to do on a rare occasion, but not today. As I pick up all of my clothes and stuff on the floor, I tell her that I'm going to jump in the shower to get ready and then I'll walk her to get a cab. I disappear into the bathroom again.

When I get out of the shower, now wearing a towel around my waist, I see she's still naked in bed. She won't leave. I dart into my walk-in closet to think. I put on a blue shirt and a charcoal Prada suit. There's no way I'm going to work, but continuing the charade is the only way I can figure to get her to leave. I slip on my socks and shoes and head back to the bathroom. I see she's still in the same position. I have to leave in five, I say firmly. Finally she gets out of bed and starts to put her clothes on. I comb back my wet hair.

She holds my hand as we walk down Laight Street. My plan is to put her in a cab and head right back to the apartment, but then she asks, "So where are you headed?"

"Wherrrrrre are you headed?" I say back to her. But she waits for me to respond. We get in the cab together. *Fuck!*

She holds my hand again as we ride in silence. When we get to her building, she gives me a kiss on the cheek and thanks me for the night. "I'll call you," I say, but I realize I don't remember her name. Did she even tell me? When she gave me her number, I entered it into my phone under "Lotus Chick." "Hi, is Lotus Chick there? It's Turney."

I tell the cabbie to turn around and take me right back to where he picked me up. He glances at me in the rearview mirror. *Whatever.* I stare out the window. Inside my apartment, Ethan and Jason are still sleeping, so I tiptoe back to my room and lock the door. Safely locked away, I pull out my cocaine and do another line on my desk next to my computer mouse. I shake the mouse for the computer screen to illuminate and I see it's creeping up on six a.m. I undress down to my boxer briefs and light up a cigarette and open my window a crack.

My whole body trembles. I need more booze. I sneak back down to the kitchen to grab whatever's in the refrigerator. I have a bottle of wine and three beers tucked under my left arm, pinned against my body, as I go back upstairs. I just need help coming down. I look at the clock again; it's a little past six. This is my window of opportunity. Melinda is probably on the desk, but she'll be the only one in the office. If

I call in sick now, she'll be the only one I have to talk to and she won't ask any questions. I stand up and start pacing back and forth, practicing my speech. Finally, I hit Dial. Melinda tells me she's sorry I'm sick but she sounds like my mother used to when she didn't believe me. When I hang up the phone, I dump out another line of cocaine on the desk and flick on the television in my room. I rent a porn movie and sit in my desk chair and turn the volume way down. I don't want Jason and Ethan to know I'm home. I'll just do a little more blow, drink a bit, and then go to bed. Then I won't party for the rest of the year.

27

AND FOR the most part, I don't party. I spend Christmas by myself in the Tribeca triplex. I was invited to all three of my sisters' houses, which are now filled with husbands and children, eight nieces and nephews, to be exact, but I didn't feel like traveling (certainly not to Paris). My parents are in Cleveland visiting my sister Kelly's family, so I couldn't go back to Maine. It's not like I'm anti-Christmas or anything. I love Christmas. But I don't mind being alone, either. Anyhow, Melinda and Rich have covered for me so many times over the past six months that I told them to take Christmas week off.

It's about four in the afternoon and I'm on the couch in sweats. I plug in the Christmas tree, throw a Duraflame on the fire, and click on the TV. There are eight wrapped gifts for me under the tree—most of them from the sell side. I light a cigarette and start to open them. I get a couple of bottles of wine, nice, expensive French or Californian cabernet. I get a Tivo box—cool—and an envelope with a gift certificate for a night's stay in the Thompson Hotel. I get a case of Don Perignon and a case of Patrón Silver. The last gift I open is from my mom. She gives me the same thing every year: a handmade calendar with family photos and dates of family birthdays and anniversaries marked so I won't forget.

I decide to open a bottle of wine. I go grab a corkscrew in the kitchen. When I get back to the couch I roll a joint and pour myself a glass of red. The Duraflame crackles in the fireplace. The tree twinkles. Through the window in the living room, Christmas night begins to fall. I hope it snows.

The next day is Friday and the market is open. I'm at work by six thirty, and alone on the desk. It's nice, peaceful—the slowest day of the year. I think back to my early time at Galleon, how terrified I was at this time of the day. And how different I feel now, and yet there's this gnawing feeling deep inside, like I'm about to be found out. Then I begin to think about my bonus. Yes, my bonus. That's it. My bonus will fill me.

The math is simple: we divide up 20 percent of the profits after expenses for the full calendar year. I also get a percentage of the management fee—the deal I worked out with Krishen. I started doing the math in October and knew I was on pace to hit my goal. November was up, as was December. Something bad could happen, of course. In 2002, Argus was heavily invested in a hospital chain called Tenet Healthcare. That November, the FBI raided one of the hospitals on allegations of Medicare fraud and unnecessary surgeries. We lost thirty, forty million in two days. It totally crushed our year. But that was last year. This year is different. And so am I.

Monday and Tuesday the following week are slow. Though trading on Wednesday, New Year's Eve, is also light—the Street is making last-minute plans or hoping to get out of Dodge—for me it's one of the most important days of the year. This is the only trading day when unrealized profit and losses count toward your performance, whereas the rest of the year positions must be closed out by either a sell or a cover to be a realized gain or loss. What happens today will directly affect my bonus.

There's something known as "ripping a stock," which is a manipulation of the stock price. Essentially, that's what I'm trying to do today. The more stocks I can rip today, the better our number will be for the year.

I begin by identifying our ten largest positions that are illiquid. By *illiquid* I mean companies that don't trade more than a few hundred thousand shares a day. It's much easier to move the price with these than, say, a stock that trades a million shares a day. I find names such as CYBX, Cyberonics, a neuromodulator company engaged in the design, development, and commercialization of implantable medical devices that provide vagus nerve stimulation therapy for the treatment of refractory epilepsy and treatment-resistant depression. *What?* I have no idea what that means and I don't care. The stock fits my criteria. Once I have all the stocks identified, I wait until the market is almost closed for the year to make my move.

At about three o'clock in the afternoon, I get a call from a broker named Tracey who works for a firm that is light on research but heavy on hustle and expense account—she's taken me on several trips. Like all of my brokers, Tracey is someone I talk to every day. But she's calling me at this moment because I ripped stocks with her on this day last year and she wants to know if I'm going to use her again. For her it's a great boost to her commission run, millions of shares to trade with no risk. Her excuse for why she needs the orders early is so she can prepare. Bullshit! The thing about ripping stocks is, the bigger banks like Goldman and Morgan Stanley won't do it. You need a firm like Tracey's that plays it fast and loose. Let me get right back to you, I say. And I hang up the phone.

In one way, I have to hand it to Tracey. She's got a lot of balls. When I used her last year, I knew she leaked my orders to another client so they could front run my trades. I knew this because the stocks began to tick up before the time I told her to put my orders in. Then her shady client was selling them back to me when I was trying to rip the stock. And now she's on the phone again this year, looking to do the same thing. But I'm not the same trader I was last year.

I still want everybody to love me. But if you're going to try and fuck me, I'll fuck you harder. Maybe it's the MDRX trade that Rosenbach had me shut out of, or maybe it's just the natural process of becoming jaded the longer you work for hedge funds. Whatever it is, Tracey has just made a huge mistake.

At 3:30, I call her back and explain how important this year is to me and how I really need her to do a great job. Then I give her the orders with an explicit instruction to not trade them until 3:55. "Not a second before," I say.

"I know," she says.

There are ten companies, and I'm shorting each a million shares. I repeat the list of ten stocks back to her. A short of a million shares of CYBX in five minutes, for example, would typically take the stock down at least five dollars, probably more.

I have the ten stocks up on my computer screen so I can monitor them. At about 3:40, they start to move a little lower until all of them are red, negative for the day. I'm sure Tracey leaked my orders again. I call her. Remember, I tell her, don't start selling any of my orders until 3:55. "Of course," she says, sounding almost insulted that I'd call to remind her. At 3:51, the stocks are still going down. At 3:52 they get hit another thirty cents. At 3:53 they are beginning to hold at their lower levels, and at 3:54 it's time for me to go to work. Whoever front ran my order is done and is waiting to buy them back when I hit the market. They think they'll make a few easy bucks. It's then that I pick up the phone. "I know, I know," Tracey says. "I'm getting ready to short all your stocks right now."

"Actually," I say, "cancel all my orders." The silence is priceless.

"What?" she finally manages to say.

"Cancel all my orders," I say. I've reminded her twice not to place the orders until 3:55. It is 3:54, and she has no out.

As soon as I hang up the phone, I call Gus and give him the real orders; they're actually buys, not sells. By 3:56 the stocks are moving higher. By 3:57 almost all of them are flat on the day. By 3:58 they're ripping—Gus and Tracey's client can't buy them fast enough, and by the closing bell I'm up a few dollars on all of them. When Gus calls back with reports, he tells me he was only able to buy a few hundred thousand of each stock. He feels bad. I tell him it's perfect. Argus just made an extra ten million dollars.

I call Tracey a couple of minutes later and apologize for the canceling of my orders. At the last minute, I say, we decided we didn't need to short any of those stocks. "Not a big deal," she manages to say, but she sounds sick to her stomach. Whoever she leaked my orders to must be livid with her. They had to have gotten crushed. Undoubtedly, they paid a much higher price than where they shorted it in front of my fake orders. Trading 101: buy low, sell high. Ooops. Nothing worse than losing a few million dollars in the last minute of the year. Happy New Year, I tell Tracey, but she's already hung up the phone. I know it's going to be a happy one for me.

28

29

EIGHT MONTHS later the city is blistering hot, concrete heat, brick heat. Opening the cab door is like opening the door of a pizza oven. There's a Mister Softee truck parked across from me. It sells ice cream, not computer software and Xboxes. The radiated heat from the street rises in front of it. It looks like a mirage. August can be brutal in the city.

There's a coffee shop with a large front window just down the block from my appointment. I go check my reflection to make sure I look okay. I'm wearing a black Armani sport coat and pants. A tie is standard-issue for a co-op board meeting, but I'm not wearing one. I've decided to live dangerously. I duck into the coffee shop to kill some time. Since I'm early, I order an iced coffee and sit at the counter. The shop is small. I imagine myself on Saturday or Sunday mornings coming in to get some coffee and all the employees saying: "Hey, Turney." I drink half of the coffee and check my phone for the time. I still have about five minutes until the meeting. I put five dollars on the counter and make my way outside.

Out in the heat, I hit my speed dial for my new girlfriend, Jenn, and wait for her to pick up. "Hey, I'm about to go in," I say.

"You'll do great," she says in her positive tone, a survival instinct she's acquired from a career filled with personal rejection. "They'll love you." There's an uncomfortable pause when she says that. Jenn has changed my life. She's been my girlfriend now for almost seven months, and we've been flirting with using the word "love" for the last couple. I've been joking with her that the first time I say it will be in a text message. She doesn't think it's funny. But I don't let that stop me. I'll text one letter at a time, I tell her. I might even let her buy a vowel. I say goodbye and hang up. I make my way to the building and knock gently three times. I can hear some commotion inside, but I'm not sure if they heard my knock. I wait.

"I" I met Jenn on a blind date. My cousin Ethan is a friend of a friend of hers—a girl who used to work with her. Jenn is a singer and backed up Enrique Iglesias on tour. She actually got fired from the gig because of jealousy. Iglesias was—maybe still is—dating the tennis babe Anna Kournikova, who, according to Jenn, thought her boyfriend's backup was upstaging her in the looks department. Jenn said that Anna even took to throwing Jolly Rancher candies at her from her seat by the stage. Jenn is so beautiful, she's caused at least one car accident I know of, and probably more. One look at her and you forget you're driving.

Back in front of the door at the co-op office, I knock a little harder. This time they had to have heard it. A few seconds later the door is opened by an older gentleman with coiffed white hair. He welcomes me in with a thin smile. The room is not very impressive. It's a cross between an unorganized office and a maintenance room. There are stacks of paper all over the desk and several filing cabinets mixed in with some tools and broken furniture. The building, 27 Bleecker, was built in 1910 as a fabric mill. In the 1980s some tenants banded together to buy it. It's seven stories high, and along with this co-op office, the ground floor houses an art studio. It makes you laugh. This is supposedly an "artists' building," but the apartments sell for a couple million apiece. It's a good guess that not a lot of the people who live here are painting portraits in Washington Square Park for a living. There are two apartments per floor—the "A" line ones are around 1,100 square feet, and the "B" apartments on the north side of the building are all around 2,200 square feet. I want 5B. It's listed at $1.8 million, but we agree on $1.75.

"I L" On the night of our blind date Jenn and I made plans to meet at Bread, a cute, tiny restaurant on Spring Street. I was dressed in a button-down shirt that wasn't tucked in, jeans, and flip-flops. My hair was long and tangled. She walked in like a vision: long, luxurious light brown hair, radiant eyes, and full lips. She was wearing a dress that was just a rhinestone or two short of an evening gown. I lost my swagger. I felt like an awkward teen talking to a girl for the first time. The restaurant was crowded and overheated. I asked her if she'd mind if we went to another place a few blocks away. She was game, and we hustled out the door. When in doubt, go to Mexican Radio. The food is great and margaritas even better. We must have had a half dozen of them apiece, but I'd begun to fall for her before I finished the first. We remember two different versions of what happened at the end of the night. She says I shoved her in a cab and ran back into the bar to drink. However, I distinctly remember telling myself that if I tried to hook up with her I might ruin the best chance I've ever had. I kissed her on the cheek, put her in the cab, and told her I'd call her the next day. The perfect gentleman. Then I walked back to the bar and got properly drunk. The very next morning I gave her a call—and every other day after that.

The co-op board consists of six middle-aged men and women who sit on one side of the table, and I take a seat facing them. I decide to take off my sport jacket and hang it on the back of the chair. I unbutton my sleeves and roll them up. I try to sit comfortably, somewhere between formal and relaxed. I want to convey that I'm professional and mature, but also relaxed and easygoing. I want to be someone they'd feel comfortable borrowing a cup of sugar from. The thought makes me laugh. On Laight Street they'd have a better chance of borrowing a cup of blow.

"I LO" I think it was on our third date when Jenn asked if I just wanted to be friends. She was concerned because I hadn't put the moves on her yet. I thought I was playing it cool. I didn't want her to get the impression that I just wanted to get into her pants; she's more of a skirt girl anyway. And all the time, she was wondering when I was going to make the move. She actually called one of her ex-boyfriends (who is now gay) to ask his advice. "We have such a great connection," she exclaimed, exasperated. Her gay ex-boyfriend's advice was to straight up ask me—so she did. I practically pulled Jenn out of the restaurant and into the taxi to her apartment.

My application sits in front of each of the co-op board members. A few pairs of glasses go on. Next to the older gentleman with the coiffed hair sits a heavyset guy in a black Megadeth T-shirt that is stretched to its limit over his belly. "So," the large guy says. "What's a Fatburger?" On my application, under "other investments" I listed the million dollars that I'd recently sunk into the fast-food franchise. It's a West Coast chain and we're bringing it east.

"Casual dining," I say, as offhandedly as I can. I tell him we had a grand opening for our first store in Jersey City last week. "There are more stores to come," I say, trying to sound businessman-like. I notice that he's hanging on my every word.

"So if we approve you, do we get burgers?" he asks.

"Of course," I say with an uneasy smile. But he's not smiling at all. He looks like he's going to eat my application.

The older gent wants to go over my salary: "At Argus?" he says, in sort of a half-suspicious, half-pretentious way. I tell him my base is two hundred k a year, but I also have a percentage of the firm's management fee. I uncross and recross my legs. I don't have to tell him the number; it's in the financials of my application. I know he sees it. Even though he's trying hard not to show it, I know he knows money isn't an issue.

"I LOV" After the first time I made love with Jenn, I knew things were about to be different. I'd never felt this way about someone before. I started thinking about her at work, and even after. I'd go to the White House and find myself wondering what she was doing. Even the guys noticed. More than once, Randy and Gus asked me what was going on. They even seemed a little worried that my life was going to change too much. A steady girl is one thing, but what if I got married and moved to Westchester? What would they do then? Who would they entertain?

The youngest person on the board happens to be a woman; she looks like she wishes it were still 1976. She's not the most attractive woman in the world, but definitely a free spirit. She's now smiling at me. I've just figured out that they are taking turns asking questions. "Tell me, Turney," she says, like she's on some kind of dating show. "What do you like to do in your spare time?" Is this where I'm supposed to talk about booze, drugs, sex, and pornography? But that was the old Turney. The new Turney has a girlfriend.

"I like to go out to dinner with my friends, read, play sports," I say.

"Oh, and I'm a huge movie guy. I love movies." She's looking at me as if she's expecting me to ask her to one.

"I LOVE" Jenn was worried she was coming between me and my roommates. "They'll be fine," I assured her. I'd lived with Jason for almost ten years—just about the length of my Wall Street career. And Ethan is family. Besides, it's not as if I'm throwing them out in the street. They both have girlfriends and plans of their own. "I just don't want them to be mad at me," Jenn said. But the thing is, I'm the one who's just a little upset. Although they never asked for it, I've spent a lot of money on them and our apartment, and I never really felt they were grateful enough. It's my own fault. I'm the one who told them not to worry. "It's all good," I tell Jenn. And it really has been since I met her.

"Why should we approve your application?" the co-op board head is saying. Good question. And just for a moment I'm quiet while I think about my answer. Ten years ago I was living as the third guy in a two-bedroom, and now I'm buying a $1.75 million apartment. At the rate I'm going, five years from now I'll be able to buy the whole building. I look at each of the board members one by one. If I'm supposed to be nervous, I'm not. My morning meetings are more stressful than this. But the last thing I want to do is come across as arrogant. The truth is, I want this apartment. I want it for Jenn.

"I understand the process, and why it's so important for you to be careful. It's not only the financial concerns—which are paramount, I know—but you've undoubtedly worked hard, and sacrificed a lot for this building, and want to protect your considerable investments. Who am I? I'm a stranger. It can't be an easy decision. I respect that. So let me put my cards on the table. I love this place, and I'd love to live here. And it's more than just how great the apartment is. It's the feeling I get when I walk through the front door of the building; it's the people, like you, whom I've already met. It's the neighborhood. It feels like home to me. I'm not going to lie. I've been single for a lot of years, working on Wall Street, and I've made good money. And I did exactly what you'd expect a single guy with money to do. But those days are over. I'm almost thirty-five. I've met a girl; we're in love. I'm ready for the next chapter in my life. And I can't think of a better place to write it than right here."

As I look around the room again, every set of eyes is trained on me. The seventies chick looks like she might cry. "I'm not going to sit here and give you a hard sell," I say. "I'd like to thank you for your time and the opportunity to meet with you. If you don't think I'm the right fit, then you should deny my application." I sit up a little straighter in my chair. "That's what I'd want you to do if I lived here," I say. "You have to be sure." At this point I'm kind of shocked that they haven't handed me the keys already.

It was Jenn who found the apartment on Bleecker. My two-year lease on the Laight Street triplex is up in October, and it's time for me to put on my big boy pants and get my own place. Jenn never really voiced her opinion about my moving. That is, until she saw me looking at fifteen-thousand-dollar-a-month rentals in Tribeca. That's when she intervened. "Why are you throwing all that money away on rent?" she asked. I just shrugged. I hadn't given it much thought.

The older gent stands up to signal that the interview has concluded. I thank each of them and look them directly in the eye as I do. Outside, the heat has abated not one bit. I walk down the block and light up a cigarette on the corner of Bleecker and Lafayette. I'm going to love this neighborhood. It's real. It hasn't lost its grittiness the way the Meatpacking District has. There's Planned Parenthood across the street, next to a homeless shelter, which is across the street from several posh restaurants. It's perfect.

"I LOVE Y" On the way home, I get a call from the co-op board. When I get there Jenn greets me at the door of the triplex holding my eight-week-old puppy, Houdini. He's a Japanese Chin who looks like Gizmo from the movie *The Gremlins*. So cute. I mentioned once to Jenn that I wanted a dog, and two days later she had a list of breeders and the types of dogs that would be good for my lifestyle. A week later we were in the car driving to Maryland to pick up Houdini. She plants a kiss on me before I even make it into the apartment. It's a long, wet, sensual kiss, a kiss I've been missing. Her smile makes me somehow feel better than I am. It's amazing. I immediately take off my sport coat and throw it on the couch, and we kiss again.

"Well?" she asks, playfully pushing me away. "Tell me how it went." I think about the call I just received and look down at the ground in front of her. "Oh, baby," she says softly as she holds me.

"I just wasn't any good in the interview," I whisper. When I look up into her eyes, the scene falls apart. There's something about her eyes I just can't lie to—even when I'm just playing with her. She sees I'm having trouble staying in character.

"You got it, didn't you?"

"They just called before I got home."

"I knew it," she says, squeezing me. "I just knew it." We kiss again and then I make my way up to my bedroom. I take off my clothes and put on shorts and a T-shirt. "Come with me," she says as she takes my hand. Jenn leads me up to the rooftop, where there's a table with a white tablecloth, a lit candle, and two wineglasses with the bottle on ice. Pink clouds blanket the sky. The sun is setting and the evening lights of Jersey City begin to twinkle on the darkening Hudson River. The water is calm as a few luxury boats idle by. We sit down at the table and uncork the bottle. I pour hers first and then mine. We toast to new beginnings. There is no need for words. I pour the rest of the wine into the glasses. The temperature has dropped a bit since sunset. I hold the glasses in one hand and take her hand with the other and lead her to the bedroom.

"I LOVE YO" I run my finger up and down and around her entire back. I can feel the electricity between my finger and her skin. It makes me feel like I'm a part of her. I close my eyes while slowly tickling her back. I lie down with her behind me. She runs her fingers through my hair. I was always on the move, always had to get to the club, the next party. I used to tell myself I didn't want to miss anything. But the truth of the matter is, I was never content, no matter where I was or who I was with. With Jenn I can just sit and talk, reach across the table and hold her hand. I like lying here next to her. I never want her to go, and I never want to leave. I don't know when that's ever happened before. It's like I'm no longer running, no longer afraid to just be . . . I don't mean to say I'm giving everything up. I'll still go out with the guys once in a while. And I'll still have to have the weekly business dinner, and maybe I'll stop at the White House every now and again. But it definitely won't be like it was. I'll just blow off some steam before I run back to my lady. I close my eyes and begin to drift off into a most comfortable sleep. Jenn is soft and warm against my back. It's then that I hear her whisper, "I love you." A tear begins to well up in my eye and then starts to roll down my cheek. It isn't hard at all for me to answer her. The words come naturally, and from a place deep inside me. And once I say them, a peace like I've never felt comes over me. I'm at the top of the mountain, and from here I can see clearly forever. I have never been happier.

"I LOVE YOU."

PART THREE

30

FOUR MONTHS later, Jennifer tells me she's pregnant. She calls me from L.A., where she's meeting with talent agents. Her voice is small, almost like a frightened child's. Although I never articulated this to her, on some level I was hoping for a pregnancy. It would settle me down, stop the top I've become from spinning. And anyhow, it's not as if it's a huge surprise. One day in the office, the conversation turned to birth control. When I revealed we weren't using any, Melinda remarked, "Ah, the old pull and pray method." "Right," I said, "except all we do is the pray part." Jenn's news is amazing. I can't believe this. On the phone, I tell her I love her and I'm thrilled.

A few weeks later, Jenn moves into my Bleecker Street co-op. Whether or not we were going to live together was never in question. But we decide there's no reason to rush out and get married. Let's get the baby thing right first. Over the next few months, evidence of my bachelorhood begins to disappear. During the day, while I'm at work,

Jenn transforms the apartment into a home. She has exquisite taste that is both bohemian and eclectic. It suits the raw building space nicely. We both have a love for Moroccan décor, and she has plenty of it from her house on Long Island, and what she doesn't have we go out and buy. The only room left unadorned is the second bedroom, which we plan to use as the nursery. Furniture, the color scheme, and toys for the room are on hold until we find out whether we're about to have a boy or a girl. We both agree on getting that information as soon as possible.

Throughout the spring and into the summer, we stay inside a lot. On weekends, we take our dogs, Houdini and M.C., for walks to Washington Square Park and sit on the benches in the dog run. I got the second dog before Jenn moved in because I felt guilty leaving one dog home alone. We watch a lot of television. Jenn is devoted to HGTV, and I buy DVDs for the first couple of seasons of 24, to which we're both soon addicted. I suffer through hours and hours of romantic comedies. But I love our eating regimen. We order in every meal: Mexican and American for me, Italian or Chinese when it's Jenn's choice. One weekend we barely get out of bed due to Jenn's morning sickness. We eat every meal while propped up in the last vestige of my bachelor days—the Charles P. Rogers sleigh bed (Jenn would soon replace it with one bought at a store called Hip and Humble)—and sleep between television shows and movies.

As idyllic as my life has become, when Jenn enters her second trimester, I feel the need to escape once in a while by going out for beers with Ethan and Jason or some of my Wall Street friends. I'm always home before midnight, and only once or twice (that Jenn knows of) do I return having had too many cocktails. But one night I come home a little after one a.m. I'm not as drunk as I am wired on cocaine; I stopped by the White House. Sleep is impossible. I crawl into bed next to my sleeping, pregnant girlfriend, facing away from her because I don't want her to catch me awake. I toss and turn. I need to fall asleep, but I tiptoe to the bathroom for one last hit, creating the cocaine paradox. It's awful. And in that forced consciousness a desire builds within me to confess to Jenn. Soon the urge is overwhelming, as if somehow an act of contrition will alleviate the torment. I can't tell her about the cocaine, I reason to myself. That would be just stupid. When I look at the clock again, it reads 4:30. I'm not going to be able to go to work. An hour goes by. I can feel Jenn coming awake. Still groggy from sleep, she looks into my eyes. I can tell by her expression that she knows something's wrong. She's not sure what to say. I did something bad last night, I mumble. She sits upright and cocks her head. I think she thinks I'm about to tell her about another woman. I had a few beers, I say, and then some guy gave me some pills. Her expression begins to sink from accusation to sadness. I tell her they were painkillers—a small lie to cover a big truth. I had to tell her something. A tear begins to roll down her cheek. She clutches her pillow and rolls away from me. Her back heaves as she gasps for air between cries and moans.

I was hoping for anger, not sadness. I begin to rub her back, but she wiggles my hand away. I sit silently, frozen in the fear that anything I say will only make things worse. Finally, she turns over and looks at me. Her eyes are red. "Do you know what it's like?" There's a quiver in her voice. I don't think I'm supposed to answer. "Growing up with a shadow that follows you all the time?" she asks. New tears begin to streak her cheeks. "When I was thirteen," she continues, "I asked my mother where my father was buried. When I found out it was only a quarter of a mile from where we lived, my heart sank. I couldn't believe I'd been so close to his grave site for so many years and never knew." Up until now, Jenn had told me little about her father. I knew that he died of drug overdose, or possibly a suicide, when she was four, but I didn't know the details. "When my mother was at work the next day and my stepfather was in the basement, I ran to the garage to get my bike." I've never been to that house, but I can see it clearly in my head. The tiny garage is cluttered with tools and junk and her bike is a pink ten-speed that has many years and miles on it. "I rode my bike to the cemetery and I found the entrance," she says. "I had no idea where my father was, so I went to the office and they told me. I rode my bike on the path through all the headstones to his grave. I was so scared, but I didn't care. I needed to talk to him; I needed to see where he was buried. When I found the spot, when I saw his name, I dropped my bike. I'd forgotten his middle name was Ira—it made me chuckle at first." Jenn takes a breath and smiles at the memory. "He's so Italian," she says, both laughing and crying. "Anyway, I lay down on the grass and spread out my arms out like I was hugging him. I couldn't stop crying. I wanted to know: Why? Why did he do this? Why did he leave me? I felt so alone. I couldn't catch my breath. I began having deep belly wails. I looked around to see if anyone could see or hear me, but no one was there. I was even more alone." She begins to cry harder. "I just wanted him to be there. Everyone told me how wonderful he was, but he couldn't quit using drugs. He left me. I had so much sorrow and grief and no one to share it with." I take Jenn's hand and squeeze it gently. "I snuck out of the house every day that summer and rode my bike to his grave," she says. "I'd spend hours there." I picture a thirteen-year-old version of Jenn sitting in a graveyard, crying, on a beautiful summer day. I begin to break down, but just then Jenn's face turns angry. "I won't allow that to happen to our child," she says. "I can't."

OCTOBER 2005

"WHAT'S A Fatburger?" Jerry, my accountant, asks. I'm talking to him on my cell as I walk through Grand Central Station. I should've involved him sooner. He sounds concerned, and I guess I understand. Restaurants are a great sinkhole for Wall Street money. But that's because too many guys go into the business for the wrong reasons. They want to be part owner of a fancy bistro or a nightclub or bar to show off, to act like the boss or have a place to bring their girlfriends. It's like paying a twenty-thousand-dollar cover charge. No thanks. For me Fatburger isn't like that. I *love* Fatburger. I had one of their burgers on my first trip to L.A. ten years ago, and every time I go to the Left Coast I plan at least one of my meals there. I look at the clock in the center of the station. It's almost six, and carpets of people are heading to the trains bound for Westchester.

Fatburger's pitch is "It's the biggest, juiciest burger you've ever seen," and they're right. The restaurants are modeled after the old roadside hamburger stand, with counters, stools you can swirl on, and rock-and-roll jukeboxes. About two years ago, a friend of mine who lives in San Francisco sent me an Internet link that mentioned Fatburger franchising opportunities. I made two phone calls—just two—and I had partners with the money and expertise to pull off the deal to bring Fatburger to the East Coast. Okay, we had the money, but saying we had the expertise might be a bit of a stretch. One of my partners' friends, John, is the operator. He's a lawyer and a day trader, but he isn't doing either right now. All he needed was a little hamburger restaurant experience, which was provided by Fatburger. They sent him to burger school.

We wanted the New York territory: Manhattan, the boroughs, and

Westchester. But Fatburger wanted a bigger player for that prime cut of real estate, so we put our bid in for New Jersey, where John lives. It came down to just us and Queen Latifah for the contract. But we got the call and went to work. We had the grand opening of our first store in Jersey City in the summer of 2004, and have plans for nineteen more. "I'm gonna need to see the paperwork," Jerry says. "Who puts a million dollars into something and doesn't tell their accountant?"

I hang up the phone and try to navigate my way out of Grand Central. Forty-Second Street is bumper-to-bumper with yellow taxi-cabs, all with their Off Duty signs glowing. I never understood why so many cabdrivers go off-duty during rush hour. I call Jesse Itzler and ask him to send our K1 directly to Jerry. Jesse and I formed a limited liability partnership a few months ago called Pink and Green. So far, we've invested in a racehorse and produced a rapper from the Bronx. It sounds riskier than it actually is. We put in only twenty grand apiece. When I hang up with Jesse, I give my cousin Ethan a call. We need a film editor badly for the movie we shot a year ago called *Holier Than Thou*. I wrote most of it, and the story is an adaptation of the Pied Piper of Hamelin legend—only set in the New York City club scene. The cool kids are sick and tired of the bridge and tunnel people infest-ing their hot spots, so they make a deal with a magical character to lead all the B&Ts out of the city. I took a week off to work on the proj-ect; we filmed twelve hours a day. I've already invested fifty thousand dollars. I just haven't had time to work with Ethan to find an editor. He keeps calling me and leaving messages. Just try and keep it under twenty grand, I tell him. Finally I call Jenn when I'm on the outskirts of the Forty-Second Street mob. As I head east and then south on Third, we chat for a few moments and her voice calms me. "I hear Mexican food and sex can induce labor," I say. We're expecting our new arrival any day. A GIRL!

31

I'VE NEVER been so stressed in my life. I need to install a baby seat in my car for the monumental ride home from the hospital. I can't seem to do it. I risk hundreds of millions of dollars every day in split-second decisions, but the installation of a car seat is beyond my comprehension. There's a black belt that looks like a seatbelt hanging from the back of the car seat. There's nowhere to put it. The buckles on the side don't attach to anything. I start to shake the car seat in the hope it will magically fall into place. The parking lot attendant at the Elizabeth Street garage is watching me and offering no assistance. I just want a stranger to stop on the street and say, "Oh, this is how you do it." That's not happening. Finally, I give up. I drive to an auto mechanic shop on Jones Street and offer the guy forty dollars to install it for me. He laughs as he takes my money. Although he's smiling, I know what he's thinking: This guy's driving a BMW 540i yet he doesn't know how to click a few buckles and tighten some straps? In no time, he gets it secured and I'm finally on my way to the hospital. I'm going to pick up my girls.

On the way, I replay the miraculous event in my mind. I can see her tiny head with her eyes tightly shut in the doctor's hands, half born for just a moment and then beautifully whole. I'm in love. I call out to her while the nurse is wrapping her in a blanket, and her head tilts my way. "I love you, Lola," I whisper. She knows her name and recognizes my voice. I've been talking to her every day for months now through Jenn's belly. I look at Jenn through watery eyes and see that hers, too, are filled with tears. We try to speak to each other, but the words come out like blubbering gibberish. The nurse gently places Lola on her mother's chest. I touch my daughter Lola Gianna Duff's tiny hand with my index finger and feel her skin for the very first time.

The Tuesday after my daughter's birth, I'm back in the office. After work I'm going to have drinks at Annie Moore's, a bar near Grand Central, with some people from Miller Tabak, a small boutique firm. The storefront of the bar is red, as is the door, to evoke a real Dublin pub. But like scores of similar establishments in Midtown, Annie Moore's is about as authentic as a green plastic derby. I see Chris and Pat, my guys, sitting at the bar waiting for me. It's not much of a Wall Street scene in here. It feels more like a rest stop on the way to broken dreams. The clientele is not quite fully broken, but close. Older men and women look deep into the bottoms of their glasses. The career bartenders are annoyed when you ask them for a drink. "Chris . . . Pat . . . Number thirty-two on the commission run, but number one in my heart," I say.

"Oh, man, really? Number thirty-two?" Chris asks. He looks upset.

"I'm kidding," I say as I shake their hands. Chris still looks upset. "You're, like, number seven." It's a lie, but I'm way overpaying him and his firm. I paid them close to a million dollars last year. It makes me one of their firm's top ten accounts. Chris orders me a beer from one of the bartenders and offers up his seat. I decline. I sit all day, I tell him. There's not much business to discuss; they just wanted to get me out and get some face time. They ask about Lola. I remember right after my daughter was born I went outside the hospital for a cigarette. When I looked at my phone, there were too many texts to count. I scrolled through and put a face to each. I have friends, Wall Street friends, Wall Street associates, and Wall Street suck-ups. Most want something in return for their friendship. Only a few don't. I give the Miller Tabak guys a detailed description of the big day. It doesn't matter if they're really interested or not. I'm glowing. Just talking about Lola makes me soft and warm inside, like doing a shot of whiskey without the consequence. I can picture her round face. Her eyes glisten and her skin is so soft. I feel myself getting a little emotional, so I suggest we do a shot. After a few more beers they ask me if I want to grab a table and get some food, but I decline. I need to get home. Jenn has been with Lola all day and I'm sure she needs a break. I can't wait to see Lola. I grab my coat and thank them for the drinks. I move across the street and start walking past Grand Central. Each step gets me closer to being home to my daughter, girlfriend, and two dogs. It's amazing how my life has changed. One minute I'm wearing cowboy shirts and out on the prowl, and in the next I have a home and a family. I walk a few blocks down Park Avenue and notice I have a slight buzz. I feel great. It's a warm October evening and the autumn light softens the city's edges. I'm gonna walk the whole way home.

And then I'm in the lobby of the White House, calling Jenn and telling her my meeting is going a little longer than expected. I'll be home in a couple of hours, I promise.

The apartment is dark and dirty. Randy and James both meet me at the door. "Look who's here!" and "There he is!" they say as they slap me on the back. And then I'm in the kitchen. The sink is filled with a week's worth of dirty dishes. My shoes stick to the floor. There are guys on the computer searching for escorts. "What's it like to be a father?" Randy asks as James taps out a hefty line on a plate and then slides it over to me. I take the rolled-up dollar bill and look down at the line. You know, I say as I bend my head down and rip the line of cocaine into my nose, then snap my head back, it was the greatest day of my life. I gasp. The cocaine burns my nose, then numbs everything. I feel a charge inside my body. It's the perfect combination of stimulation and numbness. Lola is the best thing that has ever happened to me, I tell them.

Two hours later, I'm outside the White House. I notice two men sitting in a black town car across the street. They're both wearing dark suits and sunglasses. It's dark out. They watch me as I leave the building. As soon as I begin to walk, they start their car. I check my pants pockets for coke. I didn't take any from the apartment, I know. But I check anyhow. Heat rushes to my face like I'm under a spotlight. The car slowly pulls to the end of the block as I walk toward Lexington Avenue. I see a yellow cab pull up behind them. I dart into the street and knock on his trunk. He unlocks the door and I jump in. I watch the car in front of me turn left down the avenue. We turn left. The car is slowing down and pulling over on Lex, but as soon as we pass them they pull back out and follow right behind us. I try not to look back, but I can't help myself. We're almost to the Union Square area and they're still following. Don't look again, I tell myself. The cab pulls up in front of my building on Bleecker Street. I step out onto the sidewalk half expecting to be beaten or handcuffed, or at least confronted. But when I look for them, they're not in sight.

I run into the building and to the elevator. I'm in my apartment now, holding my daughter to my chest. My whole body clenches with the thought of the promise that I made to stop using when she was born. I don't know who was in that car, but I do know it's a sign. As I look at my daughter's sweet face, I know the risk of using cocaine is far too great.

32

OCTOBER 2005–OCTOBER 2006

I WAS up all night with Lola. "I can't make it to work today," I tell Krishen.

It seems like everything is changing, changing all at once. The business is different. Newspaper headlines have taken their toll. I think the crooked CEOs of corporate America—the Lays, the Skillings, the Kozlowskis—have ruined it for everyone. Years of fraud have collapsed into cover-ups, investigations, and convictions: Worldcom, Tyco, Delphi, and Enron, and the list grows. Even Fidelity has found itself the center of a trading scandal. The Street feels like it's on high alert now. They're trying to make all hedge funds register with the SEC. It's a pain in the ass. Now brokers' expense accounts are monitored and they have to be careful how they entertain us. What we can now get away with is still pretty lavish—Vegas, VIP rooms, and limos—we just need to be more creative. Still, I've been going backwards in pay and bonuses, but it's because of our performance. Argus lost assets this year, so I'm not sure how I'll do.

At the end of October, Krishen asks me to come into the CFO's office. "I need you to sign this," he says. Argus received an inquiry from the SEC on a particular stock we bought that I traded. The stock in question was upgraded just hours after I purchased it. As I sign the document I get an uneasy feeling, the kind you get when you're sure someone is following you.

I'm spinning apart. Just as I get back to my desk, the phone rings. It's a guy from the Healthcare Mafia. He tells me about a trend happening in the generic drug sector and he's practically begging me to buy a list of stocks. I buy small and wait to see how they trade, but they're selling off. Then I buy another 25,000 shares of each, but they keep going lower. I decide to call a buddy at Morgan Stanley to ask why the stocks keep going down. When he tells me who the seller is, my hand tightens around the phone. It's my Healthcare Mafia friend who begged me to buy them: a trick so unimaginative, so impersonal, you'd expect it only from a total stranger. Did he really think he'd get away with playing me this way? He's fucked himself bigtime, because now he's dead to me. Crossed off the list. The bonds of the Mafia are frayed and pulling apart. The hot breath of the SEC, the culture of distrust, have turned us against one another. I can't trust anyone, and I can't keep it together.

A few weeks later, I walk into the office an hour late without having slept. Rich and Melinda look at me like I'm some kind of apparition. "I thought you took the day off because your parents are in town," Rich says. I don't remember telling them I was going to be out today, and my parents aren't in town until tomorrow. Their excursions to New York City are infrequent because they're afraid. They won't leave the apartment for fear of getting lost or mugged. The last time they were here, they returned to the apartment white with fear after a simple daytime trip to Chinatown. I nod at Rich and Melinda and turn around and go home.

In December, I meet Krishen in the conference room for my year-end evaluation. He forces a smile when I enter. I'm getting a bonus of $500k, he says without preface. Poor performance and lower assets are the reasons. This is the second year in a row I've been paid less than the year before. What's more, Krishen tells me, the payout structure is going to change. The firm will no longer have guaranteed percentages. Instead, five of us—me, Rich, and three senior analysts—will fight it out for 25 percent of the bonus pool. He thinks the competition will make us perform better. I think it's going to create a knife fight. We have to stab the person next to us in the back to make an extra hundred grand? This sucks. I stand up and shake his hand. "Thanks," I say.

On the first warm evening in February, Jenn, Lola, and I head out with the stroller to get some dinner. We walk in silence, not the comfortable kind. We've been struggling recently. After a few blocks Jenn starts to cry. I ask her what's wrong. She tells me how hard it is, dealing with this new life of stay-at-home responsibility, how each and every day is difficult. "Your life went back to normal," she says. Nothing could be further from the truth, I think. But I don't say a word. I go to hug her, but she stiffens. Then I notice a serious face with a pair of eyes watching me. It's a tall man with a square jaw; very fit and clean-cut. He has white hair and a Baltimore Orioles hat on. It doesn't suit him. He looks like a politician who wears the home team cap when he wants everyone to think he's a regular guy. I saw him behind us a few blocks back. He couldn't be following us, could he? He looks right at me, a lingering glance, and then looks away. I push the stroller faster. Jenn struggles to keep up.

A few days later, I call in sick to work again. "Food poisoning is the worst," Melinda says when I show up the following day. My complexion is still pale. My hands shake as I set my phone and keys down on my desk and turn on the computer. When Krishen arrives, he asks me how I'm feeling, but his words lack any sincerity. The hours struggle by. When I leave work, I see the white-haired man again. This time he's not wearing the hat. And this time I stare at him. For a second, I can see some kind of recognition in his eyes. I'm positive he's watching me. He slowly turns and walks away. It takes a few weeks for me to forget about him. Though I keep my eye out, I don't see him again. Maybe I scared him off. Or maybe he knows I'm onto him.

In late April, Rich and Krishen are already in the conference room when I come into work. Krishen tells me he wants me to go to the doctor. He thinks something must be wrong with me. "You've been sick way too much this year," he says. At first I protest, telling him that I'd told Melinda I had to take Lola to the doctor yesterday. "I know," he says. "But you keep having issues, so I think you need to get checked out."

I've missed a few days, but he doesn't understand how difficult things have been at home. I have to get Krishen off my back. So I tell him I'll go to the doctor next week. But my health issues aren't the only reason for our meeting. He wants to discuss our proprietary trading. "I want you guys to only trade healthcare names we're not involved with," he says. "Some of the analysts think you only cherry-pick their best ideas for your own trading account."

What the fuck is he talking about? That's what I do. I make us more money because the analysts don't know how to trade. It makes no sense to trade only names we aren't involved in.

"They think the reason your trading account performed better than our other funds last year is because you only pick their winners."

When I pick them, they aren't winners yet, Krishen—that's a skill.

I want to scream. Krishen stands up, I guess to let us know the discussion's over. As he heads out of the conference room, I call to him.

"I just have one question," I say. "How 'bout the analysts cherry-pick their own trades—maybe they should only put their best ideas in the portfolio?" Krishen's face turns red. He steps back into the room and pounds his fist on the table.

"How about you do your job and I'll do mine!" he screams. I've been with Argus for almost five years, and for most of that time I've been the golden boy. I couldn't do anything wrong. As Krishen walks out the door, I realize that I no longer hold that lofty position.

And things go from bad to worse. In June, during options expiration, I forget to check all of our positions at the end of the day, something I'm supposed to do every third Friday of the month. Every month options get exercised into equity positions or become worthless. When I realize it on Saturday, I know it won't be a problem—I'll just fix it on Monday. But on Sunday night I get a text from a friend, Smart Carl, about a company buying another company for an extremely high valuation. The deal is dilutive. Analysts on the Street think the company is overpaying to acquire the other. Not good for the price of the stock. Since I didn't perform my duty correctly on Friday, we actually own 100,000 shares of the company acquiring the other. When the stock opens on Monday morning, it's already down ten dollars. My error costs the firm a million bucks.

Three days after my colossal blunder, I can't work. I look like I've been crying all night. I don't even stop by the trading desk. I walk directly into Krishen's office. I know with my puffy eyes, sunken face, and trembling hands, he'll understand. "Jenn had a miscarriage last night," I say. Krishen doesn't say anything other than "Okay." He knows I'm not working today. I turn around and leave. I don't say a word to anyone on my way out.

Then I start losing money trading in my own account. The next week a pipe bursts in the apartment and I have to take another day off. The week after, I get pinkeye and call in sick again. I have the worst luck. I stop trading proprietarily. It's impossible to make money this way. Krishen wants me to fail. Why else would he limit the names I can trade? I get a call from Jesse telling me the rapper we're producing took a felony gun rap and is going to spend the next five years in jail, and our horse will no longer be racing. Too many last-place finishes. The Fatburger store in Jersey City is barely breaking even, and the plans to open the second one in the Borgata in Atlantic City might require more money. Money I don't have. Can things get any worse? At home, Jenn barely talks to me. When she does, it's mostly accusations: "You come home drunk from business dinners all the time," she says. The only good in my life is my daughter. She says her first word as she reaches to me from her crib: "Up." She's crawling all over the apartment. When I look at her, I feel peace. Her hair is growing, her eyes are China blue, and her enormous cheeks are the color of rose petals. One night, Jenn and I decide to rent the movie *Walk the Line,* the Johnny Cash story. Lola is still up, so we set her on the couch with us. We're both tired and almost ready to turn it off and finish the movie tomorrow when Joaquin Phoenix begins to sing the title track. Lola sits upright and starts to wiggle her shoulders. She does a shimmy. The thought makes me smile, even today.

In July, I decide to take Jenn to Greece. We've moved so far apart over the past months, and maybe it will bring us back together. Jenn's mom agrees to watch Lola. When I tell Krishen I'm taking a vacation, he says it's unacceptable. He says a trader shouldn't be out during earnings season, the quarterly period when the bulk of companies report their earnings to the Street. It's too late to cancel, I tell him. I already bought the tickets. I have to go, for Jenn's and my sake.

We stay at the most gorgeous hotel on the island of Santorini, called Katikies. The rooms are in the side of a mountain. It feels like a cave. They overlook the spectacular submerged volcano surrounded by a turquoise sea. One night, while walking through the quiet town, we find a jeweler. There Jenn sees a beautiful ring, a vibrant blue topaz gemstone. The next night, when she's in the shower, I run to town. We have dinner reservations at the hotel. Before we head down to the restaurant, we drink a glass of wine on the veranda overlooking the water. I get down on one knee and ask her to marry me. She says yes, and we both cry.

When summer is over, Lola enrolls in her first class—Bilingual Birdies, an English and Spanish mother-and-daughter musical class. I start planning her first birthday. I decide to charter a cruise ship for 150 people to circle Manhattan a few times. We're going to cater it with a Sunday brunch, hire a band. After a few days of securing everything and making phone calls and putting down deposits, most of the party is planned. I tell Jenn after dinner I'm going to meet some guys out and I'll be home later. But I'm not back till six a.m. and then I only have time to shower and put on my work clothes.

Things get so much worse. An hour later, I'm standing on the corner of Bleecker and Lafayette. Rich answers my call at the desk. "My friend from college tried to commit suicide last night," I say, sniffling.

"Um," Rich says. "Um, I'm sorry. Are you okay?"

"I have to fly to Ohio," I say. "Can you tell Krishen I'll be at work on Monday?" When I hang up the phone I see the white-haired man again. At least I think it's him. I'm not sure. I only see him for a moment before he disappears around a corner. Instead of walking back to the apartment, I walk south. Jenn and Lola are still sleeping. I just want to be alone. When I get home that afternoon, I tell Jenn about my friend in Ohio. She wants to know if I'm okay. She's worried about me. She thinks I should fly there, but I tell her I spoke to him and he's doing all right. I just need to rest.

Five days after Lola's birthday party cruise, I limp into the office lobby, soaking wet. I'm bleeding and have holes in my suit pants. It's almost seven a.m. The security guard gives me a bewildered look. I look away and flash my ID card. I drag my right leg along as I make my way into the elevator bank. I need to hold my body up with one arm against the wall. My breathing is erratic. It's hard to stand. I get on the elevator, thankfully alone.

I'm not sure how much farther I can go. Each time I take a step, my right leg throbs in pain. I use each desk in the office to take a mini break to catch my breath. Then I poke my head around the glass wall to see Melinda and Rich at their desks. They look up and then glance at each other. It isn't the usual *Turney's fucked up again on a Friday* look. They're scared. I try to muster some words, but can't. "I got mugged," I finally say. Rich and Melinda continue to look at me and then at each other. "I need to go to the hospital . . . my leg." I turn and start limping out of the office.

Rich gets up and follows me. "If you need anything, just call us," he says. "Are you sure you're all right?"

I get a cab. I tell the driver "107 Rivington Street." I text Jenn and tell her I fell in a puddle going to work. Then I text her that I'm going to get my knee checked out and I'll call her later. I know she's not up yet. I'm shaking in the backseat. I roll the window down. I roll it up. I blow a few deep breaths out of my mouth. I turn around to see if anyone is following my cab. I look down at my knee—it's still bleeding. My palms are raw. There are tiny pebbles lodged underneath my skin. I pull my wet shirt off my shoulders.

The Rivington Hotel lobby is dark. I hand over my license and credit card. I tell them I need a room. They look at me suspiciously but don't say a word. Why did the concierge just go in the back? Maybe I should just leave—but they have my credit card and license. I wait. This isn't good. What's taking so long? "Here you go," the gentleman says as he hands me my stuff back with a hotel key. "Take the elevator to the fourteenth floor and then take a right." I grab it and hurry to the elevator.

Once inside my room, I quickly take off my shirt and pants and throw them on a chair. I find the remote and order porn off the television. The bed is all white. I'm afraid to get blood on it. I empty my pockets and put everything on the nightstand: my keys, money, credit cards, phone, and two eight balls of cocaine. I empty one of the bags on the nightstand. I want to cry, but I can't.

Last night started so harmlessly. After work I went out for a few cocktails. I called a dealer around ten p.m. I was home by midnight. Jenn and Lola were sleeping. I was just going to have a few more bumps before I went to bed. Then I couldn't stop. I never can stop anymore. I don't have an off button. I just kept going back and forth from the couch to the bathroom. I realize I've been up for three days. This started on Wednesday. *Fuck.* What's Jenn going to say when she sees my text? I look at my still bleeding knee. I can't believe I told the people at work I got mugged. I was out of excuses.

I'm so full of shit. I didn't get mugged.

TWO HOURS EARLIER

The cab drops me at the corner of Fifty-Fourth and Park. It's not even light yet. The black sky spits the last of the rain that's left from the storm the night before. Scaffolding fronts my office building like a huge exoskeleton. The city has that just-before-dawn, post-apocalyptic feel. I'm the only one alive, and just barely. Cocaine trickles down the back of my throat as I practice my speech. I have to go to work, and they'll fire me if I do. I stand there on the street corner nearly comatose from two nights of drugs and alcohol.

My hands tremble as I light a cigarette and begin to walk around the block. Inhale desperation; exhale anxiety. I don't know how I'm going to walk into the office in the shape I'm in. I flick my cigarette, not even half smoked, onto the sidewalk. It sizzles as it hits the wet concrete and ignites a convoluted idea that my cocaine-addled brain thinks is inspired. What if I just got mugged? I feel a chill come over me. For an instant, out of the corner of my eye, I see a shadow move suddenly toward me from across the street. Just as quickly it's gone. I light another cigarette, and before I know it I've circled the block and I'm back where I started, where a huge puddle has formed in the street. I take a breath, close my eyes, and stand in front of the puddle. It's time for my mugging.

First attempt . . .

My body refuses. I'm afraid of the pain.

I stand up.

Second attempt . . .

The dive is halfhearted, but my knees dig into the pavement.

My palms burn . . .

I feel the slimy wetness on my face.

Taste it in my mouth.

Pants soaked and ripped.

My shirt is dry.

Again!

Again!

Again!

It felt as if I was pushed. I hit the puddle with such force, my face stings as it smacks the water and then the street underneath. As I lift my head I see the shadow again. It hovers over the sidewalk where I just stood. Now I'm up again—I don't even know how. I can feel blood running down my shins from the cuts in my knees—my hands are ripped and also bleeding. The shadow grows and forms into some type of being. And then I'm lying in the street water again. I can't stop.

Broken, bleeding, and out of breath, I lift my head and frantically search for my tormentor, but I see nothing, only the slick pavement and the tires of the cars parked on the side street. Somehow, I'm able to get to my feet. There's no sign of the shadow, and relief displaces fear. I've accomplished my goal. As I enter the office building, cocaine continues to trickle down my throat, but now it's mixed with a taste of blood.

I can't live like this anymore.

I never had a friend try to commit suicide. A pipe never burst in my apartment—it was a leak. Jenn had a miscarriage, but it was two weeks before I called in sick. I've been sick almost once a week, but not the kind of sick I tell work about. I've been doing cocaine four nights a week. I tell Jenn I have business dinners and then rent hotel rooms to snort cocaine by myself. I tell my friends I'm busy with work dinners. I tell Wall Street friends I'm busy being a father at home. I thought

I was going to be able to stop when Jenn told me she was pregnant. Then I knew I would stop when my daughter was born. But when Jenn and Lola fall asleep, I tiptoe out to the computer and watch porn and snort coke all night. I can't stop. Just one more line.

I'm so fucked. How'd I let it go this far? I knew I should have never taken the dealer's phone number two years ago. I'm so fucked. Just one more movie and one more line and then I'm going to flush it. I'll call work and tell them I'm still at the hospital and I'll text Jenn and let her know I'm okay. Just one more line. Just one more. Check the peephole. One more line. Check the peephole. One more line. Check the peephole.

I grab my phone. I have three texts from Jenn and two emails from Krishen. Jenn is worried. *Where are you? What's happening? Are you okay? People keep calling here.* Krishen's emails are less concerned: *You've been too disruptive this year. We need to talk, call me.* And then: *You need to come in on Monday. We need to talk.*

I look up at the clock: 2:30 p.m. Porn is still playing. I've rented more than twenty movies. There's one more line of cocaine left. I hear a voice. I know it's coming from inside my head, but I can hear it. *This is the last line of cocaine you ever have to do,* it says. My entire body shakes. This is it. This is my last line.

I'm so fucked.

33

THREE HOURS after I leave the Rivington Hotel, I'm standing outside my apartment. I have my phone, credit cards, and my license—nothing else besides the clothes on my back. I see myself in the window of the coffee shop. I look exactly like what I am: homeless. Shortly after, Ethan and Jason pull up in a cab. They wear worried expressions and approach me with hesitation. "Man, are you okay?" Ethan says. I crawl into the back of the taxi. We're going to Jason's because Ethan lives in a studio in Brooklyn with his girlfriend now and Jason has a one-bedroom apartment. I spend the night on his couch and dial Jenn the next morning. I'm not sure she'll even take my call.

After the fake mugging and my hotel stay, I walked into our apartment filled with a mixture of anxiety and hope. I'd been struck, if you believe in such things, by something akin to divine inspiration—by the belief that I was on a path to freedom from my addiction. And the first thing I needed to do was admit what I'd done. I knew it would hurt, but I reasoned it was just like pulling off a Band-Aid. Just pull it, I told myself. I told Jenn everything, at least as it concerned my cocaine use. And I promised her I'd fix what I'd broken. I begged her to stand by me.

I could see her putting the puzzle pieces together in her head. Things started to make sense. The countless sleepless nights, the manic behavior in the apartment, the continual business dinners, and the constant sick days from work started formulating a perfect picture in her thoughts. But I couldn't explain to her why I kept doing it. I wish I knew. The only thing I know is that it starts with a belief the morning after that I'll never do it again. Then later in the day it's a confidence that I'll control it next time. Finally, it comes in the form of a seven-year-old's anticipation on Christmas. I *have* to have it.

She was more upset than shocked. Tears streamed down her cheeks. I thought I hid my actions well—addicts always think that. But she'd lived the torment I'd caused. She wiped the tears from her face, which then took on a defiant expression. "I just have one question for you," she said. "A month ago when I had to go to Atlantic City with my mom . . ." Please don't ask, I said to myself. Please don't. "When you were watching Lola alone on Friday night and could barely speak on Saturday?" Her eyes burned with accusations. "Were you?"

I searched for an excuse, but I had no answer. My head hung as I stared at a spot on the floor in front of me. She grabbed her cigarettes and phone and left. "Get the fuck out" is the last thing she said to me.

On Saturday when I call from Jason's, Jenn answers the phone. I tell her I'm going to rehab. It's a holistic place in Tucson called Cottonwood, I say. The anger from the day before is gone from her voice and is replaced by a kind of detachment. She tells me she's not sure if she and Lola will be there when I return from Arizona.

I spend the rest of the morning making my confessions over the phone. When my mother hears the word "cocaine," she chokes on her words. I'm worried she won't be able to sleep. When my father comes on the line, he wishes me luck, as if I'm going off to college for the first time. "Let us know if there's anything we can do for you," he says. To a person, my non–Wall Street friends are shocked. One by one, I hear the same response: "You do cocaine?" None of them knew, but, having witnessed at least some of my odd behavior and unreliability, all of them suspected something was wrong.

The first call I make to my Wall Street world is Uncle Tucker. He's heard this type of story before but had no idea it was happening to me. He offers his assistance and compassion. Then I call Gus and Randy, both of whom seem upset. I'm not sure if they feel responsible, worried, or just mad that they've lost their best account. I call a few more Wall Street people and they all tell me not to tell anyone else. Keep it to yourself, they say. I can't do that. There's one place I must tell.

That Monday is an unusually warm fall day. I stand on the corner of Fifty-Seventh and Park Avenue. As the New York City swarm passes, I tilt my head skyward and let the sun's rays warm my face, like a kid on a sun-dappled playground. Drugs and alcohol have hollowed me out, but in the sun's warmth I'm almost whole again. I want this feeling to last forever, and I promise myself I'll never forget this moment of hope and light. It's exactly then that a guy talking on his cell phone slams into my shoulder and knocks the files I'm holding all over the sidewalk. "This isn't the beach, asshole," he says over his shoulder, without breaking stride. I gather my things and head into my office building.

The office is somber. I don't know whether my coworkers are more embarrassed or sad. Whatever eye contact exists is brief, and a few glances even feel chilly. Might be me. I'm not exactly filled with confidence right now. Regardless of the emotion, the moment is real. I walk into the conference room to see Don, our CFO, seated with Rich and Krishen at the table. The murmur I heard at the door quiets to an uncomfortable silence. I stand there with my hands in my pockets; I catch myself looking down at my shoes. I hadn't realized how dirty they are. The eye contact in the room is not much better than that outside. My gaze settles on a spot on the wall somewhere over Krishen's head, as if I'm searching the horizon. "I want to thank you for everything you guys have done for me," I say, peeking down at their reactions. It might not be my finest moment, but my words come from my heart. I tell them I know I caused them pain and brought chaos into the office. I tell them I'm truly sorry. I thought I had it under control. "I have a problem," I say. "And I need help." I tell them I'm checking into a rehab out in Arizona. "I fly out tomorrow."

Each one at the table is looking directly at me. "So the best thing for me to do, for everyone concerned," I say, measuring the moment, "is to resign. Effective immediately."

With those words, the tension on both sides of the table evaporates. I'm the elephant and I'm no longer going to be in the room. It's over. Now they don't have to fire me. Each of them has their say. I can hear the words coming out of their mouths, but they tumble over me like rapids over rocks. My face is burning and there's ringing in my ears. I know they're honestly worried about me. And I believe they truly want what's best for me. But I also know that as soon as I walk out of the office, they'll let out a collective sigh of relief.

Tuesday morning I'm alone with Lola on the bed in the master bedroom. I ask her if she knows how much I love her. She nods yes. I tell her I'm going to go away to try to make myself better, and ask if that's okay. Once again, she nods yes. Though it's impossible that she can fully understand what I'm saying, there's a glint in the depths of her eyes that assures me she does. "I love you and Mama more than anything in the whole world," I say. I hold her hand as she bounces on the bed. "I just want to go away and have them fix me so I can be a better daddy." Lola giggles, gives me a big smile, and reaches out to touch my nose. A feeling of happiness wells up inside of me. The feeling is almost overwhelming. And yet I don't cry. I'm numb still from years of drug use. All of a sudden I realize how fragile my life is, how easily drugs can obliterate my love for my daughter. *Breathe,* I tell myself. *Just breathe.* I hold Lola like I never want to let go. I hold her like that until she falls asleep in my arms.

The plane touches down in Tucson early in the afternoon. It's hot and dry. I'm dying for a smoke, but I need to pee first. I head to the bathroom in the airport, where I get a glimpse of myself. I still look like hell. My call to Jenn goes directly to voice mail. I walk over to the baggage claim and wait for my bags. When they finally come around the conveyor belt, I grab them, drag them outside, and immediately light up a cigarette followed by another. Midway through my third, an older gent with a weathered face the color and texture of a leather saddle approaches. He's been out in the sun a bit too long, I think. Like maybe ten years too long. He carries a sign that reads MR. TURNEY.

"Turney is my first name," I say by way of introduction.

"Bill's mine," he says as he reaches for my bags.

"I got 'em," I say. I must look weaker than I thought. Bill and I walk across the airport parking lot to a maroon van. It's about a thirty-minute drive to the facility. I spend the first part just looking out the window at the sights, the usual just-outside-the-airport urban sprawl of highway cloverleafs and chain stores. I can't believe I'm going to rehab.

"What's your drug of choice?" Bill asks, breaking the silence.

"Cocaine and alcohol, I guess. Do you work for the rehab?"

"I'm retired but I work for the center a few days a week doing whatever they need. I like to be around it. It helps me remember why I can't drink today."

"How long's it been?" I ask.

"Clean?" he says with a smile. "Twenty-two wonderful years."

I want to believe him, but I don't.

"It goes by, son," he says with a chuckle. Bill has a nice way about him. I like him already. "But it's just one day at a time."

I still like him, despite the cliché. The van stops at a red light.

"I'm not supposed to do this," he says, "but do you want me to stop so you can load up on cigarettes before you enter?"

With cigarettes bulging from every pocket, I feel like I'm wearing a bulletproof vest. The van pulls up in front of iron gates with a security booth. Bill waves at the guard and flashes his ID. Once we clear the first gate, there's another with more security.

"Okay, this is the end of the road for me," Bill says. "You might want to make any last-minute phone calls before entering, but I can't leave until I see you walk past the gate."

I call Jenn, but her phone again goes to voice mail. The land surrounding the center is beautiful: the mossy green and golds of sagebrush, the rust-colored cacti, some ten, twelve feet high, and the purple hue of the Santa Catalina Mountains in the distance. I walk in, and as Bill pulls away, I'm overcome with loneliness.

After intake, I'm shown to my room. Small, with four single beds, but three already have stuff on them, and a tiny bath—it's not exactly a suite at the Four Seasons. But it's not a bunk at the Bowery Mission, either. As these things go, I would imagine this clinic is high-end. It has a chef, a swimming pool, and yoga classes. The complex reminds me of a small college campus. There are multiple buildings attached by manicured walkways. I'm here to make 4.0. As soon as I drop my bags, I'm off to find the therapist assigned to me. I'm anxious to get started on getting better.

I'm two weeks into my stay before I finally get Jenn on the phone. With the time change and the center's restrictions on phone calls, I'd only been able to leave voice mails. I call from out on the patio. It's a beautiful desert early evening. "Hey," she says flatly.

"Hey, how you doing?" With fourteen days clean and dry, I have that just-sober, *Isn't everything wonderful?* glow that can be extremely annoying to people in the real world. I prattle on about how great I feel and the amazing classes I'm taking and the cool and sage counselors I've met. I tell her I've shaved my head. "I feel like I'm getting myself back, Jenn," I say. "I'm learning how to live again." There's a beat of a second or two of silence before she answers.

"You know, I think it's great and all that you love your vacation," she says. "The more I've thought about this, the more I realize how selfish of you this was. You didn't give your daughter or me a moment of consideration. It was all about you."

The rainbow over my head starts to fade.

"I opened your American Express bill to pay it for you. There's at least a half dozen charges for hotels."

I try to explain, but she doesn't want to hear a word of what I have to say. What am I going to say anyhow? I sit in hotel rooms watching porn, masturbating, and snorting cocaine for six hours a night while she sits home, worrying and taking care of Lola?

"Jenn, I never cheated on you," I say. "I promise."

I hear the dial tone and let my hand holding the phone drop to my side. I'm looking out at the mountains. The evening sky is streaked with pink and purple. A warm breeze blows in from the desert.

34

AFTER TWENTY-EIGHT days, I'm a different person. Long gone are the toxins that poisoned my body. I'm tan, have a shaved head, am clean-shaven, and look younger than my thirty-seven years. As I walk through the outside gate, I close my eyes and lift my face to the sun like I did on Fifty-Seventh Street, but here no one shoulders into me. All I feel is the warmth of another chance. When I open my eyes, my old friend Bill is standing there waiting for me, as if he just appeared. "Let me give you a hand with those bags," he says with his smile like a crease in a favorite leather jacket. I jump into his van and buckle up. "What airline?" he asks as we begin to pull away.

"Just drop me at the nearest bar," I tell him. He hits the brakes and we come to a screeching stop. He looks at me with hard assessment. The twinkle in my eyes belies my poker face. We both break up at the same time.

"The Navajos say that laughter is a sign of purity," he says as he pats me on the knee. "You're gonna be just fine."

As the elevator doors open, Jenn is standing there holding Lola's hand. Lola is not quite sure how to react. I'm crestfallen. Only Houdini and M.C. seem happy to see me. I squat down and open my arms. Then Lola breaks into a smile and toddles over. I sweep her up and hold her tightly. My baby senses my vulnerability and crawls right into my heart. It's not that simple with Jenn. She stands there, her arms wrapped tightly around her chest. She attempts to smile, but it doesn't quite form.

We spend the day together, hanging out in the apartment. The uneasiness between us is worse than a bad first date. I wonder if she feels the same as I do. And the awkwardness I feel with Jenn is only part of my discomfort. I thought it was going to be easy to put the past behind me. But everything reminds me of using: I look at the computer and I think of porn, the plates in the kitchen remind me of cocaine, the dogs remind me of sleepless nights. I place my hand on the brick wall in the living room, hoping to feel anchored. But I feel nothing.

The days struggle to pass. There are moments when the love Jenn and I once took for granted seems as strong as ever, and other times when we act like complete strangers. She spends a lot of time on the phone, sometimes with friends but mostly with her mother. It feels as though they're teaming up on me. And I have no grounds on which to fight back. I'm the one who's the addict, the guy who left for rehab and stayed there for a month. I guess Jenn's mom is just being a mom. I need to fix everything. For now, Jenn is sticking by me, but we both agree it might be time to move out of the city and start over. We decide to get through the holidays and then I'll start the process. I need to prove to Jenn and everyone else that I'm better. In rehab they told me: No major changes in the first twelve months of sobriety. But back in real life, it isn't that easy. It's Jenn's decision whether we'll stay together or not. And I need to make some money.

In January, I set up a home office for my job search. Each day I spend a few hours sending emails, watching the market online, and making phone calls. Most of the people I contact know my situation— the Wall Street rumor mill never disappoints. Those that don't aren't exactly shocked. "Turney, what do you think ninety-five percent of the sabbaticals on Wall Street are for?" my friend Rob asks. Everyone wants to help. At first I think it's because they love Turney, but then I realize the person who helps me get a job will most likely also get an indebted buy side guy to trade with—me.

Lola enjoys having me home. We go to the park and swing on the swings when it's not too cold. We eat lunch together, we watch *Dora the Explorer,* and we take naps. At night I try to hit a meeting, the ones they kept telling me about in rehab. I don't like leaving for that long. I feel like Jenn gets nervous every time I do, wondering if this will be the time I won't come back. I meet a Wall Street guy named Kevin at one of the meetings. He's tall and skinny, with the first sightings of gray hair. Though he doesn't look the part, he played Division I college basketball. He asks me questions about my daughter and the Cleveland Indians. He genuinely seems to care how I'm doing. He has a friend named Chris. I think Kevin is Chris's sponsor. Chris has a round face and wears glasses. He's in media or the Internet or something. I'm not sure how long he's been sober, but he wears an ill-fitting Sy Syms suit with a ripped pocket and has white tape on one of the arms of his glasses. He just looks happy to be alive. He's a funny guy. He follows Kevin around like a puppy. They save me a seat at a meeting every Monday and Thursday. I like them a lot.

After one meeting, they ask me to grab some coffee with them. At first, it's hard for me to open up. But when I do, I mostly talk about Jenn. Kevin tells me she has a right to be angry and I just need to focus on myself and stay in the moment. "Go to meetings, call me every day, and take care of yourself," he says. "You're doing great." Though I don't feel like I'm doing great, I soak up his encouragement. I wonder how someone from Wall Street can be so kind and serene.

Then Chris uses his breath to fog up his glasses, then cleans them, "Did you drink on the plane to rehab?" he asks out of nowhere. I shake my head no. "Smart," he says. "I did, and your boy Kevin shotgunned three beers on his flight to Minnesota." It's a funny visual, especially when Kevin pretends to perform the technique on his coffee cup. I think it's the first time I've laughed in months. The bit isn't even that funny, but Kevin keeps pretending to shotgun his coffee and I'm laughing harder each time he does.

Though much is still unsettled, on the job front things seem to get better right away. On a Monday morning in January, I sit down at my home office, turn on my computer, and see I have three emails, all from the sell side. One is from Gus, another is from a friend named Oliver, and the third is from another friend, Pat. They all have buy side leads for me. Just then, I hear Jenn and Lola preparing to go for a walk. And out of nowhere the idea of calling a dealer pops into my mind. It's insane to think I'd even entertain the thought. "Play the tape forward," they told me in rehab. I do. And the story ends with me pacing around a hotel room in my underwear, checking the peephole every five minutes. What an awful idea. I pick up my phone and follow up on the leads.

And as the week goes by, more leads and interview requests come in. I talk to a guy in a downtown boutique firm who loves me but thinks I'm overqualified. He tells me he's going to call a buddy whose firm I might be perfect for. A hedge fund called Balyasny, in Midtown, one with the same model as Galleon, wants me as their healthcare trader. They need to go over the numbers and come up with an offer. A firm, SAC Capital Advisors, up in Connecticut thinks it may have a spot for me but needs a week or two to figure out how to make it work.

My conversations with prospective employers are almost like out-of-body experiences, as if someone else is doing the talking other than me. The last time I interviewed like this, I got the job at Morgan mostly because of my knowledge of *Melrose Place*. I'm shocked now at how much I know, how poised and confident I am. In each interview, I guarantee them that I'll have the lowest SAT scores in their conference room. But, I say, if we play poker, I'll take all of your money. The line works every time. I explain the art of managing commission dollars, and how I can cut commission in half and still get them the same service from brokers as before. I tell them I'll make mistakes, but I'll never try to hide them, and my honesty disarms them. "I want to find a place to finish out my Wall Street life," I say finally. And every time I get smiles, handshakes, and promises of a returned phone call.

But alone, in my own thoughts, I'm far from confident, let alone believing someone would put me to work. I think of myself as branded with a scarlet letter, one all of Wall Street can see. I've been bad and deserve to be punished. I'm desperate to make Jenn, and the rest of the world, like me again. When I look back at that time, the fallout I was facing wasn't all that bad. Jenn stayed with me, Lola always loved me, and I still had money in the bank. It just didn't *feel* that way then. I was desperate to get a job, and willing to take the first one offered.

And in fact, it happens almost seamlessly. My lead from my friend Oliver pans out. In February, I get a call from J. L. Berkowitz, a firm that used to be called Cramer Berkowitz and was managed by *Mad*

Money's Jim Cramer. That night I'm playing with Lola in her room. I discuss the opportunity with my daughter over a pretend dinner. "I have a job interview tomorrow, Lola," I say. She smiles and flips a plastic meatball at me. "I don't really want to work there, but I guess sometimes we have to do things we don't want to, like brushing your teeth," I say. As I hear the words come out of my mouth, I can taste their contradiction. The last six weeks all I've been saying is I want a job. Lola giggles and pretends to eat. "And I also have to keep you in meatballs," I say, tickling her on her sides. Lola cackles even harder. I kiss her on the forehead. "Wish me luck," I say.

By the time I hit the street after the interview, I've already gotten two voice mails from guys who were my references telling me how much Berkowitz loves me. I'm shocked—they trade everything but healthcare, the only thing I've traded the last six years. It doesn't matter to me; a stock is just a few letters clumped together. The next morning I get a call from Jeff Berkowitz, who tells me to come in on Thursday to work out a deal. That day, I get dressed in a blue button-down shirt and khakis. My hair is still short, nearly a buzz cut. My eyes are as clear as a Maine stream. I'm about to go back to the buy side.

35

IF, PRIOR to interviewing at Berkowitz, I had any remaining hesitation about exiting the city, it was removed one day when I came
home from work. Jenn was waiting for me inside the doorway. Her
arms were tightly folded across her chest, and her face was red with
anger. She'd had yet another run-in with our next-door neighbor. A
misogynist, a racist, and an awful human being, the guy had been
the bane of Jenn's existence since she'd moved in. He kept all his crap
in our shared hallway and frequently behaved in a nasty way. "I can't
live here anymore," she said. "If you want to, that's fine. But I have
to leave." I knew she meant it. If I needed a final shove, this was it.
"Okay," I said. "Let's start looking."

Once we were in, we were all in. As if it were a full-time job—and
it nearly was—Jenn took on the task of getting the co-op ready for
sale and finding the house. She spent hours on the computer looking.

She had maps, open-house listings, and brokers' phone numbers, and she worked out our itinerary down to the minute. We hit every open house from Brookville to Cold Spring Harbor on the north shore of Long Island. And Jenn was the happiest I'd seen her since Lola was born. I realized then how selfish I'd been to her. When we'd met, she was a professional singer who'd just completed a world tour. She became pregnant just eleven months after we started dating, a pregnancy that kept her sick in bed for much of the time. With my partying and job obligations, I'd left her almost totally by herself to take care of our baby in a big apartment with a crazy neighbor. If once in a while I got impatient with her as she searched for the perfect house, the thought of how I'd treated her kept me from saying anything.

Jenn found a house online one night around midnight. "I shouldn't show you this," she said. "It's out of our price range and it's ten miles past Cold Spring Harbor." (I was up watching the remake of *Amityville Horror*. Only in hindsight do I appreciate the irony.) What can I say—a six-bedroom Queen Anne Victorian with a guest house and pool looks magnificent on the computer screen.

Jenn and I had had discussions, starting back when we were dating, about living in a house one day. But Jenn's investment in the idea was always stronger than mine. She's a Long Island girl, born and bred. For her, a house in the suburbs was a default frame of reference, what she thought was normal, where happiness lived. Though I'd grown up in a house too, I'd fallen in love with living in the city. I didn't want to live anywhere else.

But those dynamics changed when I got back from rehab. Though staying sober was my new priority, even higher on that list was keeping Jenn and Lola happy—and making a lot of money. I still loved the city, but moving into a house was perhaps my only hope of saving the relationship with my girlfriend and daughter. To get used to the idea, I

conjured images of Lola riding in the driveway on a bicycle with training wheels or playing in the backyard.

When I landed the Berkowitz job, things fell into place pretty
quickly. We knew we'd have little trouble selling the apartment. The
2006 bonus season I missed was a good one, and there was no short-
age of up-and-coming Turneys out there dying to move into a two-
million-dollar co-op.

The drive to Huntington Bay seems to last forever. The Long Island
Expressway is a parking lot. If we take the house, I'll have to make this
commute twice a day, five times a week. Finally we pull into a circular
driveway. I have to admit, the place is pretty spectacular. It might even
be worth the ride. Sitting up on a hill, the huge Queen Anne Victorian,
recently painted a brilliant white and fronted by voluminous hundred-
foot European beech trees, seems to come alive as we drive closer. It
glistens in the sunshine. The lawn and bushes are a landscaping mas-
terpiece. Along with the beech trees, there's a hybrid Japanese maple
that looks like a giant bonsai and sixty- to seventy-foot-tall buckeye
trees. Around the property's perimeter are stretches of twenty-foot
privet hedge. But the most striking feature of this dreamscape is the
house, especially the porch, which wraps around the Queen Anne like
a great silk scarf. The estate is listed at $2.4 million.

Jenn and I stand on the porch taking in the lush two acres of property. Without saying a word, we both know. I pick up Lola and ask
her if this should be our new home. She squirms out of my arms and
starts to run back and forth on the porch, blissfully immersed in her
new surroundings.

My first day at Berkowitz, I hear Jim Cramer's name evoked at least twenty times. He hasn't been with the firm since 2001, but he still haunts the office. I'm a bit confused by the firm's rah-rah attitude toward their former boss. On television he always strikes me as somewhat of a clown. I'd only met him once while I was at Galleon, and I was underwhelmed. Cramer had hired Todd-o, Galleon's options guy, to run his trading desk, and a get-together was arranged to smooth any ruffled feathers over that departure. What Cramer didn't realize was, Galleon thought he was doing them a favor, Todd-o and Gary weren't getting along. The dinner was held at a Midtown Wall Street hangout and attended by Raj, Gary, Slaine, Keryn, and me from Galleon, and Cramer, Jeff Berkowitz, and their new hire, Todd-o, from Cramer Berkowitz. As I remember it, Cramer spent the entire evening spouting off about how smart and savvy he was. It seemed to me he was desperate for Raj's approval, but that's just my take. It wasn't until the Cramer Berkowitz contingent left that the dinner got interesting. Raj and Gary mocked Cramer, mimicking his squeaky voice and making fun of his tales of trading twenty-fives and fifties. They called him an odd lot.

Though the Street still calls the place Cramer Berkowitz, Jim Cramer's name has been gone from the door for years. And despite his omnipresence in the office, he's not my boss. Jeff Berkowitz is. I like Jeff, and I think Jeff likes me even though our careers couldn't have been more different. His is the classic Wharton Business School–Goldman Sachs intern Wall Street pedigree, while mine, Ohio University–Galleon, is from the other side of the tracks. It's like, growing up, he was on the debate team and I was John Belushi. Maybe that's one of the reasons he hired me. On Wall Street you always want what you don't have. Berkowitz made a name for himself in the nineties during the hedge fund boom. And when Cramer was drawn to the bright lights of the television studio, Jeff bought the firm from him and has been running it ever since. But J. L. Berkowitz has had a few rocky years, and that's the main reason Jeff hired me: to help turn it around. Compared to Argus, my new firm—with assets only around $150 million and shrinking—is like a start-up. Working here is also a lot less exciting than the early days of Argus.

When you strip away the private jets, floor seats, limousines, and parties from the buy side, all you're left with is the job: buy and sell tickets, salesmen, and ticker tapes. Now that I'm not drinking or doing drugs anymore, work is just that: work. I guess I'm going through an identity crisis. I'm no longer the guy next to the stage at the Naughty by Nature party; I'm not the fun-master with a drink in each hand. And though I realize my old persona was wrecking my relationships and career, without it things just aren't as stimulating. It's just not that much fun. But I'm here for one reason: the paycheck. The paycheck will help pay the mortgage. The mortgage means keeping the house. Keeping the house means Jenn and Lola will be happy.

We move into the house on Memorial Day weekend, 2007. In full spring bloom, the yard is beautiful. The original owner of the house, which was built in 1906, was a landscaper from Europe and brought with him many of the trees that make the property so attractive. We agreed on a price of $2.1 million. After the broker fees, the co-op flip tax, and the mansion tax, I have $500,000 from the sale of the apartment to contribute toward the down payment. To that, I add $100,000 from my checking account, which just about drains it, and then I borrow $1.5 million from Wells Fargo. Sure, it's a lot of money, but real estate is bulletproof.

Each morning, my alarm goes off at four thirty a.m. and I'm in the car by five. The drive into the city is about an hour. When I'm a few miles away, around 5:45 a.m., the skyline starts to come into focus and I wonder: Is there a kid like me leaving Barbara's apartment right now? Is Barbara still an escort? Is she alive? Is the kid leaving her apartment freaking out? Wondering how he's going to work today? I'm thankful it's not me. The workday is from six a.m. to six p.m. With traffic, it takes two hours to get home. Please kill me. The first day is a nightmare. I'm beeping, changing lanes, and on the verge of tears when Jenn calls my cell phone. She wants me to pick up dinner on my way home. "No problem," I say. I want to scream.

The commute gets a little easier when I buy a Honda hybrid so I can use the HOV lane. But neither the fast lane nor the blare of all-sports radio I listen to all the time can drown out the worries I have about the house. The problem is, it's old. Over a hundred years old. It's older than we both realized. The list of projects needing to be done gets longer by the day: the interior needs painting, some of the floors are warped, and the wiring seems to date back to when they first switched from gaslights. With each contractor's bill I pay, money flies out one of the newly installed windows. Then we come up with the great idea of putting in a movie theater. I see myself screening my own films there. When we moved in, the third floor of the house was a converted garret with linoleum flooring, low ceilings, cobwebs, and dust everywhere. The walls were a nasty stained brown. Jenn miraculously transforms it with plush carpeting, a bamboo canopy, and movie theater seats that sit in front of a 106-inch pull-down screen. But it ends up costing $150,000, which I borrow. The plan is to use my bonus to pay it off. I'm building equity, I remind myself. But the outlay is enormous.

By the end of the summer I've found my groove at work. Over the first few months, I'd instituted some cost-cutting changes. I had unused Bloomberg terminals removed and got rid of some needless research services, and, as promised, I started to cut commission and hedging costs, a move that will ultimately add $15 million to the firm's bottom line. But it takes some time for my trading to become sharp again. I'm coming off a four-month layoff, and two years of turbulent drug use before that. I find myself getting physically tired in the middle of the afternoon. I have new systems and computers to learn. But mostly, I have to get comfortable in my own skin. Eventually it all comes back, and when it does I start trading confidently again. And begin making money.

One day, Jeff emerges from his office and tells me to sell all of our Apple position. "Lehman is in the process of downgrading it," he says. "We gotta get out." He's almost frantic and wants it done immediately. Just the week before, he'd told me Apple was one of our best ideas. But now he's pulling a complete one-eighty. I know a sell is a bad move—every fast-twitch fiber in my trading muscle tells me so. But I'm still new at the firm, and I want to be as respectful as I can, because he's my boss.

"Is there anything to the downgrade?" I ask. "Anything of substance?"

"No," he says. "It's bullshit, some valuation call—they don't know what they're talking about." I walk into his office.

"Jeff," I say, "if it's our best idea, we shouldn't sell any. We should be excited because we get to buy more." He's already instructed Heather, a junior trader, to sell fifty thousand shares.

"It's going down three to four dollars on this Lehman call," he says to me.

"Who cares?" I say. But I can see that Jeff is determined. He yells for Heather to sell another twenty-five thousand shares.

Immediately, the stock starts to drop. At my desk, I watch as it goes down four dollars, exactly how Jeff predicted. But I still know I'm right. And an hour or two later, the stock starts to rally. We don't buy any back. By the end of the day it's trading above where Lehman initially downgraded it, but now we have seventy-five thousand fewer shares. Jeff doesn't say a word to me, but I know he knows I was right. More important, I know I was right.

It's interesting, though, that almost at the exact time that I realize I've shaken off the rust, it comes to me that I have no one to tell. And almost immediately following that thought comes another—that I miss the camaraderie of the Healthcare Mafia, where I could tell the story of my being right this time and they'd know exactly what it meant to me, because we're all in the same position, we knew all the players and backstories and nuances. I have conversations, of course, with Jenn. But Wall Street stories have always made her eyes glaze over. It's even hard to talk to people in the new office. Sometimes, when the old Turney comes out—when I break out in song or pull a practical joke—my new coworkers will laugh, but mostly they'll look at me like I've lost my mind. It's different now. It's not the Wall Street I fell in love with.

Then one afternoon, Gus calls and tells me he wants to catch up and grab dinner. I haven't been on a business dinner since I returned to the Street—not that meeting Gus constitutes a business dinner in the traditional sense. Besides, he knows I'm not drinking or doing drugs. I tell him I'd love to. I need to do something besides commute, work, commute, and sleep. It's really starting to bring me down. Gus also wants to show me his new apartment on Seventy-Fifth Street. He lives with his girlfriend now. I tell him maybe another time, let's just get dinner and then I can maybe get home before Lola goes to bed.

We meet across the street from my office, at Houston's. Actually the name of the place is now Hillstone, but everyone still calls it Houston's. It's in the Citicorp building. After the spinach dip and chicken fingers, I'm about to call it a night when Gus asks if I've seen Randy or James recently. I haven't since I've been back. I talk to Randy every day because he's now covering me at my new firm, but I haven't seen him yet. I haven't even talked to James—our relationship was strictly party/business and I'm not doing business with him right now. But I miss the old times. At the meetings I was going to after rehab, they told me to stay away from people, places, and things that might trigger my addiction, but this is getting ridiculous. Just because I can't drink doesn't mean I have to lose all my friends. Besides, if I'm going to do business on Wall Street, I have to have some presence. I'm not going to do cocaine. I'm not going to drink. So what harm can it do? "Let's go see them," I say. But Gus doesn't think it's a good idea. He wants me to come back with him to see his new apartment and meet his girlfriend. Next time, I tell him.

The White House looks exactly the same, only dirtier. There are four guys in the kitchen, with Randy and James gathered around a plate of cocaine. When they realize I'm there, their expressions go from shock to guilt to being happy to see me. I hug it out with everyone, a genuine moment followed by an awkward silence. We're all looking at the plate on the counter with a healthy amount of cocaine in the middle of it. Everyone's afraid to do it in front of me. Maybe they're waiting for me to do it first. "Don't worry about me," I say, waving away the plate. But I feel uncomfortable.

I move away from the counter and light a cigarette. Randy rips a big line and then comes over to talk with me. "We're moving," he says. Before I can ask why, James bursts into the conversation.

"Didn't you hear?" he says, all coked up and manic. Obviously, I didn't. "Remember Kenny?" he says. "I do," I say. He wasn't a Wall Street guy, but a half member, half dealer to the White House. He hung out here all the time. What about him? "He got pinched," James says.

"Rumor is, he's a snitch," Randy adds. "He's not allowed in here."

It feels like the whole room starts to spin. My thoughts go to the lurker in the Baltimore Orioles hat, the dark sedans parked in front of the apartment. All the time I thought it was about underhanded dealings at Galleon. But maybe it was just the cops, looking to bust some junkie Wall Streeters. I have to leave immediately. I want to get back to Huntington Bay. I want to hold my baby.

36

A FEW days later, I'm in the office and on the phone talking to Randy. He's inviting me to the White House farewell party. It's supposed to be the last hurrah. He tells me they're having T-shirts made with a bloodshot eye on the front and a phrase I coined on the back: "We don't wait in lines, we snort them." Not sure I'm going to make the snort-fest, I say, but I'll take a T-shirt. I hang up the phone. No way I'm going anywhere near the White House. Not with rumors of someone being busted who's possibly a narc.

But the night of the party, the thought of it still resides in my head. After work, I'm in the parking garage near my office. When the attendant sees me, he flashes a smile, grabs my ticket, and runs to get my car. I get the same guy almost every day; I always tip him between three and five bucks, so he remembers me. With maybe one or two exceptions, I always exit on the Fifty-Sixth Street side of the garage so I can bang a right and jump on First Avenue and get immediately on the

Queensboro Bridge upper level. But when the car elevator doors open, the attendant, now behind the wheel, looks at me and then points to the Fifty-Fifth Street exit. Why would he do that? If I exit onto Fifty-Fifth Street, I can take a right and head over to Second Avenue, then I can drive downtown to the White House.

Despite the near certainty I will use cocaine if I go to the White House, and despite knowing that if I use cocaine my relationship with my girlfriend and daughter will disintegrate, I begin to consider it. Once the door of consideration is open, it quickly becomes an urge. I close my eyes and try to squeeze the thought from my head. Don't do anything stupid, an inner voice warns. Just go home. When I open my eyes, the attendant is looking at me curiously. I slowly wag my head back and forth and point toward the Fifty-Sixth Street exit and home.

Though a part of my brain has made a prudent decision, the rest of my body is still in revolt. My hands grip the wheel like the car has just gone off a cliff. I can feel perspiration gather under my arms and drip down my sides. I light up a cigarette. I just need to get on the bridge. Once I get on the bridge, there's no turning back. The traffic is thick. It takes me several red lights to get past Fifty-Seventh Street. I light up another cigarette. A hit of cocaine would be so nice right now, though. It would never be just a hit, I remind myself. Then my mini-fantasy goes where it always takes me: alone in a hotel room, with enough coke and porn for a short forever, and a bottle to even my world out. I look down at the keys to my house in the console. I grab them and pretend to dip them into a tiny imaginary bag of cocaine. I bring the key to my nose and snort it in one aggressive pull. My head snaps back, my eyes are closed. Then a horn sounds behind me. When I open my eyes, the cars ahead have moved along. I throw the keys back in the console. I just need to get home. At the moment of no return, just before I enter the ramp, I feel one last intense tug to peel out of the traffic flow and head back downtown. But then I realize the cars that surround me have sealed my fate. I inch up the ramp and onto the bridge.

Later that same week, I stay in the city, at a hotel on Lexington Avenue. The commute is killing me. And with Lola at her grandmother's and Jenn having plans to spend the night with a girlfriend, I take a much-needed break from the world's longest parking lot. After I check in, I call my friend Kevin. We meet at an Upper West Side outdoor café and eat french fries and drink Cokes. "Have you found any meetings out there?" he asks.

"Not yet," I tell him. "During the week, I get home so late, and my weekends are filled with Jenn, Lola, and doing things around the house. The weekend is the only time for us to really get stuff done." Kevin nods, but his expression lies somewhere between helplessness and compassion.

When I leave Kevin, I cut through Central Park to get back to the East Side. I walk past Lexington Avenue and over to Second Avenue, passing bar after bar after bar. I never realized there were so many. I guess it's only something you notice if you aren't drinking. I find my gaze lingering on each bar front. Soon I'm looking through the windows and into the welcoming darkness. I come upon one that's particularly enticing, your typical New York City dive bar. My kind of place . . . It pulls at me and I cave easily. I find an empty bar stool. A guy two seats down gives me a glance. He reminds me of Larry from all those years ago. The bartender comes and asks what I'd like. I look right into the bartender's eyes, but my mouth doesn't work. "I'll go refill the ice," the barman says. "You give it some thought." When he bends to grab a bucket under the bar, I head for the door.

37

IN JUNE, Jeff calls me into his office and says he wants to talk about the credit market. Credit market? I just got used to subprime, and now he wants to talk about credit? Since February, the talk on the Street has been all about subprime. I'd heard the term for the first time right after HSBC wrote down $10.5 billion of losses in subprime-related mortgage-backed securities. Then, over the next few months, subprime became part of just about every Wall Street conversation. The primary worry was that it would affect the homebuilder stocks and the financial sector. But by June the Street, at least my corner of it, isn't that worried anymore. Everyone says it's a housing problem for a certain group of borrowers. "It's just the minorities," I hear. "Has nothing to do with us."

But it does bring volatility to the market. And with tons of volatility, there's money to be made. I start trading the financials and homebuilders back and forth. I buy them on down days and sell them on up days. I fall into the rhythm of it. I can feel it, and it begins to work for me. Meanwhile, subprime or not, the rest of the market is driven by mergers and acquisitions. The activity is insane. Wild. Triple-digit swings in the Dow. I've never seen anything like this in my whole trading career. M&A deals maybe happened once a month. Now they're happening every day: Google buys Doubleclick; Yahoo buys RightMedia. We make a million dollars just on the rumors of Microsoft buying Yahoo. Potential takeover targets line up like dots on my old Ms. Pac-Man game. All I have to do is guide Sue (Ms. Pac-Man) through the maze. Then there's a massive ad network consolidation. One of our analysts says a digital advertiser named aQuantive is prime for the taking. We think he's right and buy it. A week later, news breaks that Microsoft is acquiring aQuantive for $6 billion. The day before the announcement, aQuantive had a market cap of just $2.8 billion. The trade makes our firm a couple million dollars. This is too easy.

But when Jeff calls me into the office, it isn't about patting me on the back. Any success I've had is considered under his direction. I sit in the chair right in front of his desk. He tells me he sees a connection between subprime and credit. He starts talking about high-risk mortgages that were bundled and sold as asset-backed securities all over the world, particularly in Europe. I have no idea what he's talking about. I think he means a derivative play on the underlying mortgages, but I'm not sure. But when he starts talking about collateralized debt obligations, I give up trying to figure it out. "What do you want me to do?" I ask.

"Start monitoring the credit markets," he tells me. "I'm a little worried." The only thing I'm worried about is how to beat the traffic on the Long Island Expressway.

Jenn and Lola are on the front porch when I get home. I beep a few times as I pull in the driveway. Things still aren't great with Jenn. Truth is, she doesn't trust me, even though I haven't had a drink or any coke in almost nine months. "I called a cover company for the pool," she says as I walk up the front steps of the porch. Lola sprints over to me to give me a big hug. "Great," I tell her, trying to sound authentically pleased. But every one of her words comes with a dollar sign. We're both concerned about having an open pool and a wandering eighteen-month-old. Despite the relative success I'm having at work, the house is a huge drain.

Over the next weeks, I try to learn more about credit than I ever hoped. My computer screen is now filled with things like TED spreads, LIBOR OIS spreads, sovereign debt, and sovereign CDS. Lola knows as much about these things as I do. But I do understand this: credit is tightening, and if banks aren't going to lend money like they have been, then the economy will suffer.

Jeff was a week or two ahead of the stampede of suits worrying about the credit crisis. But now he's like Jamie Lee Curtis in *Halloween*. He knows Michael Myers is in the house, but he's waiting patiently in the closet to poke him in the eye with a hanger. He'd rather do that than just get out of the house. Though we're keeping our long exposure on the books, we can and will get short at any point. He'd rather sell the market after it's already down a percent or two than try to be a hero and call the top.

In July we get short and Countrywide Financial, the biggest U.S. mortgage lender for single-family homes, reveals their delinquency rate has nearly doubled to almost 25 percent. As the housing prices plummet, more and more loans sink under sea level. Then, at the end of July, Bear Stearns announces that nearly all the value of two subprime hedge funds has vanished. The news is startling. It's one thing when an overseas bank, such as HSBC, has problems, but another thing altogether when a firm on the Street has them. It's like the SARS epidemic in Hong Kong. You feel sorry for the Chinese, but you'd feel a whole lot different if your neighbors started wearing surgical masks. Still, three days later, the Dow climbs over 14,000 for the first time. The peak is short-lived, though. BNP Paribas, France's largest bank, halts withdrawals from three funds while it sorts out the stateside subprime mess. Over the next two weeks, the Dow loses 10 percent. New home sales drop more than 20 percent. The market is schizophrenic.

Led by a cash infusion from the European banks and the Fed, credit steadies and the stock market corrects; by October it climbs to new highs. The rebound is driven by encouraging news from tech giants such as Microsoft, Google, Apple, and Intel. I'm not sure what to make of it. Everything around me seems to be in distress, yet the market continues to surge. I know something is wrong, but I don't want to believe it. What's wrong is that subprime isn't contained like everyone had said months before. What *is* contained is the truth of what is happening inside of some of America's biggest and most reputable banks—Citigroup, Merrill Lynch, and UBS among them. And the truth isn't pretty.

The night before Halloween, Lola wears her Snow White costume to dinner. We've decided on hamburgers cooked on the grill. The weather is mild, and this might be our last chance to eat outside. Jenn has the porch decorated in friendly ghosts, jack-o'-lanterns, and a life-size witch, one with a happy smile so as not to spook Lola. The witch hangs from the porch roof and sways in the light breeze. As we sit, I can't take my eyes off my little princess: the plastic diamond tiara in her dark hair, her skin the color of pearls. She pushes the meat out of the way; she's much more interested in the potato chips and orange soda. After a few bites, she's off to the yard to chase the dogs. Inside the white picket fence, the lawn is a carpet of red leaves from the

Japanese maple trees. Lola and the dogs run back and forth. Jenn sits across from me wearing a designer jean jacket with a fur collar.

"I'm getting nervous," I say. She tilts her head sideways, curious, and puts a little more salad on her plate. "We're spending like twelve grand a month before we even put food on the table."

"So we'll cut our expenses," she says. "We can cancel the cleaning lady, we can get rid of all the movie channels, we won't eat out, and we don't need to go on any vacations."

Though my experience tells me everything will work out—it always has—I've done the math in my head and know what's happening on the Street. I can't help but feel anxious. "With all the bills, property taxes, and a six-and-a-half-percent mortgage, it's still gonna be tight," I say. Jenn lights a cigarette but hides it from Lola; she blows the smoke toward the house. In the yard, the fallen leaves crackle under Lola's princess footsteps.

"Well, if we can't afford to live here, then we'll just sell this and move to a smaller place," she says.

"Yes, that's what we'll do," I say, smiling. But I'm not sure that's even possible.

It's November 1, 2007, and Jeff is already in the office when I get there. This rarely happens. Before I get to my desk, he yells to me about a report by Meredith Whitney. I don't know who Meredith Whitney is, let alone what he's talking about. I boot up my IM and send a message to Gus to ask if he knows, but he's not in yet. No one is in at this hour except some of the international traders around the Street. Initially I find out a few things about her: she's hot, she's a cougar, and she looks like she'd be fun to roll around with. Then I find out Meredith is an analyst at Oppenheimer and the report she's put out has Wall Street electrified. Jeff begins yelling to me to sell SPYs and QQQQs. What he wants me to do is to short the whole market. I haven't read the report, but there's no denying the urgency in my boss's voice. The market doesn't open for hours, so I start selling both the SPYs and QQQQs on my Instinet machine. The pricing isn't great, but at this point I don't think Jeff cares about my execution; he just wants to sell as much as he can. In just an hour or so, I have us short fifty million dollars, and in just a few hours the firm is net short and it looks like we're going to be for the foreseeable future.

Whitney's report, it turns out, is a scathing assessment of the very solvency of Citigroup, the biggest bank in America. The impact of it rocks Wall Street like an earthquake. Banks such as Citigroup have been considered impregnable castles where the masters of the universe live. But in the weeks to come, when their vaults crack open, only worthless pieces of paper spill out. Whitney times her report to go along with the Fed meeting, which warns of slowing economic growth. Good night. It's over.

That weekend I strap Lola into the car seat and drive the short distance to the center of Huntington Village. On the way to New York Avenue, I see a house with a For Sale sign in front, then another, and another. I follow New York Avenue to Main Street. Huntington Village is a quaint little town and one of the reasons we bought the Queen Anne Victorian. The sidewalks are red brick, and iron gaslight fixtures hold the streetlights. Main Street is the perfect setting for a homecoming parade. But on this day, I see that several stores are empty or going out of business, and I wonder to myself: Why haven't I noticed this before?

38

MARCH 2008

SIX P.M. It's snowing. I hear the melodious plucking of a harp. At first just a few tiny, wispy flakes dance and flutter to the triumphant sounds. The flakes' graceful descent is spectacular. The scene is dreamlike. The curtain of snow grows thicker. The music becomes louder, faster. I can feel the excitement building in my stomach. It's like I'm seven years old again and have just found out it's a snow day. The melody lingers in the air as the final snowflakes parachute to the ground.

The mound of cocaine rests on a polished mahogany coffee table, next to my American Express card, a glass of scotch, two packs of Newports, my lighter, and a remote control. I'm holding my cell phone as I hit Dial. I stand up to pace the deluxe suite at the Fitzpatrick Hotel. This is the hardest part. I need to call now so I can start my night. But is it too early to say good night to Jenn and Lola? Jenn never tried to be my parole officer; she wants what's best for me. She knows how much the commute is killing me, so we've worked out a deal for me to stay in the city once or twice a week. She thinks I'm at Gus's, though, not in a four-hundred-dollar suite. When she answers I try to act casual but tired. She'll believe tired. "How'd you do today?" she asks first thing. It's a question she's been asking a lot lately. Now the whole world knows what's happening to Wall Street.

"We're doing better than most," I tell her. "We're still up on the year."

"I'm glad," she says. "We need you to be up." I ask if I can say a quick hello to Lola. Jenn calls her, but she doesn't want to get on the phone. Then Jenn starts talking about Lola's preschool, but I'm not listening anymore. I'm staring at the mound of cocaine. I need to get off the phone.

"I'm gonna crawl into bed and watch a movie," I say. "I might fall asleep, so if I don't talk to you again, have a great night. Kiss and hug Lola for me."

"Okay," she says, but she sounds a little annoyed. Did I cut her off? Did she have more to say about Lola's preschool? Or is she suspicious?

But my questions are quickly displaced by the harp music that begins to play again. I roll a twenty-dollar bill and gather enough cocaine with my American Express card to form a hefty line. I order my first porn movie with the remote. I light up a cigarette. I snort the entire line and the rush immediately flushes to my head and then all over my body.

It's maybe a few days later, I can't be sure. I'm at work, though, and I get an email from Gus. It's a picture of a two-dollar bill taped above the Bear Stearns logo at their corporate headquarters. That's how much J. P. Morgan paid for Bear's stock, a stock that was worth $171 just a year before. I look around our office. The analysts are sitting silently, glued to their screens. Heather, the other trader, has a worried look on her face as she slumps low in her chair. Jeff looks like he hasn't slept in months. I imagine all of Wall Street looks the same. It doesn't matter: sell side, buy side, fixed income, equity, or private equity, we're all screwed.

I send an IM to James, with whom I started trading a few months ago. *Let's meet at 4:15*, it says. Our code. Since 4:20 is synonymous with smoking weed, we thought meeting at 4:15 was only appropriate for cocaine. I trade a ton with James today, all day. After the market closes, I'm on the sidewalk, smoking a cigarette. Midtown is already a sea of people heading to Grand Central, nearly all of them with a cell phone pressed to their ears. I can hear their conversations: a woman with a thick Long Island accent, a guy whispering to his sidepiece, a boss screaming at his secretary. Across the street from me is a bike messenger. His bare legs are purple with tattoos; he wears a locking chain across his chest like a slave. When I look at him, he looks away and begins touching his nose, and I know it's some kind of a signal. I'm convinced he's watching me. Just then, James comes waddling up Third Avenue. I hand him my pack of Newports and he puts it into his coat pocket. "Fucked up out there, dude," he's says. "All my accounts are freaking out."

"I know, I know," I say. "Fucking brutal." But all I can think about is the bag he's surreptitiously sliding into my cigarette pack. James asks about my plans for the night. I tell him I have a dinner with some research guys. "I need this," I say, as I hold up the Newport box he just handed me, "just to get through the night." He laughs at the thought of my being all jacked up sitting around some Wall Street stiffs. As I begin to turn away, I feel another bolt of paranoia. "This is just between you and me," I say. No one can know, not even Randy or Gus.

"No problem," he says. "I'm a vault." I search his face for any sign of deceit. His eyes dart away from my assessing glare. I give him a gentle fist bump to his shoulder and walk away.

And then I'm in a room in the Fitzpatrick again. Hank Paulson is on the television screen. I pour out the coke onto the coffee table in front of me. I rip a line, hit mute on the remote, and watch Paulson's lips move for a few moments before I order porn.

It's after work, a week later, maybe two. I go to an informal charity event at a bar in Midtown. It's to raise money for Wounded Warriors. When I walk in, a few people call out my name—they're surprised to see me. I go to the bar to order a Coca-Cola. "I don't drink anymore," I tell the bartender. He didn't ask, but he tells me I'm probably better off. I stand with my back to the bar, looking out at the crowd. All of a sudden it dawns on me: they're all younger than I am. My ten years on the buy side flash before my eyes, and I think of Galleon with Gary and Raj. I ran into Raj at one of these charity events not too long ago. He acted like he didn't even know me. I laughed at his phoniness. I guess I was dead to him. The last time I saw Gary was at a fortieth birthday party for a mutual friend. They had Usher play for the entertainment. I alluded to the MDRX trade with the courage of cocaine within me. I said that I didn't know who said what, but I was sorry for my part. He looked me in the eye and shook my hand. I think he thinks I was apologizing for something, but that was fine with me. I believed it was behind us.

At the Wounded Warriors party, I see a friend of mine from Credit Suisse walk in. Stephen looks like he just got off a beach. He's tan and his long hair seems highlighted by the sun. He grew up in a Wall Street family, but surfing is more important to him than his job. He gives me a big hug and asks how I'm doing. When he notices the soft drink in my hand, he smiles. "I'm proud of you, man," he says. I know the remark is genuine, but I'm a phony. And then we're surrounded by four or five young Wall Streeters who know Stephen. "My boy Turney here is legendary," he says. "His parties were epic." He tells them about

South Beach and Susquehanna: "His skin was green when he came back from that trip," he says to peals of laughter, but the laughter recedes to a subtle soundtrack of memories. I think of September 11 and the Twin Tower Fund's party and my birthday bash. I think about all the money I spent and all the money I've made just by being myself, or who I thought I was. Who was I, anyhow? How far away my childhood and Maine seem now. An image of my father comes to me, him shoveling the driveway, not nearly keeping up with the heavy flakes that keep piling higher. And yet he works on, and on, until the day runs out of light. As I look around the room, I wonder who in this crowd came from where I did, and who has the same path ahead of them. And in that instant, I feel sorry for myself. As the memories fade and the moment again comes into focus, the laughter has ended. This pending doom on Wall Street has everyone feeling sorry for themselves. A pall hangs over us. It's like a party after a funeral. No one is smiling.

But Stephen continues to talk about me. He tells his audience about the time I gave his coworker Brian a hundred thousand shares for doing a cartwheel on the trading floor. "Brian turned his ankle and was limping around for a week," he says. The young traders look at me with eyes wide with wonder. But Stephen's words of admiration sound to me like a eulogy. I excuse myself and tell him I'll be right back. And that's when I see James standing in the entrance of the bar.

It's six a.m. the next morning, or maybe it is the following week. I'm staring down at a toilet in the office bathroom, which is filled with puke. I can taste the scotch I drank the night before. I throw up again, nothing but bile. I grab some toilet paper to wipe both sides of my mouth. I flush and sit on the toilet, trying to catch my breath. When I stand, the floor spins beneath me. When I look at myself in the mirror, I'm repulsed. My face looks raw-red, and the blood vessels in my nostrils are inflamed. I resemble a guy who just ran out of a burning house. I splash some cold water on my face and stare again, hoping I'll magically look presentable. I look the same. Somehow, I get back to my desk. Heather asks me if I'm okay. I tell her I'm sick, I might have the flu. She tells me I should go home. "Go," she says. "Take care of yourself." But I shake my head no, playing the brave man. It feels like an eternity for the market to open. When it does, my screen goes bloodred; everything is down. I feel something drip from my nose, water from the sink or perspiration, I think. Then I see a red drop between the letters K and L on my keyboard. Another falls to the exact same spot. There's blood on my keyboard.

On Thursday, Gus is watching *SportsCenter* when I get to his apartment on Seventy-Fifth Street. His girlfriend, Lori, is in the kitchen. She's somber and orderly, the opposite of Turbo. Gus's place reminds me of my apartment on Sixty-Seventh Street, a high-rise cookie cutter with two bedrooms. I can't afford to stay at the Fitzpatrick anymore—besides, I'm constantly worrying that Jenn will open my American Express bill and see that I've been staying there instead of at Gus's. Lori waves at me. She feels sorry for me. She thinks I was crazy to buy a house so far away from the city, a house that's about to drown in a mortgage, with payments that are set much higher than what the house is worth. I throw my overnight bag into the guest bedroom and join Gus on the couch. He wants to talk about the market.

The next hour is excruciating. I have a bag of coke in my pocket. I call Jenn and Lola to say good night. After an hour of watching television, I yawn. "I think I'm gonna call it a night," I say. Gus and Lori exchange a look. "I'll talk to you tomorrow," I say to Gus. "Thanks again for letting me stay here."

Sometime past two a.m. I need alcohol to bring me down. Earlier, I saw a bottle of wine in the refrigerator. I tiptoe out to the kitchen. I can't see anything. It's pitch-black. I use my hands to feel for the dining room table. I know it's right in front of my bedroom. My eyes start to adjust. I can feel the change from wood floors to tile on my bare feet. I wave my hand to feel for the refrigerator. I pull the handle slowly, careful to make as little noise as possible. But the seal breaking sounds like Velcro ripping. A triangle of light spills from the fridge. I grab the bottle of wine from the bottom shelf, pull out the cork, and lift it to my lips. I chug as much as I can, and then take another hit. As I put the bottle back in, I feel someone behind me. I turn to see Lori standing there watching me. She doesn't say a word. She runs back into her room. Jesus, she scared the shit out of me.

Five minutes later, I'm back in the bedroom and there's a knock on the door. "You have to leave," Gus says. He's fucking joking, I think. It's two thirty in the morning. "You can't do this in my apartment anymore."

"Do what?" I ask.

"Turney, we know you've been doing coke—you've been doing it every time you stay here."

"So what?" I say. "You and me have done a ton of blow together."

"It's different now. You've been to rehab, and you've admitted you have a problem. I want you to be okay, and I'm not going to let you do it here."

"Fuck you," I say to him. "Without me, you wouldn't have this fucking apartment."

"I'll let you stay until the morning," he says. "Then you have to go."

How long ago was it that Gus introduced himself as Turbo and climbed into the back of the limo? How long ago was it that I gave him his first order and promised Rich and Melinda he wasn't a squirrel? Fuck him.

I'm driving home from work a week or so later. I haven't used much in that time. I know I have to stop. My biggest fear is Jenn finding out, and yet all I can think about is having one last run. I had a conversation with my accountant. I told him that my partners stopped paying rent on our Jersey City Fatburger location. "That'll get your landlord's attention," Jerry said. I see my million-dollar investment in my rearview mirror fluttering down the Long Island Expressway, as if someone had opened a suitcase and emptied it out of the back window. I can't believe this is happening to me. I need to tell Jenn. I need someone to feel bad for me.

Jenn is in the garden when I pull into the driveway—not in the vegetable garden down by the pool, the one so fertile that it sometimes produces another round of crops again after a harvest; not in the nearby butterfly bush garden, the one with electric-pink flowers, wild strawberries, and a hybrid apple tree; and not in the rose garden, which has seven or eight different colored roses and blooms as big as softballs. No, she's in the flower garden near the house, the one with a mind of its own, the one that sprouts types of flowers we don't remember planting. She's kneeling in the dirt and wearing clam-digger jeans and one of my old white button-downs. She holds a gardening spade in her hand, and her forehead glistens a bit from perspiration. I get out of my car and walk toward her. "I think my Fatburger investment is a zero," I say. No response. "I'm gonna lose a million dollars, I think."

"That's too bad," she says as she pulls a giant weed out of the ground.

"Where's Lola?" I ask.

"At my mom's," she says, wiping her brow with the arm holding the spade but not looking at me.

"Cool," I say with a hopeful smile. "What do you want to do?"

"I have plans," she says as she digs around a hydrangea. "There are some leftovers in the fridge."

I'm Christopher Walken in the last scene of *The Deer Hunter*. Behind Jenn, the sun is beginning to set. The garden and lawn glimmer in the softening light.

I think she knows I'm using again.

39

ON MONDAY, September 29, 2008, I'm in the office watching CSPAN as Congress votes on whether or not to rescue Wall Street: one vote yes, then a no, a yes, a no, a no, and another no. About ten minutes into it, I look at Jeff slumped at his desk. We'd thought it was a layup. There wasn't a chance that Congress wouldn't pass TARP. And now we both know the bailout vote is going to fail. We're positioned with very little exposure—short slightly with some long positions mixed in. As each no vote comes in we start to short more and more. I'd insisted, after a round of conference calls with my Fatburger partners, that we short commercial real estate stocks, and the firm stands to make money on this calamity. But Jeff is far from happy.

There's a saying on Wall Street that those who have a short bias were abused as children. Rooting against the rest of the Street is isolation in its purest form. I'd spent so much of my buy side career flying above the fray, making money without trampling on anyone. And here I am in the place that I'd for so long despised. Lehman Brothers, the fourth-largest bank in America, has already filed for bankruptcy. People I've known and partied with are now taking subway rides, carrying cardboard boxes filled with what's left of their working careers. Merrill Lynch has been sold for 50 percent of the value it held just months before. And I'm shorting the market, no longer playing the game for the game's sake but for keeps—for the money. I feel hollow. I lost my innocence a long time ago, but this feels different. Any remnants of a soul I possessed seem to be disappearing with the market.

As the congressional vote concludes, Jeff sits quietly, looking at the television in disbelief. He realizes before I do that being long or short doesn't matter anymore. Wall Street money is worthless now. After the vote, the bottom falls out of the market. The Dow has its worst day ever. The next day the cover of the *New York Daily News* has a large red arrow pointing down with the number 777 emblazoned across it.

After work on Tuesday, I get on the shuttle at Grand Central. The subway rattles and screeches. A homeless man sits directly across the car from me. He wears layers of torn and soiled clothing. He has black plastic bags for shoes. He scratches his crotch as he stares at me. His eyes are like brown marbles: glassy and hard. I try not to make eye contact, but I can't help myself. Every few seconds, I'm drawn to his burning glare. He sees into my soul, and the intimacy is unbearable. Finally, the train pulls into Times Square. I stand by the door, waiting for it to open. I turn one more time to look at him. "You're not alone," he says in a deep, resonating voice.

I walk up to Hell's Kitchen, where James now lives. His apartment is elegantly dirty. There are empty beer bottles sitting on coffee and end tables, the ashtrays are filled to overflowing, and there are porn magazines strewn about. And yet, somehow, it doesn't seem offensive. It feels a bit unreal, like the set of a play. It's also filled with all of James's Wall Street toys: a huge flat-screen, an Xbox, golf clubs, expensive wristwatches, photos of him in the Hamptons, and the keys to his Porsche hanging from a cabinet in the kitchen.

Along with his girlfriend, who sits tightly next to him on the couch, James has already started in on the cocaine. He introduces me to Jessica, who looks like a stripper: fake blond hair, huge fake boobs, and tons of clownish makeup. I just want to get my coke and get out of here. I sit down to be polite. They slide a plate full of cocaine over to me and I snort three quick lines. James tells me Jessica has some friends she can invite over. "Nah, I'm okay," I say. "I need to go meet some people." I know they know I'm lying, but fuck them. I don't care. Just give me my cocaine and leave me alone.

Thirty minutes later I'm out the door. I'm wandering around Hell's Kitchen looking for a bar where no one will know me. On Ninth Avenue I find a hole-in-the-wall. When my eyes adjust to the darkness, I realize I'm the youngest person here by twenty years except the female bartender, who looks tired and lonely even in the bar's dim light. When she smiles at me, I see that her teeth are brown and crooked. There are a half dozen or so men at the bar. I sit next to a guy who holds on to his longneck with two gnarly hands. He peels at the label with a ragged, dirty thumbnail and mumbles something to the bottle. I order tequila on the rocks—I don't care what kind. There is no music playing. This isn't so bad.

40

JULY 2009

AFTER WORK I'm on Fiftieth Street when someone grabs my arm. I get pulled away from the crowded sidewalk. It's Slaine. I haven't seen him in years. His shirt—it's loose. I've never seen him in a shirt that wasn't skintight. There are rumors on the street—Gus had told me— that the SEC is investigating Raj, that they have or had someone on the inside of Galleon wearing a wire. Is Slaine wearing a wire? He asks me how Berkowitz is treating me. He knows Jeff from the old days, he says. Then he asks what kind of trades I'm working on, if I have any tips for him. It's a normal question under any other circumstance, but as I look again at his shirt, I can't get away fast enough. "Hey, man, it was great to see you, but I gotta go to a meeting."

"This is how you treat the guy who gave you your start?" he says.

"I'm sorry," I say. I'm afraid to say anything, and James is waiting for me with my coke.

Later the same night I'm back at work. The conference room is dark. Lights from the offices across the street cast weak shafts across the floor. I know I can't sleep, but I have to stay somewhere. It's around three a.m. I crawl under the large table and set the alarm on my phone for six a.m.: just in case. I close my eyes. I place my hands on top of my shaved head. I can feel the tiny stubbles on my fingers. What happened?

In March, Jenn finally told me she'd had enough. We put the house up for sale. She said she couldn't do it anymore, that she wanted me out of the house. But I can't afford to rent an apartment, let alone a hotel room for a night. I've been sleeping on couches, driving back and forth to get new clothes and spending the weekends in Huntington Bay.

Chase closed our home equity loan. I'm out of money. Even though the firm did exceptionally well in 2008, up 10 percent, my bonus was tiny compared to what I'm used to. We don't manage enough money. My salary doesn't cover our mortgage, and I still have to feed our family.

I can't sleep. I get up every fifteen minutes. I walk around the perimeter of the office. I go into the bathroom to look at myself. I have to look presentable when everyone shows up to work. My face is drained, my eyes are bloodshot, but with my shaved head and clean clothes in my overnight bag, no one will know I didn't shower.

We haven't had a single offer on the house. We can't give it away. I need to go home. I'll go home tomorrow after work. I need to see Lola. I need more clean clothes. I wouldn't be in this mess if Gus hadn't kicked me out of his apartment. Last week I tried to stay there without his permission. The doorman doesn't know I'm not allowed up. But when I got there at three a.m., the apartment was locked. I tried to sleep on the cold tile of the bike room off of the apartment. The room where everyone throws their garbage down the trash chute.

Everyone has turned their back on me. I've stayed with two different friends who don't work on Wall Street. Both are named Kelly. After a week, they both told me I had to leave. They told me they weren't going to enable me. They told me I had to tell my boss and go back to rehab. They're wrong. I'm going to quit, starting right now.

I go back to the conference room to lie underneath the table. I need a cigarette. I grab my ID off the table so I can get back into the office. Downstairs I make my way over to Third Avenue to light up. I need to come down. I need alcohol. I need something. I'd better smoke two while I'm down here. I light up a second one. A few blocks away I see a man riding a bike. He looks much too large to be riding it—like seven feet tall. He's an African American with a huge afro. He's shirtless and he's pedaling up Third. He's getting closer and closer, and he stares at me. He's about ten feet away when I see him pull something out of his shorts pocket. He's almost to me. Then I see his phone. He points the camera directly at me. We're a foot away from each other and he snaps a picture.

Back underneath the conference room table, I'm terrified. My body shakes. My hands tremble. Why did he just take a photo of me?

41

OCTOBER 16, 2009

I'M IN my underwear and white T-shirt, shivering, standing barefoot on the front porch of the Queen Anne. The temperature is in the low forties, and the dampness makes it feel colder. It's still dark out, but I know I have to leave for work soon. There are two empty cocaine bags on the outside dining table, and I open a third. I dig my house key into the bag, scoop as much as I can onto the key, and then snort. Dig, scoop, snort. Dig, scoop, snort.

There's half of a still-lit cigarette hanging in the ashtray, but I light up a new one. I can feel my heart palpitating. It's going to explode. I know it. I chug some scotch from the bottle. There's about a third of it left and I down the whole thing.

The sun begins to rise. I can't stand to look at it. Inside, the house is only half furnished. There's one couch, the television, which is still on, and a chair in the living room. I need more cigarettes. I go upstairs. I walk by where Lola's room used to be. It's empty. I can't look at it. Then I walk over to the master suite closet. Jenn's side is completely empty—I try to ignore it. I rummage through several coat pockets until I find my Newport cigarettes. I run back downstairs. Without Lola, Jenn, and the dogs around, the house feels dead. I need more coke.

When I check my phone for the time it reads 5:30 a.m. I have to lie down. I grab a pillow from the couch and press it hard against my chest, trying to hold my heart in place. I'm going to die. Next time I look at the clock it's 5:59 a.m. I have to go to work. I run up to the shower and jump in. My whole body vibrates, and my hands shake like I have palsy. I drop the shampoo and pick it up. I try to squirt some out and the bottle again slips out of my hand. I give up and now stand on the cold tile, naked and dripping wet. I hold my arms tightly to my chest.

Forty miles away, in his Sutton Place co-op, Raj, my old boss from Galleon, is riding his exercise bike, looking out the window onto the East River. He wears a shiny tracksuit and a white towel, which is wrapped around his neck like a brace. Perspiration pours from his forehead. I've never been to his apartment but know people who have. They say it's beautiful. Worth millions, it's modest, I guess, for a billionaire's apartment. Judge Judy is one of his neighbors. Of course, he also has an estate in Greenwich. Raj has a trip planned later in the day to England to launch a new $200 million fund. He keeps pedaling.

Still soaking wet from the shower, I pace the nearly empty living room and stare at the phone in my hand. I practice saying hello, but each time I sound like I'm high. I *am* high. I can't do this. Finally, somehow, I summon the courage, scroll to Jeff's phone number, and hit Send. With each ring, I fight the urge to disconnect the call. And then I hear his voice: "Yeah," he says.

"I can't come in today," I say.

"Are you okay?" Jeff asks.

At precisely 6:30 a.m., the doorbell to Raj's apartment rings. No doubt, he's surprised by the sound. If you live in a Sutton Place co-op, the doorbell almost never rings unannounced. But he's far more surprised when he opens the door. Standing there in the hall are a half dozen or so federal agents, some wearing FBI windbreakers.

"No," I tell Jeff. "I'm not okay." I don't know how much Jeff knows about my drug use, but I suspect more than I realize. He seems concerned but not shocked. He tells me he'll call me back. "Jeff, I can't come in today," I say again. "Or ever," I mumble. I hang up the phone and do some more cocaine. I know it's going to make it worse, but I don't have a choice. I grab the empty bottle of scotch and suck out the last drops. I make my way back out to the porch and light up another cigarette. The morning sun now bathes the front yard. The lawn hasn't been mowed since early summer, and the gardens are overrun with weeds. I notice a car parked near the end of my driveway. I saw it drive by the house earlier. I go back into the living room, turn off the television, and shut all the shades.

Under the watchful eyes of the agents, Raj puts on a white dress shirt, open at the collar, a green cardigan, and a blue blazer. When he finishes dressing, an agent tells him to put his hands behind his back. He feels the cold steel on his wrists and then hears the click of handcuffs locking. The agents ask Raj if he has a gun, if he has any drugs in the house. He thinks they might plant something. His wife and kids are there. It's a sight they'll never forget. The agents tell him he's under arrest for insider trading. They lead him from the apartment and then out of the building.

I'm almost out of cocaine. When my phone pings with a text, I nearly jump off the couch. I can't look at it. Instead, I clutch the pillow again in fear of my heart exploding. I creep to the living room window and stand, hidden by the curtain, looking out to the driveway and street beyond. A dark sedan, the same one that was parked in front earlier, I think, slows as it passes by. The driver looks right at me. I stand there frozen, both afraid he can see me and afraid to look away.

Raj sits in an FBI interrogation room. His lawyer is not yet there. He doesn't need a lawyer. Ethnically, Raj is a Tamil from Sri Lanka. Soldiers in the Tamil Tigers wear chains with cyanide capsules around their necks. They'll kill themselves before they're captured. Raj won't admit a thing. He won't cooperate. The interrogation goes on for hours. The agents play back wiretaps of Raj's phone conversations that implicate him. But Raj says nothing.

My cell phone dings again. Then again and again. Texts. A few seconds go by and then the phone dings a few more times. What the fuck is going on? Jesus Christ. I pick up the phone to look at the first message—Raj has been arrested, it says. The next one is the same thing and then another says the FBI has raided Galleon's office. My phone continues to ding as the messages come flying in.

I'm numb. Oh my god. It all makes sense. The FBI is coming to get me. I run to find the plate with evidence of cocaine on it, furiously scrub the plate in the kitchen, then run to the bathroom and flush the remaining cocaine. It can't be about Galleon. I did nothing wrong. A catalog of trades flips through my thoughts. Nortel, I think. No, it can't be that. I didn't know anything. It was so long ago. Am I guilty of insider trading? They've been watching me. They know I give out commissions for drugs. The White House! Fuck, that's it. The rat Randy told me about. They have photos of me getting the handoffs from James on street corners. I'm so fucked. They're coming for me.

I look out the window again. I see two dark sedans driving slowly up the street. There are a few guys in the car. I see the turn signal come on. They're pulling into my driveway. Holy shit, run! I think. Where?

I have nowhere to go. Maybe if I pretend I'm not home. The cars are halfway up the driveway. I know it's the FBI. I'm going to jail. This is it. Don't admit anything. You didn't do anything wrong. But I did *everything* wrong. I look in the mirror in the entrance area near the front door. I'm rail thin. I'm still in my underwear and T-shirt. My eyes bulge above the black rings below them. This is who I am; this is what I've become. I hear car doors slam.

I can see three men in suits get out of the car. I have to face them. I open the door and walk outside. The angle of the morning sun now almost blinds me. I can barely make out the three figures walking up my driveway. I'm too high to cry. I no longer have any fight, and in this surrender I feel the slightest of comforts, like a drowning man who gives in to the inevitability of his watery death. I've long since lost control of my life. I've lost everything during my time on the buy side: my relationships, my money, and, most important, my self-respect. Now my freedom. I thought I was good at my job but I was wrong. Real success on Wall Street is measured not in bonus or salary but in photographs on desks of children wearing soccer uniforms and caps and gowns. Success on Wall Street is measured the same way it's measured by a factory worker, a math teacher, or an engineer with four children in Maine.

When the three figures walk into the shade cast by the house, I can finally make out their familiar faces. Relief quickly collapses into dread. A fractured memory of texting Kevin last night spills from my thoughts. When he looks me over, in my bare feet and underwear, a small smile of concern and empathy comes to his face. He's here with Chris, and another guy named Jim whom I'd met at meetings. "You need to go away," Kevin says, his crystal-clear blue eyes holding me like some type of force field. I can't stand the truth of them, but can't look away.

My mind immediately starts searching for an excuse: I can't go for thirty days, I think. What about my job, the mortgage? How will I explain it to Lola? Yet "Okay" is all I manage to say, and with that one word I feel an overwhelming sense of relief.

"A guy goes to rehab once and everyone's rooting for him. A guy goes to rehab a second time and people start to drop off," he says. His words are honest and genuine. I believe what he's saying. "We'll always be here for you, man. But I promise you, if this keeps going on, people are gonna drop and drop fast." I feel like they already have.

Somewhere, deep inside, I know it's over, all of it: my drug use, my drinking, and the Turney I created for the buy side. I think of my daughter and all the moments I've already missed in her life. "Everything's going to be okay," Kevin says as he puts his arm around my slumped shoulders. I want to believe him, more than anything.

42

THIRTY DAYS CLEAN

AS THE taxi from LaGuardia Airport nears the house, I'm excited when I see Jenn's car parked in the driveway. My muscles tense. I'd spoken to her just yesterday from the Recovery Place, a rehab in Fort Lauderdale, and asked if I could see Lola when I got home. They've been staying at her mother's house. But as I pay the cabbie and then pull my large bag from the trunk and throw it on the porch, my stomach knots. I don't know how my daughter will react when she sees me. The thirty days I've been gone seem like an eternity.

Through the screen window, I can see Lola and Jenn playing in the kitchen. As I open the front door, Lola looks up and recognition brightens her face. She rushes toward me. "Daddy!" she screams, a sound as beautiful as any I've ever heard. I hold her tight. She radiates a warmth so pure, it instantly dissolves my anxiety. How could I have ever jeopardized something so precious? Jenn once asked me if I loved cocaine more than Lola. I answered with righteous indignation: "How can you ask that?" I never thought it was one or the other. I thought I could control it; I'd just do a little. It'd be different the next time. It never was. And each high dragged me further from my daughter. I believe the things they told me in rehab and meetings, that I'm powerless over drugs and alcohol and once I start with either, I give up control of my life. But there's also right and wrong. As I hold Lola, I never want to make the wrong choice again. Out of the corner of my eye, I can see Jenn starting to cry.

The next day, the day before Thanksgiving, I call Jeff to tell him I'm ready to come back to work. I'd spoken to him a few times when I was in Florida, and he was very supportive—he paid me the whole time I was away. I tell him I'll be in on Friday. I remember when I moved to the city in 1994, Larry, the guy in the Raccoon Lodge, said, "Always work the day after Thanksgiving: it makes you look like a hero." I'm ready to be the hero. But Jeff tells me to take the rest of the week off and he'll see me on Monday. I can tell by his tone something is up.

On Monday morning, I'm at the office early, scrubbed clean and pressed. Everything looks a little sharper, a little brighter to me, as if the building has changed the lighting to a slightly higher wattage. And I'm nervous. Over the last ten years or so, my life has been a kind of bipolar existence, with wild swings from false bravado to the lowest self-esteem. Rehab and recovery from drug addiction stuck a pin in the bravado, leaving me vulnerable and in self-doubt. I'm worried about how people will treat me, especially Jeff.

I'm there less than fifteen minutes when my boss calls me into his office. Jeff begins by asking how I'm doing. He's very kind, saying how much courage it must take to face my problem, how proud he is of me. But then he begins to talk about business and the state of the firm, which isn't great. Our assets under management are back to what they were when I was first hired. Investors used us as a source of funds and withdrew money despite our performance in 2008. It's then I know the purpose of this meeting.

Being fired doesn't make me want to use. Negative circumstances usually didn't send me directly to a drink or a drug. In a way, being let go is a relief. I'm not ready to be back on the buy side. And as I walk out of Berkowitz's office for good, I wonder if I'll ever be.

Although the house is going into foreclosure, Jenn and I are not getting back together, and no firm wants me as their trader, the next few months have a graceful simplicity to them. I attend an outpatient program at a place called the Realization Center and go to a few meetings a week. A colleague on Wall Street offers me a job selling his geopolitical research—I used the product at Berkowitz. All it entails is picking up the phone and leveraging what is left of my contacts. But the best part of the job is, I can work from home. It allows me the opportunity to take Lola to preschool three times a week. It also gives me time to write.

I'd started writing in rehab. And the words came out of me in a kind of Kerouac flourish—the quantity, that is, not the quality. To be honest, most of what spills onto the page isn't pretty. And yet there's something utterly perfect about it. It's as if I've opened a door to a room that's been sealed shut since college. I'd tried to pry open the door a few times during my Wall Street career—writing those movie scripts and working on that rap song. But even though it was my fantasy to chase profits and inspiration, my job (and, I guess, my addiction) had always pushed my creative urges into a dark corner. I wasn't alone. Some of the funniest, most creative people I've ever met work on Wall Street. But, like their bonuses, their talent is sealed in bank vaults. Here in early sobriety, however, when anything seems possible, I begin to allow myself to dream. In the real world it's not that easy, though. And the buy side isn't about to turn its back on me.

I'm pitching my geopolitical research to a new behemoth hedge fund named Pioneer Path when they ask me to come in and meet them. The office is gorgeous. New everything. The receptionist greets me and offers me coffee or water as she leads me to a conference room. As I'm laying out my research on the table, a light-skinned black guy named Deric walks into the room wearing a huge smile. I knew Deric when he traded for Lehman. Although we weren't super tight, I do remember several fun dinners we had together. I remember too that he's a big poker player, and I like him. He comes over and gives me the Wall Street hug. It's only my third pitch meeting, so even with the friendly face across the table, I'm a little nervous and not as smooth as I'd like to be. But I explain to him, as honestly as I can, how I used to use the product, the value I found in it, and how it helped me trade when I was on the buy side. Though he watches me intently, he seems to be feigning interest in what I say. The smile never leaves his face. When I close the presentation, he just sits there quietly looking at me, nodding slightly. "How much you gonna get paid this year?" he asks. I look around the room, stalling and trying to figure out why he asked the question. Nothing comes to me. I know my earnings this year will be awful. Maybe thirty grand.

"About three hundred grand," I say. I just lied. "Actually, probably less."

"What if I could double that?" he says. His smile grows even wider. The amount of money dances in front of me, beckoning. "Come back and see me next week," he says, standing and reaching his hand out to shake mine. "We're looking for a new healthcare trader."

Ten minutes later, I'm on the street with an appointment reminder on my cell phone for a meeting with the HR person at Pioneer Path the following week. My mind spins with scenarios. With that type of guarantee, I could make a stick with my eyes closed. I could even save the house, maybe move back to the city, get an apartment in Tribeca. If I can stay sober, I'll have more money than I can spend.

The interview with HR goes flawlessly. I'm emboldened by my sobriety. I answer her questions with honor and integrity and try to convey that I have the work ethic of a Boy Scout. At the end of the interview she asks me to come back the next day to meet with some traders. "Be happy to," I say.

The following day, the traders quiz me on Obama and healthcare reform. To help me prepare for my interview, I called an old Healthcare Mafia friend named Chris, who still trades healthcare. Chris filled me in on what I'd missed, and all I already knew comes back. I hit every question the traders throw on the barrel of the bat. It feels almost surreal, the clarity I have and how confident I feel. In my heart, I know I'd be a great hire for them—*if* I can stay sober. But is this what I'm supposed to be doing? They tell me to come back for a final interview.

In the car on the ride home I call Jenn, Kevin, Uncle Tucker, and my parents to ask their advice. Although the responses vary—from Jenn's "It's your decision" to Uncle Tucker's enthusiasm—most of their advice boils down to the same thing: I have to do what I think is right for me.

"You're ahead of your skis," Kevin says. "They didn't offer you the job yet." He reminds me that all I really have to do is not pick up a drink or a drug. "If you do that, everything will work out the way it's supposed to," he says.

That night I can barely sleep. I know they're going to offer me the position, and if they do, I don't know how I can turn it down. I need the money, but it feels like I'll be signing my own death certificate. I don't know what to do. I've never been a big God person in the traditional sense. I remember going to Sunday school as a kid a couple of times, and as a family we went to church when we lived in Ohio. But once we moved to Maine I don't remember ever going back. One time—it might have been Thanksgiving or Christmas, when we were all together—my sisters told my mother they didn't believe in God and they were all going to vote Democratic. "We failed, we failed," my mother laughingly cried. But from a very early age, I've thought there is something greater at play in the universe—something both good and bad. I've felt those forces my entire life. I experienced the worst during my active drug addiction and saw the best in Lola's eyes. An image of my daughter's eyes is the last thing I remember before I finally fall asleep.

The next day I'm seated in the same conference room I've visited three times before. A man, sharply dressed, very Wall Street, walks in. He's holding a copy of the résumé I'd brought on my second visit. There are some noticeable pen marks up and down the sides. I shake his hand firmly and look him in the eyes. We chitchat about the markets, my house, his house, my daughter, sports, and New York in general. He smiles across the table. "So I hear you're a great healthcare trader," he says. Then it hits me. I can't believe no one noticed it on my résumé.

"Actually," I say, "I haven't traded healthcare since 2006 when I was at Argus." His eyebrows arch as he considers my statement. "Yeah," I say, "we traded everything but healthcare at Berkowitz."

"Oh" is all he can manage to say.

"Yup," I say, "I haven't traded one share of healthcare in four years."

For a moment he looks away. Maybe he thinks I'm nervous. I'm not nervous. I've never been calmer in my life. He begins to explain the duties of the position. Then he explains how Pioneer is a global firm and the traders alternate holidays and take turns working at night. I interrupt him.

"Yeah, I'm not sure I can do that," I say. "I have a four-year-old daughter and I just can't see missing the holidays or losing a few nights a week." I see a hint of a smile on his face. It's like he's sharing this special moment with me. I think it's safe to say he's never had an interview quite like this one. "I just don't think I can make that commitment," I say, smiling as I do. In fact, I can't stop smiling. This is the best interview I've ever had. He caps his pen and smiles with me.

"Do you have any other questions or anything else to say?" he asks, closing this most untraditional interview in the most traditional way.

"No," I say. "I don't. Thank you for your time and consideration."

It's around nine thirty a.m. when I walk out of the building and the last gasp of Midtown's morning workforce rushes by me. It's cold and overcast. I look up at the gray sky between the tall, shiny glass buildings. I'm on Fifty-Fourth Street and Lexington Avenue, exactly halfway between the Berkowitz office and the puddle I jumped into to fake a mugging. In this magnificent moment, I know my buy side career is over. I'm not sure how my next chapter will read—but wherever I'm headed, I'm ready.

EPILOGUE

I'M SITTING in my kitchen at 8:06 p.m. on April 28, 2012. I've got on my pajama bottoms and an old white T-shirt—I know: stylish. Unfortunately, I washed the T-shirt with something red and it now has a pinkish tint to it. This is pretty much what I've been wearing in my apartment for the last twelve months, though yes, I regularly do my laundry. The view out my window is thought-provoking. Midtown rises from the rocks of Manhattan like a kingdom of money and power. In some ways, especially at night when the lights come on, it seems like a scene from my book. I gaze across the East River several times a day, especially during writing breaks, thinking about how many stories are taking place there.

I'm living in Long Island City in a one-bedroom apartment, smaller than the one I lived in when I moved to the city in 1994. It works for me. I have everything I need. I haven't had a drink or a drug in two and a half years now. It hasn't been easy and some days are harder than others. My goal is no longer happiness but serenity. I have joint custody of my daughter, speak to her every day, and write every day. Though most of my money is gone, I've never been happier.

Six months ago a friend told me that if I write this book it will be the final nail in the coffin for my Wall Street career. At which point I said, "Give me the hammer." To me, this book represents a beginning, a middle, and a new beginning. I wrote it for myself. Writing it is something I *had* to do. I don't blame Wall Street, the buy side, drugs and alcohol, or anyone for my struggles. Writing about my experiences has shined an even brighter light on what's wrong with this business. But when I look in the mirror, I don't see Wall Street.

I felt no anger while writing this book. I've met so many amazing, intelligent, honest, and friendly people while working in the financial industry. It was not my intent to paint an unflattering picture of them. Good and bad people exist in *every* industry. Wall Street is no different.

But if you run a firm on the Street and for some reason you see me in a couple of years knocking on your door asking for a job, do me a favor. Just smile and say, "Not hiring."

AFTER THE CLOSE

Every time I sit down to write, I close my eyes, put my hands over my heart, and say, "Acknowledgment, Intention, Gratitude, Humility."

ACKNOWLEDGMENT

It's not always our job to understand the universe, but we *should* acknowledge it.

Among the stars who populate *my* universe are Julie Flanders, Nathaniel Tilton, and Brian McDonald. Julie, your intuition, coaching, and kindness helped guide me back to my writer-self. I ended up in your office by chance and by chance I started writing again. Nathaniel, we started writing rhymes together back in the eighties. When we discovered we were both writing books at the same time, I felt I had the support of my childhood friend all over again. Brian, you taught me how to write a book proposal and saw something in between all of my fragments and run-ons that others may not have been able to. You're a friend, mentor, and big brother.

Another glittering star is Lisa Leshne, my agent. Lisa, your determination, insight, and hard work brought life to this project. Everyone told me how hard it is to find an agent, especially a great one. I'm lucky. Your passion, honest feedback, and expertise helped me carry this book forward. You made it better.

Also shining bright is Rick Horgan. Rick, your sterling reputation as an editor frightened me at first, but your gentle and knowledgeable hand inspired and infinitely changed the scope of this book. I'm so grateful you believed in this story and pushed me to my limits. I wanted to cut a vein and leave it on the page because of you. *Wow.*

INTENTION

Help, heal, and entertain . . . The one question I've been asking myself the last few years is *How do I get to keep writing?* My intention is to do so.

GRATITUDE

There are so many friends and family who support me—here's a short list: Lola Duff, Mom and Dad, Debbie, Kristin, and Kelly, Tucker Sine, Ethan and Lenore Duff, Rob and Eliza Sine, Gretchen Berg, Suzanne Turner, Jennifer and Claire Scully, the Gutkowskis, Jason and Lauren Kondi, Keith and Brooke Savitz, Dave and Sara Roter, Steffen and Meg Kondi, Scott and Michelle Levy, Pete and Ruth Cocozza, Scott Friske, Sam Sebastian, Dave DeWalt, Brad Cochran, Monday Men, Don Bosco Hewlett, Kevin Breznahan, Todd and the McWilliams, Writing Sober, Perry Hodge, Kevin Weir, Mike Breheny, Jayme and the Caseys, Chris Lottridge, Peter Young, Kevin O'Keeffe, Chris Langel, Kelly Dillon, Kelly Schwartz, Mike Elovitz, Patrick Grady, Sean Farley, Francesca Kimpton, Joe Foster, Dave Fromm, Sara

Blakely and Jesse Itzler, Steve Ehrenkranz, Kelli Deveaux, Marisa Polvino, Dan Purnick, Rob Lubin, Jennifer Kalish, Ric and Lauren Weisgerber, Ross Peete, Dan Simon, Dave Morris, Liz Wintrich, Patty Donaldson, Katie DiMento, Johnny Hong Kong, Bob Cook, Buckles, Caroline Cofer-Golin, Charlie Della Penna, Jon Fox, Chris O'Connor, Heather O'Hara, John Latino, JT, Kia, Lauren Tant, Lillyan Manus, John Lewin, Lisa Bloomquist, Michelle Debusschere, Joe Assad, Joel Morgan (1973–2004), Lori Carson, Pete Murphy, Matt Candel, James Karabelas, Megan Basten, Kathleen Reardon, Kim Duda, Jim Heins, Amber Senn, Billy Gaus, Chris Arena, Dan Fox, Jaime Meagher, Jeff Bennett, Jen Bingler, Jeremy Bronfman, Joey Raia, Keryn Limmer, David Slaine, Todd Harrison, Krishen Sud, Jeff Berkowitz, Pat Shevlin, Chris Birch, Roger Meilleur, Austin Graham, Dr. Errol Gluck, Carly Novich, Mike Masiuk, Dave Osh, Oliver Wiener, Steve and Judy Taylor, Brian Volpe, Steve Starker, Andrew Walker, Matt Walton, Fred Berman, Zandy Reich, Mary Vogt, Joe D., Danny Breen, Rich Giroux, Melinda Loiacono-Zech, Kevin Debbs, Collin Henne, Bruce Cacho, Dan Hess, Ted Pratt, Christina Carathanassis, the Wenja, Nicole, Eric, Dr. Kondi, the Recovery Place, the Realization Center, Cotton Wood de Tucson.

Also, thanks to the entire team at Crown Books and Random House Publishing for enthusiastically getting behind this book—especially Tina Constable, Tara Gilbride, Paul Lamb, and Mark Birkey.

HUMILITY

Progress, not perfection . . . I'm trying.

A COMPLETE LIST OF THE BOOK'S PSEUDONYMS

Darlene

Looks Like a Larry

Baby Arm

Mr. Whisper

Nate

Peter and Kevin from Barneys

Randy

James

Adelina

Gus

Dr. Fish

Lily

Robert and Vinnie—Gus's bosses

Roger and Trevor—Hedge Fund Mafia

Sam

Victor

Lotus Chick

Tracey

Bill from rehab

Kenny the narc

Jessica—James's girlfriend

Lori—Gus's girlfriend